CAIRO 1921

CAIRO 1921

TEN DAYS THAT MADE THE MIDDLE EAST

C. BRAD FAUGHT

YALE UNIVERSITY PRESS
NEW HAVEN AND LONDON

To Neil Nevitte and Trevor Lloyd

For information about this and other Yale University Press publications, please contact:
U.S. Office: sales.press@yale.edu   yalebooks.com
Europe Office: sales@yaleup.co.uk   yalebooks.co.uk

Set in Adobe Caslon Pro by IDSUK (DataConnection) Ltd
Printed in Great Britain by TJ Books, Padstow, Cornwall

Library of Congress Control Number: 2022939647

ISBN 978-0-300-25674-1

A catalogue record for this book is available from the British Library.

10 9 8 7 6 5 4 3 2 1

CONTENTS

ILLUSTRATIONS

7. View of the Pyramid complex at Giza, *c.* 1920–33. Matson photograph collection, Prints and Photographs Division, Library of Congress, LC-DIG-matpc-15590.

8. Cairo in the 1920s. Chronicle / Alamy Stock Photo.

9. Cairo cityscape, *c.* 1920–33. Matson photograph collection, Prints and Photographs Division, Library of Congress, LC-DIG-matpc-15589.

10. Cairo Conference delegates, March 1921. Gertrude Bell Archive, Newcastle University PERS F 005.1.

11. Cairo Conference group at the Giza Pyramids. Gertrude Bell Archive, Newcastle University PERS F 004.

12. Dining room of Semiramis Hotel, Cairo, 1920. Matson photograph collection, Prints and Photographs Division, Library of Congress, LC-DIG-matpc-03818.

13. Winston Churchill, T.E. Lawrence and Prince Abdullah, Jerusalem, 1921. Matson photograph collection, Prints and Photographs Division, Library of Congress, LC-DIG-matpc-20843.

14. Faisal I, King of Iraq, by Bassano Ltd, whole-plate glass negative, 19 September 1919. © National Portrait Gallery, London.

15. Jafar al-Askari. archivist 2015 / Alamy Stock Photo.

16. Gertrude Bell with King Faisal, 1922. Gertrude Bell Archive, Newcastle University PERS B 018.

17. Gertrude Bell, Sir Percy Cox and Ibn Saud, 1916. Gertrude Bell Archive, Newcastle University Photographs W 056.

18. T.E. Lawrence and Gertrude Bell. Gertrude Bell Archive, Newcastle University Photographs F 001B.

19. Churchill with Bishop MacInnes of Jerusalem, 26 March 1921. Matson photograph collection, Prints and Photographs Division, Library of Congress, LC-DIG-matpc-08801.

20. Winston Churchill with Sir Herbert Samuel, March 1921. Matson photograph collection, Prints and Photographs Division, Library of Congress, LC-DIG-matpc-04699.

21. Winston Churchill, Clementine Churchill and Prince Abdullah, 1921. Matson photograph collection, Prints and Photographs Division, Library of Congress, LC-DIG-matpc-08805.

Map

The Middle East in the early 1920s.

ACKNOWLEDGEMENTS

This book has been especially enjoyable to research and write, mainly because of its subject, but also because doing so provided a welcome task during the Covid-19 lockdown. Everyone had to come up with their own way of enduring the upheavals of those un-lovely months; working on this book about the Cairo Conference of 1921 was mine.

As always in book-writing, many thanks are due to a number of people and institutions. First, I should like to thank Yale University Press, London, and my editor, Joanna Godfrey. I have known and worked with Jo for a number of years now and she is simply one of the very best in the business. I would like to thank her for having taken up the idea for this book with her usual enthusiasm, and for guiding it through every step along the way to publication. My thanks, also, to the other excellent staff at Yale, for their ready help and expert work, especially Katie Urquhart, Felicity Maunder and Lucy Buchan. Additional thanks to Jacob Blandy.

Archives and libraries of course are indispensable to good history writing, so my thanks to all of those – and to their superb staff, and in many cases their online resources – that I used in researching this book: The National Archives, Kew, London; the Liddell Hart Centre for Military Archives at King's College London; the Churchill Archives Centre, Cambridge; the Gertrude Bell Archive at Newcastle University; the Parliamentary Archives, London; the National Records of Scotland, Edinburgh; the Middle East Centre Archive, St. Antony's College, Oxford; the Bodleian Library, Oxford; the J. William Horsey Library at Tyndale University, especially Hugh Rendle, University Librarian; and the John P. Robarts Research Library at the University of Toronto. Also, a sincere thanks to my brother, Wylam Faught, and his wife, Katie, for providing their cottage in Lanark County, west of Ottawa, in order for me to do some intensive work on the book. I am very proud to have been the first 'White Lake Writer-in-Residence'.

I have dedicated this book to two former professors of mine, one a political scientist and the other an historian, who throughout their long and highly productive academic careers were exemplary teachers and scholars. But their mentoring and friendship shown to me personally over the years has been of even greater value. Acknowledging University of Toronto Emeritus Professors Neil Nevitte and Trevor Lloyd in this way is but a small token of my appreciation for them both. Lastly, I would like to thank my wife, Rhonda Jansen, for her constant support, for always indulging my need to look at most things in life through the lens of history, and for my equal need to write books: all done with unfailing grace and good humour.

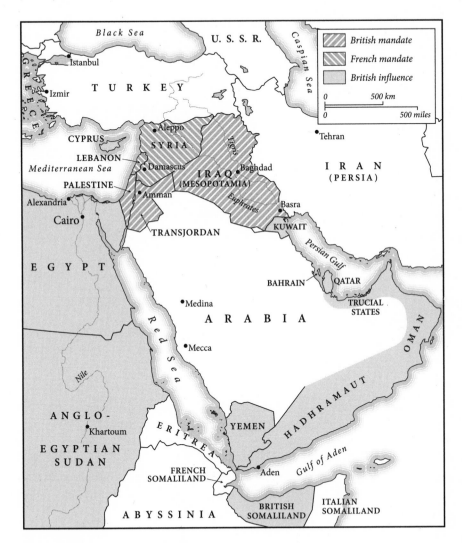

The Middle East in the early 1920s.

PREFACE

On Sunday, 20 March 1921, a group of delegates attending the Cairo Conference on the post-war geopolitical future of the Middle East were invited by their host, the British colonial secretary Winston Churchill, to join him for a special outing. The conference delegates' visit to Giza, the site of the ancient pyramids and the Sphinx, and a short drive from their hotel across the River Nile, had been designed by Churchill to provide them with a capstone event to celebrate their time together in the Egyptian capital. Though a few formal dinners remained, the visit to the pyramids would prove to be a social highlight of the ten-day conference.

One of the photographs taken that day (reproduced on the cover of this book) would later become an iconic image in the modern history of the Middle East. Directly in front of the Sphinx, the invited delegates sit alongside one another on camelback. To the left can be seen Churchill's wife Clementine, wearing a flowing white ensemble and a pair of sunglasses, a kerchief sheathing her head; her husband is to her side, in a trench-coat, a homburg hat and sunglasses. Then comes the long-time Arabist Gertrude Bell, wrapped in a long coat with an unlikely fur collar; on her head is perched an elaborate feathered hat while in its shadow her steely eyes stare straight ahead at the camera. Next to her, the already legendary T.E. Lawrence sits diffidently atop his camel, wearing a suit and tie and a homburg, and looking distinctly unlike 'Lawrence of Arabia'. Finally, beside Lawrence is Churchill's bodyguard, Walter Thompson, squinting into the camera. Famous though the photo would become, the scene it depicts is nevertheless faintly ridiculous; at best decidedly touristic in the manner of the day. Of course, in spite of their attire, Bell and Lawrence, veterans both of long passages in the desert, had in the past spent many months riding camels, so the staginess of the moment would not have been lost on them. (Churchill and Clementine, on the other hand, had never ridden a camel before in their lives, and in the former's case this fact would soon be embarrassingly revealed.)

The Cairo Conference stands as a watershed moment in the modern political history of the Middle East. It was called by Churchill in the aftermath of the 1919 Paris Peace Conference – and one of its cognates, held in 1920 at San Remo, Italy – to determine the nature and scope of the newly created international Mandate System. At its conclusion the Cairo Conference would set in motion the creation of two new Arab states, Iraq and Jordan, as well as influence deeply the direction taken in the future by Mandatory Palestine, forerunner of the modern State of Israel. Although the Cairo Conference has been featured in a number of studies of the history of the Middle East in the early twentieth century, it has not before been examined comprehensively in the manner attempted by this book.[1] Recently, as I was finishing work on a biography of General Edmund Allenby, I began to think that a close examination of the Cairo Conference might bring a new and valuable perspective on the events and purposes of those ten important days back in 1921.[2] In Allenby's private letters, written in the spring of that year when he was British high commis-

2

sioner in Egypt, he made a number of references to the expected arrival in Cairo of 'Mr. Winston Churchill' for a special conference convened to concentrate upon the geopolitical future of the Middle East. Indeed, Allenby had been contacted by Churchill only a few weeks earlier asking for his recommendation as to the right hotel – he would suggest the luxurious Semiramis in central Cairo – in which to house the delegates and hold the conference sessions.[3]

Over the last half-century, the private papers of the Cairo Conference's main participants – especially those of Churchill and Bell – have become more readily available for study. As I began to look closely into accounts of the conference, I could see that their contents would allow for a deeper penetration of both its proceedings and results. As I read about how the conference had come to be, how it had been run, about its plans and the personalities of those who had been involved, it seemed to me that a comprehensive examination of it might contribute to a more substantial understanding of the diplomatic history of the post-First World War period. It was an era marked by a firm belief in the efficacy of international summitry – of what may be called conference culture – to solve the problems created by the highly destabilizing impact of the war.

The Cairo Conference – together with a contiguous few days for a select number of its participants that would follow in Jerusalem – took place therefore within a tradition that had been created by the European diplomatic conferences held at Vienna in 1815 and Berlin in 1878 and 1884, and which would continue at Paris in 1919 and then again at San Remo the following year. Moreover, and in a similar vein, British colonial and imperial conferences had been held regularly since 1887, and they too had reinforced the conference culture of the time. The distinctive purpose assigned to the delegates at Cairo, however, was to remake and reorder some of the vital constituent parts of the Middle East in the aftermath of the colossal upheavals brought about by the First World War and the concomitant defeat of the Ottoman Empire.

Such a fundamental regeneration naturally carried with it the heft of European geopolitical interests, as well as the equally weighty ones of certain nascent Middle Eastern states. But that is not the same thing as saying the latter's interests were simply subsumed by those of the Euro-imperial centre represented especially by Britain and, to a lesser degree, by France. Even though the Cairo Conference was overwhelmingly a British government event, present at it too were a handful of leading members of the government of Iraq, both Iraqi and British nationals. Their participation goes some way in suggesting that local voices were sought, and counted for something in the conference's deliberations. In other words, it will be contended in this book that the Cairo Conference was not merely a 'rubber stamp' or a 'purely theatrical' event, descriptions of it which have been offered by some historians in the past.[4] During this era, the idea of Great Power trusteeship as a more progressive successor to traditional forms of empire had become one of high international standing within the chancelleries of Europe, as well as in the United States, especially when empire remained in place as the principal organizing feature of contemporary international relations.[5] Indeed, in the evocative words of a leading historian of global empires, John Darwin, Britain's *imperium* in the Middle East 'was a volatile salient in the middle of the world'.[6] Today, the Middle East continues to bear the indelible mark of that era's attempt to refashion the region according to the state-building imperatives undertaken by its chief politicians and diplomats.

As I moved more deeply into reading the letters of the main participants at the conference, into assessing its documentary record, and into understanding the framework undergirding what it intended to accomplish in the Middle East, the seriousness and comprehensiveness of its proceedings became that much clearer to me. Nevertheless, even Gertrude Bell, then an official in the Iraqi government, was reluctant initially to attend its deliberations for fear that it would be little more than a show put on by the British Colonial Office, made

4

that much more appealing by its being held in the unique atmosphere of the Egyptian capital city of Cairo. 'I was not at all anxious to go', Bell would write to her stepmother, Lady Florence Bell, while travelling from Baghdad to the conference in late February of 1921. She went on to explain her doubts 'as to the wisdom' of being away from a restive Iraq just then. But if reluctance to go to Cairo had been Bell's first impulse then it would be replaced a month later on the journey back home by a more considered position: 'I'm really glad to be going back to Baghdad with this wonderful job before us'.[7] Indeed, Bell's sanguine view of the Middle East's future in the spring of 1921 and her role in it was representative of the vast majority of the participants at Cairo, especially Churchill and Lawrence. All of them would leave the conference committed to enacting its decisions and completing the political remake of the Middle East that had commenced with the comprehensive defeat of the weakened Ottoman Army in Arabia, Syria and Palestine in the autumn of 1918 (a victory had been spearheaded by Allenby's Egyptian Expeditionary Force). As an airily confident Lawrence would write home to his mother in Oxford near the conclusion of the conference: '[we] agreed upon everything important: and the trifles are laughed at'.[8]

The essential task of this book, therefore, is to answer this question: how had Churchill and some of his Cairo Conference colleagues come to be sitting atop camels in front of the Sphinx on that March morning in 1921? To them, the conference represented an ambitious and progressive attempt to fashion a new post-war geopolitical paradigm for local governance in the Middle East. In the short term its plans necessarily included a certain level of continued British mandatory supervision as required by the new League of Nations, which had been recently launched at Paris. However, the clear understanding of all those concerned was that such control would dissipate gradually in favour of genuine national independence. Was their privileging of the idea of the nation-state as normative a reasonable approach to post-Ottoman imperial control in the Middle East? The

Cairo Conference's dominant 'Sherifian Solution' – a plan designed to monarchize two heirs of the Arab Hashemite dynasty, Prince Faisal and Prince Abdullah, by placing them on the thrones of Iraq and Transjordan, respectively – was its answer. But were the Cairo Conference's prescriptions really those which ultimately would give the people of Iraq and Transjordan the kind of political and economic stability they desired? Moreover, would Palestine, the most complicated of the political situations under discussion, also find the right way forward through the conference's capacious plans?

In the intense geopolitical crosswinds of the early 1920s, the delegates at Cairo would make an attempt to fashion a lasting statist solution for various Arab peoples, as well as for the Jews of Palestine. Having Arabs engage the modern world politically through the formation of newly engineered states was no different in aspiration than what had been undertaken two years earlier at the vastly larger Paris Peace Conference.[9] In short, the Cairo Conference would come to provide a powerful and representative example of the determination of Britain and the post-1918 international community to fashion a new order in the Middle East out of the destruction of the old.

A note on nomenclature

In the pages that follow I use the term Ottoman to refer to subjects of the Ottoman Empire, although Turk or Turkish was often used at the time by the British and other Europeans. In the spelling of the names of persons, places and events, I have used what is standard practice in the West today; however, I have not altered the way in which such words were used and spelled in quotations from the period. So, for example, Transjordan is used instead of Jordan; sherif, rather than sharif, and so on. The context in which such terms appear should help also to clarify their usage for the reader.

1

THE FIRST WORLD WAR IN
THE MIDDLE EAST

In the autumn of 1918, as the catastrophic First World War wound down along the Western Front, far to the east in the Syrian capital city of Damascus a rapturous celebration of the country's newly won liberation from four centuries of Ottoman rule broke out. On the morning of 1 October the Australian Desert Mounted Corps, a part of General Edmund Allenby's combined British and imperial force, had led the way into the still-burning and chaotic city. Soon thereafter, and in a respectful nod to the impending arrival of the Arab Northern Army fighting in the name of Prince Faisal of the Hashemite dynasty of the Hejaz region of Arabia, the Australians would withdraw from the conquered city in order that the Arabs alone might enjoy their supreme and historic moment of triumph.[1] And enjoy it they did. Amidst shouts of joy and piercing ululation, the vanquishing of the Ottomans was savoured throughout the city of 300,000 that had served historically as the focal point of pan-Arab society. Revelling in the experience also was the young British officer, Lieutenant-Colonel T.E. Lawrence. Having started out as an Arab Bureau deskman in Cairo early in 1915, the intrepid Lawrence had gone on to become Faisal's chief military adviser. In the process he had become a heroic figure to most Arabs. Known to them as 'Aurens', later on that first day of October he drove into Damascus in his armoured Rolls-Royce, nicknamed 'Blue Mist'. Wearing full Arab dress as usual, Lawrence was 'cheered by name', as he recalled later, 'covered with flowers, kissed indefinitely, and splashed with attar of roses from the house-tops'.[2]

Belying the celebratory nature of Lawrence's welcome in Damascus, however, was the utter exhaustion he felt by this late stage in the war. After some two years of life amidst the harsh desert battlefields of Arabia, Palestine and Syria, Lawrence was both emotionally and physically spent. He had fought hard, led desperate men, and endured a severe beating and rape at the hands of Ottoman captors, while all the time nursing the supreme hope of helping the Arabs achieve their independence from Ottoman rule.[3] But over the next forty-eight hours in Damascus that persistent hope would begin to falter in the face of the even stronger persistence of Anglo-French realpolitik. Two days after Lawrence's arrival in the city, Faisal would make a triumphant entrance of his own – on horseback, followed a few hours later by Allenby.

The charismatic Arab sharif, or prince, and the stern British commander had agreed to meet that afternoon at a local hotel in order for Allenby to inform his counterpart of the British government's uncompromising plans for the newly liberated Syria, plans that would put paid to Faisal's hopes for immediate Arab independence. Despite being allies in the struggle against the Ottoman Empire for the preceding two years, neither man had met the other in person before. Upon their meeting, Allenby was impressed immediately by Faisal, judging him to be, as he wrote later to his wife, 'keen', 'fine', 'straight in principle'.[4] To Faisal, according to Lawrence's description, Allenby appeared as 'gigantic and red and merry, fit representative of the Power which had thrown a girdle of humour and strong dealing around the world'.[5] Over the course of a briskly tense thirty-minute meeting that day, the two men would set in motion a burgeoning plan for a new style of Middle East governance.

The Hotel Victoria, the site of their meeting, no longer stands in the centre of Damascus, having given way long ago to the city's twentieth-century urban development. But in 1918 it was the only 'A-class' hotel in the city and for half an hour on the afternoon of 3 October its luxurious interior became the scene of a remarkable late-wartime encounter between Allenby and Faisal. Lawrence, as Faisal's main British adviser, was present also, and the meeting's controversial outcome was of such great disappointment to him that he abruptly quit the war at that very moment and headed for home. The meeting would prove to be a rigid exercise in intra-imperial wartime enforcement.

Allenby had come to it with instruction from the British government to make clear to Faisal that the future of Syria was one that necessarily required the presence of formal French supervision, a state of affairs necessitated by the Anglo-French Sykes–Picot Agreement, arrived at by both countries two years earlier in 1916 (see below, p. 28). 'But did you not tell him that the French were to have the Protectorate over Syria?' So asked an exasperated Allenby of Lawrence after Faisal had balked when told of the restrictive condition that had been placed upon future Syrian independence. 'No, Sir, I know nothing about it', Lawrence had replied, according to the account of the proceedings offered later by the Australian general Harry Chauvel, who was also present at the meeting. Disingenuousness is rarely a useful tack in negotiations, and certainly Allenby was angered by Lawrence's feigned ignorance over the provisions of the Sykes–Picot Agreement. Allenby became angrier still when Lawrence said he would refuse to work in tandem with the French liaison officer who must now be assigned to Faisal. Instead, Lawrence indignantly stated, he was due for leave and was therefore going to take it immediately. An obviously upset Allenby shot back: 'Yes! I think you had!', and with that a dejected Lawrence left the meeting.[6] Outside the hotel he met up with Lieutenant-Colonel Pierce Joyce, one of his close colleagues from the desert campaign, who found him at that moment to be 'a depressed and insignificant figure in dirty unwashed Arab clothes'. After a brief exchange, Lawrence said, 'I am going home for my work is done'.[7] By the next evening he had left Damascus altogether – a city to which he would never return – and was on his way to Egypt and from there a return to England.

Later, in *Seven Pillars of Wisdom*, his highly personal memoir of the Arab Revolt, Lawrence would express regret for the manner of his peremptory departure from the Middle East: 'at once I knew how much I was sorry'.[8] But if subsequent generations are inclined on occasion to go looking for a moment when the term 'Middle East' began to enter the lexicographical front rank of international affairs, the Damascus meeting of Allenby and Faisal followed by Lawrence's abrupt and regretful farewell serves well as a candidate. Very soon thereafter however, and in light of the fact that he believed the Arabs to have been betrayed at Damascus, Lawrence would embark on a protracted attempt to convince both the British and French governments that Faisal should be allowed to keep and govern the land that his Arab forces had helped to win for the Allies: 'fighting King Faisal's post-war political battles', as Joyce described it later.[9] For the doggedly committed Lawrence this campaign would run all the way until March of 1921, when it culminated with ten days of crucial policymaking at Cairo.

The nature of what Lawrence, together with a number of other leading figures of the day, would attempt to achieve at Cairo had sprung directly from the collapse of the Ottoman Empire in the Middle East during the First World War. Its defeat had clear and wide-ranging ramifications for British – as well as for French and Russian – imperial interests in the region. As the Victorian era drew to a close in the late nineteenth century, the British Empire had found itself in the midst of a complicated and ever-changing geopolitical environment.[10] A unified and imperial Germany had emerged as a clear rival, its industrial manufacturing capacity having grown to exceed that of Britain's own, while its navy posed an equal challenge to the supremacy on the high seas long enjoyed by the Royal Navy. Meanwhile, the centrality of the Suez Canal and the route to India to British imperial strategy – the so-called 'swing door' of empire – had recently come in for a moment of severe challenge by the similarly competitive French. Anglo-French rivalry had increased in the region over the preceding generation. The Berlin West Africa Conference of 1884–85 had resulted in a speedy delimitation of most of sub-Saharan Africa by a small number of European states with Britain and France in the forefront of this partition. In an era when controlling the headwaters of the Nile was of high importance to Europeans, one of the key zones of Anglo-French contest was the territory on either side of the Upper Nile. Accordingly, only a last-minute British mission – sent to the remote outpost of Fashoda and led by Earl Kitchener in the aftermath of his successful Sudan campaign of 1898 – would smooth the ruffled feathers of Anglo-French diplomacy. If Kitchener were to have failed in this mission it was believed in both London and Paris that war would have been the likely result. As it was, however, shortly thereafter the Anglo-Boer War emerged to embroil the British in a three-year-long conflict in South Africa. So costly was this war that the acknowledged bard of empire, Rudyard Kipling, concluded that Britain had been taught 'no end of a lesson'. The fact that Germany had been an active sympathizer with Boer geopolitical aspirations against Britain during the war would only deepen the sense of concern about the prevailing state of British imperial affairs.[11]

At the same time, in the lands of the Middle East, presided over by the Ottoman Empire for the previous four centuries, the British looked on with growing concern. Supported traditionally by Britain as a means to check regional Russian expansionism, especially along the North-West Frontier of India, the Ottoman Empire appeared to have entered a period of terminal decline. To some extent, the so-called 'sick man of Europe' had been viewed as ailing for years. But by the turn of the twentieth century such fears were being clearly borne out, as independence movements in the Balkans along with Russian expansionism in the Caucasus struck hard against Ottoman imperial integrity. Additionally, France had made a move on Tunisia, taking it away from the Ottomans in a manner that the British themselves had employed earlier when occupying both Cyprus and Egypt. Meanwhile, another of the rival European empires, the Austro-Hungarian, would annex Ottoman Bosnia-Herzegovina in 1908, just as resurgent Italian imperialism would assert itself in Libya in 1911. All told therefore, in the years leading up to the outbreak of the First World War, the Ottoman Empire's decline would push the British to reassess fundamentally their traditional policy of bolstering it in the service of strengthening their own imperial position.[12]

British imperial policy in the Middle East had always been comprised of an amalgam of methods and plans used to achieve particular ends. Traditional diplomacy, through which the British employed an integrated system of consulates and residencies to further their interests, was the first of these methods. Next came informal spheres of influence, characterized by economic, financial and military penetration that were designed to win favour with local indigenous elites. The most long-lasting example of these was known as the 'Great Game', a protracted exercise in intrigue, subterfuge and collaboration played readily by Britain and Russia within Persia and Afghanistan.[13] Third, the British created buffer zones or curried favour with client states to ensure that their vital interests, contingent upon the integrity of the Suez Canal, remained safeguarded. Egypt of course had become the fulcrum of this policy since its occupation by the British in 1882. Highly important too was the nearby transit port of Aden, a key station along the route to India. Lastly, from time to time Britain believed it necessary to launch military or naval operations to ensure that the security of its regional position was maintained. The Second Afghan War of 1878–80 is a prime example of this phenomenon, as is the Gordon Sudan Expedition of 1884–85. Altogether, these aspects of imperial strategic policy meant that during the first decade of the twentieth century Britain would achieve a pronounced degree of domination in those areas in or near the Middle East that bore most directly on ensuring security over the vital Suez passageway to India.[14]

Despite the effectiveness of this strategic quadrilateral for the British, the picture was never necessarily a clear one. Centre and periphery were always shifting in their relationship with London's best-laid plans, inevitably coming up against unpredictable local realties. Indeed, the regional situation had been complicated further still by the rise of a more assertive German foreign policy during the 1890s on a trajectory that would continue throughout the first decade of the twentieth century. Under the control of the young and ambitious Kaiser Wilhelm II, imperial Germany had begun to make evident its own ambitions in the Middle East to rival those of Britain, as well as of Russia. Among the ways in which these ambitions were demonstrated was a state visit to Jerusalem and Damascus by the Kaiser in 1898.

More substantial though was the key role taken by the German state in designing and building the Hejaz Railway, which would open in 1908. One of the Kaiser's closest advisers at the time, Max von Oppenheim, would help to persuade him of the idea that pushing German influence eastwards might result in an enhancement of the country's imperial reach. As a former attaché at the German Consulate in Cairo, in Wilhelm's estimation von Oppenheim spoke with authority on this attractive potentiality. Equally strong on the point was the German ambassador at Constantinople, the imposingly patrician Adolf Marschall von Bieberstein. One of the chief outcomes of these influences was the Kaiser's decision to back the building of what would become an 800-mile-long railway stretching from Damascus to deep inside the Arabian desert before terminating at the Islamic holy city of Medina.

For years the Ottoman sultan, Abdulhamid II, had dreamed of just such a railway running from Damascus all the way to Mecca as an iron road to ferry the Muslim faithful on their annual Hajj pilgrimage. In addition, it would serve to highlight the Sultan's devotion to the duties of being caliph of the Islamic world as well as providing clear evidence of Ottoman imperial power. As a prelude to building the railway the Ottomans would construct a telegraph line along the same proposed route. Once strung, it served as a persuasive demonstration that building a railway was also achievable. Accordingly, in May of 1901, construction on the *Hamidiye-Hijaz* – 'praiseworthy' – railway began. It was expected – and in most places within the Ottoman Empire enforced – that contributions from devout Muslims worldwide would be forthcoming to make travelling on the Hajj easier, safer and cheaper.

The successful construction of the Hejaz Railway came to depend largely on the labour of Ottoman soldiers. It relied also on foreign, especially German, technical expertise. Its manager, for example, was an engineer from Leipzig named Heinrich August Meissner who had served in various places throughout the Ottoman Empire as far back as 1886. To the British, meanwhile, the new railway was considered an Ottoman-German strategic provocation, and potentially threatening to their regional interests. The security of the nearby Suez Canal was their chief concern of course, informed by the Mahdi's revolt in Sudan in 1884 to which General Gordon had been unsuccessfully dispatched.[15] But an ongoing jihad in Somaliland was of great concern also, as had been an earlier rising along the North-West Frontier of India. Once the railway opened in 1908, British suspicions would be exacerbated by the appointment of a number of German nationals to various levels of its operations, including as consecutive directors-general between the years 1910 and 1917.[16] All told, the British feared that the railway was a means by which to solidify an Ottoman-German imperial axis in the Middle East.

In the last years before the outbreak of general European war in the summer of 1914, these imperial rivalries and challenges would be put into even sharper relief. The Ottoman Empire continued to decline in the face of internal revolts such as what occurred during the First Balkan War of 1912–13 and which resulted in the loss of virtually all of its remaining territory in Europe. For Britain, meanwhile, to the longstanding importance of the Suez Canal as the so-called 'spine' of empire was added the recent discovery of oil in nearby Iran.[17] Shortly before the beginning of the war the Royal Navy had switched from using coal to oil to power its fleet, and thus had become highly dependent on liquid 'black gold' to keep it fully operational as the primary sword-arm of trade and empire. To this end, Winston Churchill, as first lord of the Admiralty, had moved decisively in June of 1914 to purchase for the British government a controlling stake in the Anglo-Persian Oil Company to guarantee security of supply for the navy in the future.[18] The modern Western-directed oil industry was rising fast and the Middle East's central place in it was in the process of being made abundantly clear. For Britain, this new geostrategic reality added yet another important dimension to its broad-based regional interest. Accordingly, there was little doubt in London that the looming war in which the Ottoman Empire would very likely come to support the Central Powers of Germany and Austria-Hungary meant that the potential for a cardinal geopolitical reconfiguration of the Middle East was at hand. And the British, it may be argued, were better prepared for this sort of fundamental change than any other great state in Europe.[19]

Only a few years before Allenby and Faisal's fateful meeting in 1918 in Damascus, the groundwork for the circumstances that would make such a meeting possible had been put in place by the British high commissioner for Egypt, Sir Henry McMahon. A lifelong British diplomat and servant of empire, in 1915 McMahon had been sent to Cairo as successor to Lord Kitchener, whose brief three-year tenure as high commissioner in Egypt had come to an abrupt end upon his hurried appointment as British secretary of state for war in August of 1914.[20] Although McMahon was understood to be an experienced and cautious imperial hand, one might well have questioned the latter attribute once he decided to open up a potentially provocative correspondence with Sharif Hussein. The ageing Hashemite dynast ruled over western Arabia's Hejaz region, containing within it both Mecca and Medina. Meanwhile, the vast majority of the rest of territorial Arabia fell under the competing dynasties of the House of Saud and the House of Rashid.

It may well be that the British high commissioner in Cairo had acted provocatively in replying in August of 1915 to the sharif's introductory letter sent to him a few weeks earlier. But if so, it was only because the way forward in this regard had been charted by Kitchener's earlier interview of one of Hussein's sons, Prince Abdullah, in Cairo in February of 1914. In that brief but important meeting Kitchener had attempted to gauge the Arabs' willingness to support the British against the Ottomans should war come to pass in the region in the near future. Indeed, later, in March of 1915, Kitchener would inform his fellow members of the War Council in London that 'should the partition of Turkey take place ... it is to our interests to see an Arab Kingdom established in Arabia under the auspices of England ... containing within it the chief Mohammedan Holy Places, Mecca, Medina and Kerbala'.[21] Pre-war tensions in the Hejaz between the Arabs and the Ottomans had been on the rise for years, a situation exacerbated by the building of the Hejaz Railway. To the Bedouin Arabs who lived in much of the territory traversed by the railway its construction had portended a tightening of Ottoman control over the Hejaz, an especially unwelcome development in the eyes of Hussein and the Hashemite royal family itself. Making the prevailing situation even less appealing to Hussein was the menacing presence of a 10,000-man Ottoman garrison at Medina. Indeed, by this point in 1915 the sharif and his four sons had agreed already amongst themselves that an Arab revolt against Ottoman imperial rule in the Hejaz was the correct course of action to take. And it could begin, they had surmised, as early as June of 1916.[22] To all of these real and potential developments in the Hejaz the British Foreign

Office, under its assiduous and long-time secretary Sir Edward Grey, would give its ready assent.

A couple of months after Kitchener had made plain his aspirations for the rise of a British-influenced Hejazi Arab state in the post-Ottoman Middle East, in May of 1915, during a visit to Damascus, Prince Faisal was given by the representatives of two key Arab nationalist secret societies – al-Fatat and al-Ahd – the document that became known as the 'Damascus Protocol', and which would serve as a pretext for his father Hussein's initiation of the protracted correspondence with McMahon.[23] In the protocol, the conditions required by the nationalists for Arab support of the Allies in their war against the Ottomans – a war which by then was well underway – were spelled out. Once accepted, this document would seal the Hashemite royal family's decision to raise a revolt in the future against their Ottoman overlords.

A few months later, on 14 July 1915, Hussein's initial letter would land on the high commissioner's desk in the British Residency overlooking the Nile in the centre of Cairo. The highly charged correspondence between them would run until March of the following year and number ten letters in total, five from each man. These letters formed the core of the way in which the British as well as the Allies more generally would react to the sharif's decision to pit his Hashemite Arab kingdom against the considerable modern might of the tens of thousands of Ottoman troops deployed across Arabia, Syria and Palestine. The letters did not constitute a formal treaty or a binding agreement between the British and the Hashemites. But their contents did show a clear willingness by McMahon to take (Hashemite) Arab nationalist aspirations seriously. Moreover, they acknowledged that potential Allied battlefield success would be linked to support for the post-war creation of an independent Arab state.[24] In the letters Hussein showed himself to be ready and willing to sacrifice his own men and money in a bid to win independence from Ottoman control. His position aligned well with the British ambition to topple the

Ottoman Empire altogether, which would have the effect of sundering its regional control and damaging severely the war-making capacity of the German-led Triple Alliance.

For some eight months the McMahon–Hussein correspondence went back and forth between Mecca and Cairo until concluding on 10 March 1916. On that date the high commissioner delivered his final letter to the sharif, in which he agreed to the various requests for British help that had been made – including the provision of a stockpile of weapons and the payment of £50,000 in gold sovereigns – and acknowledged that the Arab Revolt would begin a short time later in June.[25] And begin it did, the first shot fired by Hussein himself from his palace window in Mecca at dawn on the tenth day of the month.[26] That single shot, which split the antebellum quiet of an early morning in Islam's holiest city, would set off more than two years of fierce desert warfare between the Arabs and the Ottomans.

Over 100 years on, the resultant Arab Revolt continues to fascinate. The leading figure in this conflict is T.E. Lawrence, or 'Lawrence of Arabia' as he would be called at war's end, by when the story of his charismatic leadership of the Bedouin during the revolt had turned him into a global celebrity. Born in Wales in 1888 during a peripatetic period in the life of his unconventional family, by the age of eight Lawrence lived with his parents and three brothers (a fifth and final brother would be born in 1900) in a large house in the leafy precinct of north Oxford. Number 2, Polstead Road, the Lawrence family home, would be the focal point for many years to come in the life of the intellectual and retiring 'Ned', as Lawrence was called in his youth. Indeed, his parents, Thomas and Sarah, would provide him with a small study at the base of their home's back garden so that he could enjoy the privacy and solitude he craved as a sensitive and bookish adolescent. Within a fully kitted-out retreat equipped with electricity, a telephone link to the main house and a fireplace, the teenaged Lawrence would read voraciously and, later, as an undergraduate, write extensively.

Lawrence's student writing would culminate in a thesis, the capstone of the three years that he spent reading for a degree in modern history at Jesus College, Oxford. His undergraduate thesis had come about as the result of a growing interest in the history of the medieval Crusades. His abiding interest in the field would yield a couple of long summer vacations spent touring first through France by bicycle and then later on foot in Syria. In both places Lawrence investigated and sketched the Western architectural heritage of the Crusader castles that had been constructed mainly during the twelfth century. Indeed, so engaged was Lawrence by this work that during the summer of 1909 he would walk solo from the top of Syria to the bottom, covering altogether about 1,000 miles in the process. During this meandering walk he recorded his findings meticulously, learned to speak Arabic, and began to nurture a passion for the people, society and culture of the Middle East that would come to dominate the rest of his life.

In 1910, the year that Lawrence was awarded a first-class degree at Oxford, the keeper of the university's Ashmolean Museum, D.G. Hogarth, offered him a job working as an archaeologist in Syria. The location was to be at Carchemish, a 3,000-year-old Hittite site rich in both significance and artifacts. Lawrence leapt at the opportunity to join the dig. Indeed, a return to the Middle East is just what he had desired above all else during the first months after graduating from Oxford, even if it meant turning down the offer of a postgraduate scholarship. Before departing for Syria, Lawrence spent part of that summer in camp with the Oxford University Officers' Training Corps and then once again in cycling through France. Finally, in November Hogarth confirmed Lawrence's appointment as an archaeological assistant and he was off. Initially he went to Lebanon, where he stayed for two months to work on his Arabic. In February of 1911 Lawrence then moved on to the ancient city of Jerablus in northern Syria. The Carchemish site that would be his professional home for the next three years and 'the best life I ever lived', as he called this period later, was located next to Jerablus.[27]

The Carchemish dig occupied a large site on the west bank of the Euphrates River very close to the border with Ottoman Turkey. In addition to the Hejaz Railway, the Ottomans had also constructed the Berlin–Baghdad railway line, which ran right alongside Carchemish.[28] Begun under German supervision in 1903, this line would remain unfinished until completed by others many years later in 1940. But during the period of Lawrence's three-year residency at Carchemish the line would become increasingly controversial in the context of regional imperial rivalries, which the discovery of oil in Iran and the high probability of its existence also in Mesopotamia would do much to intensify. Meanwhile, the recently fully operational Hejaz Railway had become an arrow pointed at the heart of Arabia, and as such clear evidence of the power and reach into Arab lands of continuing Ottoman suzerainty. Little did Lawrence know in 1911 upon his arrival in northern Syria that six years hence he would begin to plot how best to blow up and generally disable the Hejaz Railway in the service of the Arab Revolt.

The years that came between these events would see Lawrence develop first as an accomplished archaeologist, and second as an even more able British intelligence operative and leader of Arab irregular forces in the field.[29] Lawrence's first months at Carchemish saw him create a circle of friends, many of them local Arabs, establish a work and social routine, and from time to time be introduced to passing notables. One such person was forty-three-year-old Gertrude Bell, who by that time had become a well-known desert traveller. Her capacity for long-range expeditions together with a remarkable linguistic facility, a keen eye for photography, and an evocative writing style, had made her the most famous European woman in the Middle East. Like Lawrence, Bell was an Oxford graduate in modern history, and from their first meeting in May of 1911 – 'he [Lawrence] is an interesting boy', she wrote home, 'he is going to make a traveller' – they would be linked together permanently as part of the wartime British political and military vanguard in the region.[30]

Until the summer of 1914 Lawrence's life continued to revolve completely around the Hittite dig at Carchemish. During this period, he would also make occasional trips home to Oxford as well as travelling locally and into neighbouring Lebanon. Meanwhile, the weakening Ottoman Empire continued to fray at the seams. Just a few years earlier in 1908, for example, the Young Turk Revolution had forced Sultan Abdulhamid to restore the Ottoman Constitution of 1876 and transfer more power to the Chamber of Deputies. For some radical nationalists however, such as the Young Turks who were in favour of constitutional reforms, these concessions had come too late and were of unsatisfactory scope. Consequently, in April of the next year, the Sultan would be deposed by force. In the aftermath, political instability grew in the Ottoman capital of Constantinople as well as throughout the empire.[31] Lawrence too was caught up in the pre-war turmoil, writing to a friend, for example, 'down with the Turks. But I am afraid', he commented knowingly, 'there is not life, but stickiness in them yet'. In particular, he hoped that independence might come to the subject Arabs should the Ottoman Empire be brought down from within.[32]

Beginning in 1914, Lawrence's increasing expertise in understanding the region along with his advanced language skills would be made use of by the British War Office. In January of that year, for example, he commenced a special map-making expedition under the auspices of the London-based Palestine Exploration Fund (PEF). Together with a close colleague of his from Carchemish, Leonard Woolley, as well as Captain Stewart Newcombe, a member of the Royal Engineers who would figure prominently in the Arab Revolt to come, they traversed the rugged Sinai Peninsula. They did so under the guise of being wandering archaeologists. In truth, however, they were operating as British spies and gaining a detailed geographical knowledge of the area, including that of the forbidding Negev Desert. Acting at the behest of Lord Kitchener as secretary of state for war, their survey had been undertaken in anticipation of what the impending European conflict might mean for Great Power politics in the Near and Middle East. Get it done 'p-d-q [pretty damn quick] as whitewash' is the way Lawrence described his map-making task, in a style typical of the man.[33] The survey would be published later by the PEF as *The Wilderness of Zin*. Its completion in the autumn of 1914 acted as a suitable moment to mark Lawrence's entry into the kind of life which was going to be his now that the war was underway. The halcyon days of the Carchemish dig thus came to an end, and with their passing Lawrence's life was about to be given over to the dangers and vicissitudes of the Great War and the resulting Arab Revolt.

Years later, in *Seven Pillars of Wisdom*, Lawrence would write of having dreamed early on of 'hustling into action' a new Asia, specifically in the form of an Arab uprising against their Ottoman overlords.[34] By December of 1914, such 'hustling' might be said to have begun in a nascent way already: in that month Lawrence was sent to Cairo by the War Office as a junior intelligence officer. As of late October the Ottoman Empire had entered the war formally on the side of the Central Powers. The stage was set, therefore, for a decisive conflict in the Middle East, the outcome of which – as anticipated keenly by Lawrence – would spell the end of 400 years of Ottoman imperial power across the region.

For Lawrence however, until well into 1915, his desk-bound intelligence post in Cairo would leave him 'BORED', as he would write home despondently in June of that year.[35] Still, he was good at his job, especially editing the *Arab Bulletin*, a key British intelligence organ. But as time wore on the prospect of any sort of effective Arab rising appeared to him to be distressingly remote. This inert state of affairs he blamed on the five men of the Hashemite royal family in the Hejaz who were not yet completely united over whether sponsoring a revolt was the right way forward for the Arabs in the context of the expanding European war. During that first full year of the conflict however, the inchoate nature of a prospective rising had

begun to congeal for the Hejazi Arabs, spurred by the correspondence undertaken by Sir Henry McMahon and Sharif Hussein.

Towards the end of 1916, however, and then in the middle of the
following year, two important events would take place that altered
the trajectory of the war in the Middle East. The first of these was the
sending of Lawrence, along with a small party of British intelligence
officers, from Cairo to Arabia in October of 1916. They would go
there to interview the elder three of Hussein's four sons (the youngest
was only in his teens) to determine under which of them a much
more effective Arab military campaign might be waged against the
Ottomans. Lawrence himself said that he was looking for the one son
who had 'the necessary fire' for such a task, as he described it in a
letter home.[36] This special mission to Jeddah in the Hejaz would
introduce Lawrence to Prince Ali, Hussein's eldest son, Prince
Abdullah, who came next in line, and finally to Prince Faisal himself.
Disappointingly, Lawrence found both elder sons, especially Abdullah,
to be unimpressive as potential military leaders. However, this feeling
was manifestly not mutual, at least as far as Abdullah was concerned.
Upon meeting Lawrence, he was impressed by his erudite display of
local knowledge, not believing that any non-Arab could know as
much as did he about tribal relations and the region's trackless desert
geography. Moreover, Lawrence seemed to be highly informed about
Ottoman troop movements in the Hejaz. Equally impressive was that
Lawrence had conveyed all of this local knowledge to Abdullah in
fluent, even colloquial, Arabic. 'Is this man God', the Hashemite
prince is reported to have exclaimed in disbelief during his meeting
with Lawrence, 'to know everything?'[37]

Notwithstanding Abdullah's fulsome praise, Lawrence would
leave their meeting at Jeddah unsatisfied in his quest. Consequently,
he moved on to interview the third of King Hussein's eligible sons,
Prince Faisal. After riding hard on camelback for 100 miles inland
from Jeddah, Lawrence arrived at Faisal's remote desert encampment

in late October. Upon his arrival, however, Lawrence's rough journey was proved worth making. 'This was the man I had come to Arabia to seek', he would write later in *Seven Pillars*. As far as Lawrence was concerned, if Faisal took clear charge of the Bedouin of the Hejaz the Arab Revolt had a real chance at success. He would do so, and during 1917 the slow-to-develop uprising against the Ottomans began to coalesce, with both Faisal and Lawrence at its heart.[38]

As a consequence, over the first half of that year the nascent Arab Revolt became less of a nationalist dream and more of a battlefield reality. One of the main reasons for the revolt's increased effectiveness was Faisal's ability as a leader to recruit and then to hold his men long enough in the field to make progress against the Ottomans. Commanding an army comprised essentially of irregular troops was not an easy task, but as the revolt slowly gained ground in the spring of 1917 – owing especially to successful attacks on the Hejaz railway – the prospects for its success brightened. To the British official mind, the Bedouin had much potential as warriors. They are 'wonderfully good and silent', Pierce Joyce emphasized in a report, 'at getting into position for dawn attacks'.[39]

The second momentous event that changed the course of the Arab Revolt in its early stages was the arrival in theatre in mid-1917 of General Allenby as the new commander-in-chief of the Egyptian Expeditionary Force (EEF). Lately transferred from the enervating atmosphere of the Western Front, and determined to succeed, Allenby would be rejuvenated immediately by his new command. Not least in this regard was the impact on him of his initial meeting with Lawrence, a revealing encounter between two men of vastly different experiences and of clearly diverse temperaments drawn together nonetheless through the exigencies of war. Indeed, not long before meeting Lawrence, Allenby had arrived in Cairo as successor to the ineffective General Archibald Murray. As a career cavalryman Allenby had been ground down especially by the relentless inertia and enormous losses of the Western Front. His relocation to the vitality of Cairo followed by the open spaces of the Palestine and Syria campaigns to come would give him a fresh start. In June, at his send-off in London, Allenby had been given an emotional charge by the prime minister David Lloyd George to deliver Jerusalem as a Christmas gift to the nation. The British people were starved for a clear battlefield victory, he was told. It was up to Allenby therefore to deliver one, and he was determined to fulfil the task.

Accordingly, Allenby could not have been greeted by better news than that which was brought to him in Cairo by an exhausted Lawrence himself on 12 July 1917. Immediately upon completing a hurried two-day trek across the desert, and still attired in his distinctive Arab dress, Lawrence arrived at the new commander-in-chief's headquarters as the bearer of good news. He was there, he said, to report on a stunning Arab victory over the Ottomans that had occurred just a few days earlier at the strategically important Red Sea port of Aqaba. Moreover, Lawrence himself had conceived the plan of attack. He had then proceeded to lead the successful assault on Aqaba at the head of a collection of Arab irregulars, the most prominent of whom was the fierce Howeitat chieftain, Auda Abu Tayeh. Now, drained physically but elated emotionally – and looking nothing like a British officer might be expected to appear – the physically unimpressive 5′ 5″ Lawrence stood before the commanding 6′ 2″ Allenby and recounted his tale of an unlikely Arab triumph of two days earlier.

Allenby, known as the 'Bull', and taciturn at the best of times, was even more reserved than usual that day as the oddly dressed Lawrence began to recite to him the events of the preceding week. The Arab defeat of the Ottoman garrison at Aqaba had been total, its defenders having been chased almost literally into the sea. The only account of their seminal meeting on that July day at British headquarters is from Lawrence's *Seven Pillars of Wisdom*. But it is hard to imagine how it might have been improved upon – or Lawrence's gift for descriptive prose exceeded – by anyone else. To the 'large and confident' Allenby my 'littleness came slow to him', it begins. Nor, given the way that Lawrence was dressed, could the general 'make out how much was genuine performer and how much was charlatan'. Still, there was no doubting that a singular victory had been won, and, regardless of Lawrence's evident unorthodoxy of dress, more of the same might be expected if the British were to offer their unreserved assistance to the Arabs in the field. Allenby concurred, and his readily offered support would end the meeting, a promise, Lawrence wrote, that was more than 'enough for his very greediest servant'. As Allenby had told him, 'I will do for you what I can', and with that assurance Lawrence would go directly back to Arabia to continue the fight.[40] 'Lawrence's activities among the Arabs', as Allenby informed the chief of the Imperial General Staff in London, William Robertson, 'promise great things'.[41] And so they did.

Meanwhile, Allenby's own campaign that autumn would take him directly across to Palestine. After General Murray's two earlier failures, a victory at Gaza was to be had at last and then another at Beersheba before Allenby turned northwards and began to march across the rugged Judean Hills to Jerusalem. As winter in the Holy Land approached the campaign would become a tough and tenacious slog for his Allied troops against an Ottoman enemy that was determined to hold out against them for as long as possible.[42] 'The rocky and mountainous country they fought over is indescribable', Allenby wrote wearily to his wife.[43] Still, by early December it was clear that Jerusalem was indeed going to be won by the Allies in time for Christmas. A last stand for the Holy City was made by the Ottomans, but on the ninth day of the month they were finally dislodged and sent fleeing north-eastwards in a rapid retreat into neighbouring Syria.[44] Formal Allied occupation of Jerusalem would come two days later on 11 December when Allenby strode purposefully through the Old City's Jaffa Gate. Standing at the Citadel beneath the ancient Tower of David, he read out a proclamation guaranteeing civil and religious freedom to all of the city's residents for as long as it lay under British occupation.[45]

First Gaza, then Beersheba, now Jerusalem: the military domi-
noes had fallen fast and hard for Allenby in the hot pace he had set
in 1917 against the Ottomans to secure Palestine and Syria for
Britain and the Allies. Meanwhile, on his right flank, having rolled
up from Arabia through southern Palestine and into Syria, was
Faisal's resurgent Northern Arab Army. Under his inspirational leadership and with Lawrence playing an imaginative and decisive role
in guerilla operations that would disrupt and damage the ability
of the Ottomans to operate effectively – especially via the Hejaz
Railway – the Allies were poised now for imminent victory. 'It is all
such sport', Lawrence was known to say to his fellow officers. But to
the Bedouin, according to Pierce Joyce, Lawrence very soon became
'a byeword [sic] in the desert' owing to his 'individual bravery and
endurance'.[46] Throughout the winter and spring of 1918 this powerful
and determined combined force of Allies and Arabs would continue
to push back the Ottomans, who nevertheless fought desperately
under the command of their resilient and canny German general,
Otto Liman von Sanders. Steadily however, they were forced to
retreat north as well as east across the Jordan River to the city of
Amman and then well beyond.

The decisive victory in this latter stage of the Palestine campaign
would come in September at historic Megiddo – known for its designation as the Bible's apocalyptic site of 'Armageddon' – which cleared
the way for a final Allied move against Damascus, achieved not many
days later at the beginning of October. For Allenby and the EEF the
campaign would prove to be a ringing success. To the winning of
serial victories with comparatively light Allied casualties was added
the surrender of some 75,000 Ottoman soldiers, almost the full
number of troops that Liman had at his disposal.[47] Indeed, by the end
of October all that was left of the Ottoman Army was a small remnant
of men who had fallen back on the northern Syrian city of Aleppo.
Defeated subsequently there too by Allenby, the Ottomans made a
last desperate stand at nearby Mouslimmiye under the command of

their charismatic hero of Gallipoli, Mustafa Kemal (later to be known as Ataturk). Following their defeat the Ottomans would make a complete surrender according to the terms of the Armistice of Mudros, which was signed on 30 October.[48] Accordingly, after almost half a millennium of rule over the lands of the Middle East, the Ottoman Empire ceased to exist. The terms governing its epic demise would now be consigned to the diplomatic deliberations to come at the post-war Paris Peace Conference.

In the aftermath of the successful Arab Revolt and the comprehensive Allied victory over the Ottoman Empire in the Middle East, Britain and France would be left, however, with a geopolitical situation scarcely less complicated than what they had encountered in the region prior to the war. In 1916, in anticipation of an eventual Allied victory in the Middle East, the two countries had negotiated an unofficial agreement between them which had taken the combined surnames of its chief negotiators, Sir Mark Sykes and François Georges-Picot. Indeed, although the Sykes–Picot Agreement had been ratified just a few weeks prior to the start of the Arab Revolt, its negotiation and ratification had been carried out in secret. Very few people, therefore, knew about the scope of its provisions, least of all the leading Hashemite royals, Hussein and Faisal. Its provisions would privilege Anglo-French interests in the Middle East over the granting of Arab independence after the war.

The progenitor of the Sykes–Picot Agreement was a thirty-six-year-old titled aristocrat from Yorkshire. Sir Mark Sykes, 6th baronet, was rich, much-travelled in the Middle East and strongly opinionated, although to some observers – both during the 1910s and afterwards – he amounted nonetheless to little more than a self-serving opportunist. Such was certainly the view of Lawrence, who later wrote scornfully that Sykes had been nothing but 'a bundle of prejudices, intuitions, [and] half-sciences'. Still, in 1915–16 all three of these attributes were highly persuasive in the febrile atmosphere of the wartime Middle East.[49] Initially brought into government service by Kitchener to act as his personal adviser on Arab affairs, Sykes had quickly become the moving spirit behind Britain's determination to be a decisive presence in shaping what it was assumed would be a post-war Middle East freed from Ottoman rule. Initiated by the Asquith government's creation of a parliamentary committee chaired by Sir Maurice de Bunsen of the Foreign Office, by late 1915 a grand diplomatic plan had begun to gain traction in London and Paris to divide Ottoman-controlled Mesopotamia and Syria between Britain and France once the Ottomans had been ousted.[50] The irrepressible Sykes was in the vanguard of this plan, which he had begun to construct in minute detail along with his French diplomatic counterpart, Georges-Picot. Together, at a series of meetings held mostly at the French Embassy in London, they had worked out the parameters of what such a redrawn regional map might look like. A grid which contained a red (British) 'A' Zone and a blue (French) 'B' Zone was the result, a territorial division that placed Mesopotamia and what would become Transjordan under British control, with Syria going to France. In essence, Sykes–Picot was a pointed exercise in Anglo-French geopolitics without regard for local autonomy. But neither was Sykes–Picot created with the idea of Great Power mandatory supervision in mind, something that would come to pass only with the convening of the Paris Peace Conference. The future of Palestine, however, could not be agreed upon by Sykes and Georges-Picot, nor could clarity of thinking be found over that of Lebanon, although it was assumed that it would fall to France. But the essential plan was agreed nonetheless, and on 3 January 1916 Sykes and Georges-Picot shook hands on the deal.[51]

Soon one more state was to be added to the Sykes–Picot Agreement in the form of late-imperial Russia. By 1916, the 300-year-old Romanov dynasty had begun to totter under the weak leadership of Tsar Nicholas II in advance of its crumbling altogether in the successive revolutions of 1917. For now, however, Britain and the Allies were desperate to keep the ailing Russian bear in the fight against the Central Powers and this strategy included making the Russians party to the Sykes–Picot Agreement.[52] The intricate diplomacy required to do so was completed in May. The potential territorial delimitation represented by Sykes–Picot, however, had not been made according to what McMahon had effectively promised to Hussein in their recently concluded exchange of letters. Nor had it anticipated the Mandate System created at Paris. Rather, McMahon had endorsed an undefined Arab independence to come. And therein lay the rub. Promises made – or not made – to the Arabs would become a persistently thorny issue for Britain and France over the next five years. In particular, McMahon's promise of Arab independence as understood by Hussein would be described later as having been mere 'lip service'. Still, there is little doubt that the tripartite Sykes–Picot Agreement's chief motivation was to secure British, French and – to a lesser extent – Russian geopolitical interests in the region once the Ottoman Empire had been defeated. This calculation was made with little regard as to the place occupied within it by the Arabs.

Meanwhile, for the British, a secondary issue was also at hand. But it was one of increasing urgency. The longstanding demand of Zionists – made by the head of the London-based Zionist Organization, Chaim Weizmann – for a Jewish national homeland to be created in Palestine was reaching its climax.[53] British diplomatic representation in Palestine stretched all the way back to 1838, when a consulate had been established at the urging of the Anglican evangelical social reformer Lord Shaftesbury.[54] Indeed, throughout the last years of the nineteenth century, and into the early years of the twentieth, culminating in the First World War, international Zionism had become a political lobby of first-order importance in Britain. In December of 1916, after over eight years in office, Herbert Asquith had succumbed to the intense political pressures of a catastrophically costly war, as well as to the accompanying Fleet Street machinations, and resigned from office. Into the resultant breach at 10 Downing Street stepped the charismatic and canny figure of David Lloyd George. And in the person of the new prime minister Zionism had found a determined political champion. Raised in the chapel-based Baptist evangelical Christianity of his native Wales, Lloyd George was accepting of the imminent end-times view of Zionism held by a great many millenarian Christians. They understood the return of diasporic Jews to Palestine to be a harbinger of the apocalyptic second coming of Christ.[55] This firm belief, however, sat uncomfortably beside the protracted persistence Weizmann had maintained of eschewing any British territorial offer other than Palestine (such had included Uganda or Saskatchewan) for a Zionist homeland. The Zionist demand would open up yet another avenue for British influence to be exercised in the Middle East beyond its putative alliance with the Hejazi Arabs.

The year 1917 proved to be a watershed for Britain's public commit-ment to international Zionism. Weizmann's protracted championing of the Zionist cause led him to undertake a journey of political advo-cacy during which he held a series of interviews with important British policymakers. He met with the former home secretary Sir Herbert Samuel, the future high commissioner for Palestine. Samuel was both Jewish and a strong Zionist. Sykes, the subject of a subsequent inter-view, was easily convinced of the geopolitical advantage to Britain of helping to establish a Jewish homeland in Palestine. The zoologist and politician Lord Rothschild became another key ally. Decisively, Arthur Balfour, even though years removed from his brief premiership, continued to hold high office as foreign secretary, and was a long-time acquaintance of Weizmann's. Altogether, the many years of having pressed the Zionist cause would pay off for Weizmann. His dream was about to become a reality. On 2 November 1917 Balfour sent a letter – henceforward called the 'Balfour Declaration' – to Rothschild in which he made it clear that the British government would support the creation of 'a national home for the Jewish people' in Palestine.[56] The letter was careful to state 'that nothing shall be done which may preju-dice the civil and religious rights of existing non-Jewish communities in Palestine'. But its promulgation was evidence nonetheless that the British government had staked a claim to post-Ottoman Palestine, as well as to the necessary presence within it of a Jewish homeland. For their part the French simply would have to be made to accept that Palestine was a special British case. To the Arabs, however – and to their key supporters amongst the British, most notably Lawrence – the Balfour Declaration would be an infinitely more challenging commitment to square against the angular geopolitical and sociological reality of the post-war Middle East.

Indeed, once news reached Lawrence of the Balfour Declaration he regarded it as evidence of a further betrayal of the Arab cause. If the Sykes–Picot Agreement had offered a blueprint for the achievement of Anglo-French paramountcy in the Middle East – and concomitant Arab subordination – then to Lawrence the Balfour Declaration was a regrettable addition. Altogether, both policies would cause 'great strain' to the Anglo-Arab alliance, as well as to Lawrence's own mind, as his authorized biographer Jeremy Wilson later put it, rather too mildly. Because Lawrence during this period of time remained fighting in the field and was thus far from the halls of political power, there was little that he could do about his situation other than to carry on with completing the campaign in the desert. His abiding hope was that an ultimate Allied victory over the Ottomans would lead to a fair result for the fighting Arabs, on whose behalf he was daily risking his life.

Allenby's victory in the Middle East – his 'great exploit', as King George called it in a breathless telegram sent to him in September of 1918 – would be celebrated by Britain and its Allies.[57] The triumph over the Ottomans brought him a peerage as 1st Viscount Allenby of Megiddo and Felixstowe, as well as sustained personal popularity. To be sure, in both territorial and symbolic terms, Allenby's victory had been complete. But geopolitically the victory had been disjointed in what it had delivered to its various combatants. If expectations for the post-Ottoman Middle East were high among the Arabs, they were scarcely less lofty, if differently conceived, in London and Paris. The Allied wartime diplomacy that had delivered the McMahon–Hussein correspondence, the Sykes–Picot Agreement, and the Balfour Declaration would now be forced by the victories of the preceding year to yield a new and potentially comprehensive settlement across the broad and varied territory of the Middle East. The Ottoman Empire was gone but a large and unruly diplomatic lacuna existed in its place. Of this state of affairs Lawrence in particular had been left in no doubt. From Cairo on 14 October 1918, on his way home to London following his precipitous departure from Damascus, he would sum up in a letter his time spent fighting in the desert. Written to Major R.H. Scott, the base commandant at Aqaba, in it Lawrence adopted a nostalgic air. His Arab Bureau and British military colleagues were, he wrote, 'an odd little set and we have, I expect, changed History in the near East. I wonder how the Powers will let the Arabs get on'.[58] As Lawrence would very soon find out, at precisely the same time a great number of other people were asking exactly the same question.

2

'WHAT A DIFFICULT WORLD THE WAR HAS BEQUEATHED TO US!'
MIDDLE EAST DIPLOMACY AFTER 1918

The Allenby-led victory over the Ottomans and their German allies in Palestine and Syria in October 1918 had been overwhelming. Against expectations, the Ottoman Empire had been removed as suzerain of a vast domain over which it had ruled for centuries. Indeed, in an era replete with world-historical events, the fall of the Ottomans in the Middle East would prove to be one of the most important and longstanding outcomes of the Great War. In the centuries-long history of foreign empires dominating the dusty plains and serrated hills of Palestine, for example, most had chosen to adopt divide-and-rule policies in order to effect control. The most recent example of this approach had been the Ottomans' own *Vilayet* system of provincial administration, used in Palestine and throughout Ottoman territories in the Middle East. Dating from the mid-nineteenth-century era of Tanzimat reforms, which emerged during a concerted era of attempted Islamic modernization epitomized by the work of the Egyptian-born jurist Muhammad Abduh, the *Vilayet* system was rejected by British as inherently parochial. They attempted to replace it with the creation of a group of new states whose future was understood to include the eventual achievement of genuine Western-style national independence.

While aware of the sweeping nature of what had been accomplished under his command, Allenby would find little time to ruminate upon its long-term implications. The speed of contemporary events was such that it forced him to follow up the fighting with a series of immediate diplomatic actions. As he wrote to Clive Wigram, King George's assistant private secretary, on 5 October, 'things look very different now to what they did 6 months ago; both here and in Europe'. Symbolically, Allenby's signing of the Armistice of Mudros with the Ottomans at the end of October had come exactly one year to the day after his triumph over them at Beersheba, which had put the whole Egyptian Expeditionary Force on the road to victory in Jerusalem. The armistice would serve also as a prelude to an intense preoccupation with what the victorious campaign portended for the future of geopolitics throughout the Middle East.

Though intensely satisfying initially for the Arabs, the prevailing geopolitical situation in the newly conquered Middle East was to prove highly complicated for the Allies. Faisal felt that the Arabs should be allowed by right of conquest to remain in control of Syria. The British and the French, however, had bound themselves to the Sykes–Picot Agreement and therefore everything that would transpire subsequent to the conquest of Syria was viewed through its geopolitical lens. On the ground and in the moment it was up to Allenby to act both as military commander and civil administrator in Syria, and to do so with due regard to Faisal's claims and sensitivities. As Allenby informed the War Office on 6 October from Damascus: 'an Arab administration was in being and the Arab flag was flying from Government buildings'.

During these early postbellum days in Syria the political situation remained relatively calm. But the complicated political reality, both European and Arab, militated against Faisal achieving all that he wished to, and, critically, all that to which he believed his people were entitled. Earlier, during their testy meeting at the Hotel Victoria on 3 October, Allenby had informed Faisal of the formal recognition that the British government had granted to the Arab forces fighting in Palestine and Syria.[1] Such recognition meant a reserved place for the Arabs during the peace negotiations to come in Paris. Certainly, as Allenby told Faisal on more than one occasion, the making of the peace was the time during which the Arab position would be clarified. He recognized that Faisal was 'nervous about the peace settlement', as he wrote to his wife. 'But I tell him he must trust the Entente powers to treat him fairly'. Still, Allenby never laboured under the illusion that Faisal and the Arabs would achieve *all* that they thought was their due. Indeed, while pleased that at Damascus an Arab 'civil government is making progress', as he informed his wife, 'there are many conflicting political interests, which to some extent keep back our reorganization'. A little while later, on 23 October, Allenby maintained in a report to General Sir Henry Wilson, the new chief of the Imperial General Staff in London, that 'the Arab Government is getting to work satisfactorily'.[2] But shortly thereafter he followed up this report with a message confirming the creation of the new European-supervised Occupied Enemy Territories Administration (OETA), which at a stroke undercut the Arab administrative position. Altogether, therefore, the political situation in the newly conquered Arab lands would remain fluid and unresolved.

The OETA – subdivided into three administrative sub-units, North, South and East – would prove to be an exercise in indirect rule. This form of colonial governance had become the accepted British standard. Accordingly, as Allenby explained to the War Office, 'as far as possible the Turkish system of government will be continued and the existing machinery utilized'. Demonstrative of imperial collaboration, indirect rule's usefulness as an interim measure in the Middle East was one that came naturally to Allenby. Consequently, the former Turkish administrative areas and their records were to be used to smooth the way forward for the new European supervisory regime. It was a regime that needed to operate apolitically, however, as Allenby emphasized, if it were to be successful. Accordingly, all officials tasked with running the OETA were prohibited from engaging in 'any political propaganda'. Nor, he added, were they to 'take part in any political questions'.[3]

The OETA's boundaries were exclusive of Mesopotamia and the Hejaz but otherwise they corresponded closely to the provisions of the Sykes–Picot Agreement, meaning that OETA North was to be French-run and that OETA South would be administered by the British. OETA East was centred on Damascus and therefore intersected with Faisal's new Arab administration, at least for the time being. There was little doubt in Allenby's mind that the provisions of the OETA were meant to be temporary. Still, the mere existence of the OETA carried with it the prospect of inertia and at least semi-permanence. In this situation, and like his fellow British colleagues, Allenby distrusted the French implicitly but without ever saying so in public. Allenby could see plainly Faisal's similar distrust of the French in Syria; they meant, said the Arab leader prophetically, 'to get hold of the country'.

While Allenby was required to maintain a scrupulous fairness in his public utterances about the new provisional political arrangements, in private he wrote and spoke forthrightly about the prevailing situation, especially as it concerned France. Allenby regarded the co-author of the Sykes–Picot Agreement, François Georges-Picot, who was under consideration to become the French governor of OETA North, as being nothing more than 'a superficially clever man, but shallow & transparent. I know him well, & he knows me', he wrote to General Wilson on 9 November. As Allenby saw it, the overriding problem with Georges-Picot and the French was that if they were allowed to achieve all that they wished to in the Levant there would likely be 'sudden trouble'. In an especially transparent message to Wilson, Allenby described at length his view as to the prevailing post-war situation in the Middle East. 'The future', he forecast, 'when martial law no longer prevails, is not so cloudless. Distrust of the French is not, in any way, abated'. Conversely, at this early stage Arab faith in the British remained strong, Allenby believed, because of their mainly trustful wartime relationship with Faisal. Without this faith however, 'there would be blood, fire & ruin throughout all Arabia ... If we act up to our declared principles regarding the rights of self-determination of peoples, we shall retain that confidence. If not, there will be chaos'.

On 11 November 1918, just two days after Allenby wrote these words to Wilson, the Allies and the Germans brokered a general armistice signalling the end of the First World War. After more than four years of almost incalculable death, destruction and dislocation, all appeared to be over at last. 'That closes the war', Allenby wrote simply but in great relief to his mother, 'except for the inevitable troubles that will arise during the rearrangement of nations and borders'.[4]

In Allenby's mature view the Sykes–Picot Agreement had come to fit very badly the prevailing geopolitical situation in the post-war Middle East. In adopting this stance, he would be joined by a number of others such as General Sir Reginald Wingate, the British high commissioner for Egypt during the previous two years and the man whom Allenby would succeed in March of 1919. Wingate wrote to him in November to say that 'it [Sykes–Picot] requires much alteration if not complete scrapping'. Even more earnestly, however, T.E. Lawrence had begun to dispute the agreement worked out between Mark Sykes and François Georges-Picot almost three years earlier in 1916.

Lawrence had arrived back in London in late October 1918. Once back home he began immediately to champion the Arab cause.[5] Lawrence would be clear in telling the Lloyd George government – specifically the members of its Eastern Committee, which was responsible for British policy in the Middle East – they could count on Faisal's support for Britain's imperial position in the region but only for as long as they remained anti-French. 'Our whole attitude to the

French is hardening here', wrote David Hogarth, Lawrence's old archaeology colleague, now also returned to London. 'TEL has put the wind up everybody and done much good'.[6] Lawrence was keen – as he had shown upon meeting the touring American film producer Lowell Thomas earlier that year – to use his own prospective celebrity, as well as the press, to support the Arab cause. Accordingly, he wrote immediately to Geoffrey Dawson, editor of *The Times*, to say 'that the Arabs came into the war without making a previous treaty with us, and have consistently refused to listen to the temptation of other powers. They have never had a press agent, or tried to make themselves out a case, but fought as hard as they could (I'll swear to that) and suffered hardships'.[7] Indeed, British claims to suzerainty over Palestine and Mesopotamia had drawn no opposition from Faisal. But in his view, reciprocity for this was British support for his own claims to Syria and Lebanon against those being made simultaneously by the French.

As a result, throughout October and November of that year Faisal would attempt to enact a policy of capacious Arab administration in the region. As it pertained to Lebanon and its port access specifically, the policy provoked immediate French resistance, and a commensurate move by Allenby to calm both Britain's wartime allies and the Arabs themselves. The prominent local Arab leader Shukri Pasha Al-Ayyubi, having been replaced as military governor of Damascus, was put into Beirut by Faisal to fill the same position there. The French objected strongly to this unilateral appointment, arguing that it violated the provisions of their 'B' Zone of the Sykes–Picot Agreement, which, in their view, had placed Lebanon under French control. For the time being and to keep the peace Allenby agreed reluctantly with the French and pressed Faisal to have Shukri step down. But Faisal resisted such overt pressure. Accordingly, on 10 October British officers in Beirut were instructed by their commander, General Sir Edward Bulfin, to remove the Arab flag from all public buildings in the city. Unsurprisingly, Faisal reacted angrily to this starkly symbolic measure, and could not be appeased. He sent a tersely worded cable to Allenby protesting that

'I see no need to explain or elaborate to you what disgrace befell the Arab flag in Beirut, the very same standard of the nation that you told me recently was included by His Majesty King George V as part of Britain's allies'.

As civil administrator over these newly occupied Arab lands, Allenby had discovered quickly that operating in this ever-shifting politico-diplomatic world was thankless and elusive of a decisive outcome. To him, as a career soldier, such was almost the complete antithesis of what he had experienced during his long military career. In response to Faisal's protest over Beirut, Allenby repeated what he had said earlier: until the peacemaking deliberations at Paris took place and binding judgements were rendered for the future of the region, it was his responsibility to ensure that military rule would continue to be enforced effectively in Lebanon and everywhere else his authority held sway. Still, Allenby recognized both the need for and usefulness of Faisal exercising greater governmental control over both his people and the territory in question. Accordingly, on 21 October he granted Faisal full political control under supervisory British military rule in zones 'A' and 'B', as delineated in the Sykes–Picot Agreement. As a result, a few weeks later Faisal went to newly liberated Aleppo to demonstrate that Syria, in his view, had become in effect an independent Arab state. On 6 November Faisal entered the city in triumph and on the 11th gave a rousing speech in which he appealed to Arab generosity and patriotic determination to create in Syria a new post-Ottoman pluralist state. 'The Arabs were Arabs before Moses, and Jesus and Muhammad', he emphasized to his listeners, 'and anyone who sows discord between Muslim, Christian and Jew is not an Arab. I am an Arab before all else ... I ask my brothers to consider me as a servant of this land'.[8]

Faisal's insistence on an Arab-controlled Syria had been emboldened by a new Anglo-French Declaration, made just two days earlier, in which both Britain and France appeared to supersede the Sykes–Picot Agreement by promising 'the complete and final liberation of the peoples so long oppressed by the Turks and the establishment of national governments and administrations deriving their authority from the initiative and free choice of the native populations'.[9] On the same day that Faisal had entered Aleppo, Georges-Picot himself had arrived in Beirut and insisted immediately that Syria be turned over to the French. Very quickly his expectations in this regard were to be dashed, with the impact of the declaration of 9 November effectively nullifying the Sykes–Picot Agreement. Still, its full text had included an undefined 'functional' role for both Britain and France in the future political development of the Arab Middle East.

The exact nature of this prospective functional role remained anybody's guess, although what can be discerned in its wording is a move towards formal mandatory supervision, as would later be confirmed at Paris. However, for Allenby the Anglo-French Declaration was precisely what he had been seeking to ease tensions both in the Arab street, as well as in his personal diplomatic relationship with Faisal. As he had written to General Wilson on 19 October: 'If a statement, by the Governments, French & British, could be published – to the effect – that, after the war, the wishes of the inhabitants could be considered in deciding on the form of Government in conquered territories – it would do much to restore confidence'.[10] In this instance Allenby had got exactly what he had asked for.

Meanwhile, on 8 November, Lawrence cabled Faisal's father Sharif Hussein, informing him that Allenby would be in touch shortly about Hejazi representation at Paris. Already, the Foreign Office had asked Allenby whether the time was right to have the Arabs represent themselves directly at the Peace Conference, to which he had replied with an enthusiastic yes. Lawrence told the sharif that the obvious – really the only – choice to fulfil this role was Faisal. Hussein agreed readily with Lawrence's advice and instructed Faisal to proceed immediately to the French capital to act as his plenipotentiary. Once there, the sharif emphasized, Faisal was to remain closely in line with 'our loyal ally Great Britain' to achieve the best possible diplomatic result for the new Arab nation. In late November 1918 therefore, after having laid the groundwork for an Arab administration in Syria, Faisal departed for France and the impending commencement of the Paris Peace Conference. Concurrently at Westminster, Lawrence continued to argue the Arab case persuasively in front of the Eastern Committee.

Altogether, at least as far as Allenby was concerned, by the end of November the initial political and diplomatic challenges generated by the Ottomans' recent defeat had been met. His counsel was being accepted at the highest levels of the British government; he had effected a concordat with Faisal; and he was doing his best to maintain civil relations with the French. To this latter point can be added the person of Sir Mark Sykes who, like Georges-Picot, had arrived in the Middle East in November. A short time earlier in London, Sykes had put together a small mission with himself at the head and had convinced the Foreign Office of its potential efficacy in obtaining for Britain 'as satisfactory a settlement of Middle Eastern questions as military and political circumstances will permit'. On 30 October he had set off for Palestine.[11] Having arrived he would report to Allenby, as Georges-Picot had done; both men were operating in the capacity of 'political adviser' to their respective governments. Any and all communications that they would make with their home governments, therefore, were required to go through Allenby as presiding military commander. It seems that Allenby liked both men well enough, telling Wilson, for example, that he was glad Georges-Picot had come, 'as now I have someone to whom I can talk plainly'. Allenby had never met Sykes before but anticipated that he would fall into much the same category as Georges-Picot. Wilson, however, was not so sure. 'I hope Mark Sykes behaves himself', he wrote in a letter to Allenby in early December. 'He is a good fellow but cracked and his blessed Sykes–Picot Agreement must be torn up *somehow*'.

In effect, the 'tearing up' of the agreement had begun to happen on the day of the publication of the Anglo-French Declaration a month earlier. Still, the exact aspirations for national self-determination that the declaration contained were a long way from being fulfilled in the Middle East, if they were to be met at all. In the meantime, Allenby remained at the centre of affairs, travelling around his temporary military fiefdom and taking its political temperature while trying simultaneously to control the potential for an anti-European uprising by the Arabs. The likelihood of such an event was one that Allenby continued to lay principally at the feet of the French, as he explained in a note to Wilson on 14 December: 'I'm just back from Aleppo, Beirut etc ... Feeling of the Arabs towards French is still bitter, and the French don't do much to soften matters'. All the same, Allenby was pleased to inform Wilson that Sykes 'has been decidedly useful & helpful' and, he added, actually 'gets on well with Picot'.[12]

Adding another layer of complexity to the tense situation in the Middle East over which Allenby presided was the continuing pressure exerted by Chaim Weizmann and his fellow Zionists on the British to fulfil the promise contained in the Balfour Declaration. As Allenby recognized, an insistent Zionism was something that would clash irreconcilably with the almost 600,000 Arabs who were resident permanently in Palestine; the vastly smaller Jewish resident population was just 66,000. As he wrote to the War Office in December, 'it must be realized that [the] Arab nation's ambitions count for little in Palestine where [the] non-Jewish population is concerned chiefly with maintenance in Palestine itself of a position which they consider Zionism threatens'. In other words, Palestinian Arab nationalism was clearly of secondary concern to most Zionists in their drive to make good on the Balfour Declaration. Allenby was under no illusions therefore about what lay in store for the peacemakers who would soon be gathering at Paris.

In the New Year of 1919, as the Paris Peace Conference got underway, Allenby continued to spend a great deal of time in consideration of the geopolitical future of the Middle East. He toured his vast regional command in order to see that the provisions of the Armistice of Mudros with the Ottomans were enforced. Alas, as he complained to General Wingate on 15 January, the defeated Ottomans were being 'dilatory' in fulfilling its terms.[13] In early February, therefore, Allenby spent thirty-six hours in Constantinople, during which he demanded and received full compliance with the armistice, specifically the requirement that all Ottoman regiments in the region be disbanded immediately. Compliance was duly made.[14]

Throughout February – punctuated on the 16th by the unexpected death of Sykes, who had contracted Spanish influenza, in Paris – Allenby continued to preside over the shifting sands of Anglo-French politics and diplomacy in the Middle East that maintaining his military command in Palestine required. Indeed, in one of the final documents composed by Sykes, written for the British delegation on 22 January, he had praised Allenby for being the 'key note' of the Great Powers' position in the Middle East. 'His splendid character, his popularity, his readiness in emergencies, and the background of victory', Sykes continued, combined to make him 'an immense asset'. Therefore, he concluded, Allenby should be consulted on all points by those who just then were beginning their deliberations at Paris.[15] At his command headquarters, meanwhile, Allenby continued to resist attempts by the French to assert a more pronounced military presence in either Lebanon or Syria.[16] He would not waver in this stance despite the steady demands of Georges-Picot that the resident French military detachment should be allowed to increase its size. As Allenby explained to Wilson, he had refused the French diplomat's overtures on grounds both military – 'I already have sufficient troops . . . [and] do not recognize Monsieur Picot as having any right to give an opinion as to the number of troops necessary in my theatre of operations' – and political. 'Should more French troops arrive while the Peace Conference is sitting', Allenby continued, 'it will convey to the inhabitants, who are openly suspicious of French intentions, the impression that the future of Syria has already been decided on'.[17]

There is little doubt that Allenby now felt himself to be in the hothouse of international affairs, a not disagreeable place to be, necessarily, but clearly not his normal military milieu. Certainly, as he wrote to a friend at the beginning of March, 'there is plenty to do and plenty to think about. All nations and would-be nations and all shades of religions and politics are up against each other and trying to get me to commit myself on their side. I am keeping up my end, so far; but there is need to walk warily'.[18]

A few days later, on 12 March, and in keeping with his new administrative role, Allenby was asked to come to Paris to apprise the US president Woodrow Wilson and the other leading statesmen of the Peace Conference directly of the prevailing political situation in the Middle East. Just at that time, early in March, they were beginning to give over their full attention to its close examination.[19] 'Don't you think it would be a good plan to get Allenby to Paris as soon as possible', Philip Kerr, David Lloyd George's private secretary, had written to his chief on 28 February. 'He can speak with much more authority about Syria, Palestine and Turkish questions generally than anybody else and his advice ought to be invaluable when it comes to military questions involved'.[20] The prime minister agreed. Allenby was invited to Paris shortly thereafter, and arrived on 19 March.

Over the next forty-eight hours Allenby lived within a whirlwind of high-level diplomatic talks. As Margaret MacMillan points out in her comprehensive history of the Peace Conference, 'for six months in 1919, Paris was the capital of the world', and Allenby was welcomed there as the conquering hero, if not of the biggest battlefield in the Great War, then certainly of one of its most legendary.[21] He took up residence at the Hotel Majestic, one of the two main sites occupied by the British delegation at the conference. 'With a most comfortable suite of rooms & a motor car at my disposal', Allenby then proceeded to bring a dose of what he regarded as realpolitik to the delegates' understanding of the geopolitics of the post-war Middle East. Amused rather than over-awed by the popular attention his arrival in

Paris had generated – 'I have been interviewed & snapshotted, cinematographed and stared at continually', he reported home – Allenby addressed the conference's Council of Four on the 20th.[22]

On that day Woodrow Wilson, David Lloyd George, Georges Clemenceau of France and Vittorio Orlando of Italy listened carefully to the man who had been lionized just a few hours earlier in the streets of Paris as something none of them had ever been: a victorious military commander. Allenby's reputation had preceded him. As usual he spoke with directness and brevity. Clemenceau, in particular, did not much appreciate Allenby's bluntness in explaining why he believed that imposing a French mandate upon Syria would court military disaster. Even less did he appreciate Allenby's answer to the question, which had been asked earlier and elsewhere by President Wilson, of why it appeared that French interests were being shunted aside in the Middle East in favour of those of both the British and the Arabs. Allenby had expected such a question and he chose to answer it colloquially. 'When I was at school, if I saw two boys fighting, the one big and the other small', he recounted, 'I first kicked the big boy, not the small one'.[23] The implication regarding the French position in Syria had been made clear, and coming from a proven warrior like Allenby it seemed to have the desired effect on most of those who heard it.

The major outcome of the Council of Four's session with Allenby, however, was for Wilson to suggest that an Inter-Allied Commission on Mandates in Turkey – known later as the King–Crane Commission – be sent to Syria to investigate the situation. Its task would be to determine the wishes of the people in a manner that accorded with the Anglo-French Declaration made the previous November. By this time the US president had little regard for whatever was left of the Sykes–Picot Agreement. Would not a proper commission, Wilson queried instead, based on the emergent principle of national self-determination as contained in his recently authored Fourteen Points (a guide to a new post-war world order), be the right way forward?[24] Unsurprisingly, the French, who were keenly aware of the depth of

Syrian animosity towards them, flatly rejected Wilson's idea. At the same time too, however, Wilson managed to annoy the British by suggesting that such a commission's remit should be expanded to include both Mesopotamia and Palestine as well. The commission was duly formed, but, owing to strong Anglo-French reluctance to participate in both its formation and subsequent deliberations, the Americans would be its sole members. In the end, the King–Crane Commission's recommendations would not be published until 1922 and when finally made public would be regarded by both Britain and France as moot.[25]

During Allenby's brief and busy stay in Paris, dominated by his meeting with the 'swells', as he described the members of the Council of Four to a friend, he also found time to hold an important luncheon party. Included among his guests that day were both Faisal and Lawrence, the latter of whom had arrived in Paris in early January and had been in constant contact ever since with both the British and the Arab delegations. But by the time he met with both of them over lunch, Allenby's attention had been drawn by the Foreign Office towards another pressing matter. Although the conference proceedings were otherwise all-encompassing for the prime minister – 'Wilson and Lloyd George struck me as being the leading men, by a long way', remarked Allenby – the political situation in British-controlled Egypt had deteriorated significantly and required Lloyd George's attention. Indeed, during the waning days of the war a nationalist rebellion had broken out in Egypt accompanied by widespread acts of public disorder.[26] Egyptian nationalism had roots at least as far back as the British occupation in 1882, which the war had heightened, and was further exacerbated by Britain's exile of the nationalist leader Saad Zaghloul in 1919.

In response to the situation in Egypt, the British government had begun to consider employing a firmer hand in Cairo. General Wingate was absorbing the blame for having not done enough to prevent the conditions that had spawned such disorderly outbreaks in the first place. His recent recall to London by the government for consultations over the crisis had been made for precisely this reason. In considering who might replace him in Cairo, the prime minister had had his high view of Allenby confirmed by Lord Curzon, the former viceroy of India, who would be named foreign secretary that October. Curzon regarded Allenby as 'the most prestigious British official, civil or military, in the Middle East'.

On the morning of 20 March therefore, Allenby was informed that the British government wished to appoint him as its special high commissioner for Egypt and the Sudan. He accepted the appointment without a moment's hesitation, in large part because he believed that it would be a temporary one lasting only so long as Wingate was required to remain in England.[27] 'Now I return to a restless Egypt', Allenby wrote to his wife on the 21st, the day of his departure. 'This Egyptian complication is a new one', he continued. Allenby believed that his presence there would 'have a calming effect; but the unrest has got a deep root, & there will be hard work to do'.[28] He reached Egypt on the 25th, and once there plunged immediately into his new role of imperial proconsul while at the same time remaining, for the time being at least, commander-in-chief of the conquered Allied territories in the Middle East.

Following Allenby's swift departure for Egypt, the Paris Peace Conference convened for a further three months until concluding its meetings in June. But it did so without ever resolving the geopolitical situation in the Middle East and the demands made for Arab independence. Faisal, with Lawrence constantly by his side, argued strongly for Syria's independence as an Arab state but neither France nor Britain were prepared to allow it. Nor was the United States. Faisal did not contest the plan for Palestine to include a Jewish homeland; nor did he choose to dispute France's determination to exert post-war control over Lebanon. As MacMillan notes, 'France had historically been the protector of the Christian communities throughout the

Ottoman Empire but it had particularly close ties to the Maronites' of Lebanon.[29] Faisal decided therefore not to push for control over the country. But on the question of Syria and Mesopotamia and the rest of the Arab world, Faisal continued to insist upon the right to self-determination. Indeed, in March of 1920 Faisal and the new General Syrian Congress – which thereafter would be regarded as Syria's first parliament – would proclaim the founding of the Arab Kingdom of Syria. This declaration would fall on deaf ears, however. Both Lloyd George and Clemenceau refused to acknowledge the newly declared Syrian state. Wilson, meanwhile, believed that the only workable solution for the Arabs was to employ the constitutional gradualism of the Mandate System being put in place by the conference under the newly established League of Nations. Accordingly, Faisal's early departure from Paris in April was a bitter one, as it was for Lawrence also.[30] In the aftermath of the conference both felt an acute sense of having been betrayed by the Allies, especially the French. Allenby saw Faisal in Damascus a short time later in May and afterwards informed General Wilson that he 'is as bitterly anti-French, after his stay in Paris, as he was before he left Syria for Europe ... He told me plainly that he would have no French in Syria'.[31] Still, from the perspective of both the British and French states, if the Mandate System could be used as a first step on the path towards Arab independence then all might yet not be lost. The San Remo Conference of the Supreme Council of the Allies, which would assemble in Italy the following year to consider the implementation of the Mandate System, might become the means to achieve just such an outcome.[32]

Held in April of 1920, the San Remo Conference brought together the members of the Allied Supreme Council for a week of deliberations over the Mandate System as it had been laid down in Paris the previous year. The conference would be attended by Lloyd George and a number of other world leaders, diplomats and ministers, including the prime minister of France, Alexandre Millerand. While there they focused their attention on the so-called 'Class A' mandates – that group of former Ottoman territories comprised of Syria, Mesopotamia and Palestine. The first two of these mandatory territories would be recognized by the conference provisionally as constituting full-fledged states, while Palestine was not accorded the same status. The French, meanwhile, acknowledged this action grudgingly but only in anticipation of the soon-to-be confirmation at San Remo of their mandatory control over Syria. For the British a similar situation would prevail in Mesopotamia and Palestine. For Faisal, however, the confirmation of the French mandate over Syria in April at San Remo left him in an extremely tenuous position as the country's recently proclaimed king.

The San Remo Conference acted to operationalize one of the chief outcomes of the Paris Peace Conference. The result – under the Permanent Mandates Commission of the League of Nations as formally established in December – was to solidify European supervision over, and to harden the borders of, the three former Ottoman territories under consideration.[33] In so doing, the continued presence of both the British and the French in the Middle East was made inevitable, as was the creation of a Jewish homeland in Palestine.[34] Both of these outcomes were fraught, however, with potential for continued violence. 'Unsettled and dangerous' the region would remain, Major-General Sir William Thwaites of the War Office reported to Allenby in the spring of 1920. He stated flatly that the situation owed itself to the 'willful disregard by the Allies of the wishes of the people of Syria and Palestine by foisting the French on the former and the Jewish National Home on the latter'.[35] Indeed, France's assertion of complete control over Syria provoked Faisal to fury. He urged Allenby to inform Lloyd George that the French commander in Syria, General Henri Gouraud, was leading a punitive military expedition in the country. Faisal accused the French of conducting nothing less than a full-fledged war against the Syrian people, of which the decisive Battle of Maysalun in June would be the centrepiece. 'French Artillery and aeroplane explosives', he told

Allenby, had been used, 'promiscuously and without pity destroying the villages and tearing to pieces the defenseless inhabitants'.[36] Following this comprehensive military defeat would come Faisal's swift deposition from the Syrian throne in July, and his subsequent expulsion from Damascus. His ignominious termination as king of Syria would mark the end, in the words of his biographer Ali Allawi, of 'two and a half tumultuous and event-laden years in which Faisal had sought an independent state for the Arabs in Syria'.

Faisal had implored the British government 'to ask the French to stop these harsh measures'. But Lloyd George had ignored him, remaining more greatly concerned with the mandate that the British state had assumed over Mesopotamia, which was comprised of the three former Ottoman provinces of Baghdad, Basra and Mosul. Henceforth the country was to be known as Iraq, in reference to its ancient foundational Sumerian city-state of Uruk. There Gertrude Bell had become a political officer (with the title of 'Oriental secretary') on the staff of the recently appointed British high commissioner, Sir Percy Cox. Both were engaged closely in analysing Iraqi society and in making recommendations to the British government as to the form its mandatory governance should take. Indeed, Bell saw her role in Iraq as extending beyond immediate mandatory considerations to that of advising on its eventual independence. Her inveterate Middle Eastern travel and archaeological work along with her deepening political experience had yielded a voice to be reckoned with concerning the future of Iraq. She was to write a number of key memoranda for the British government to that end. In January of 1920, for example, she had already sent one such document to Edwin Montagu, secretary of state for India and therefore at that time responsible administratively for Mesopotamia. In what was a measured but insistent disquisition, Bell set out what she understood to be the means to be adopted by the British as well as the ends to be achieved in undertaking mandatory responsibility for Iraq. 'We are, I suppose,' she began, 'near the time when we shall be able to set up a civil Government here – a moment I daily pray for, for it will cut the bottom out of most of the discontent here. That is to say, it will do so if the new institutions are conceived on wise and generous lines; otherwise we shall create a permanent state of what is technically called sedition which will lead us, and that before long, into much the same place in which we stand in Egypt or Ireland'.[37]

Ultimately, Bell would come to argue persuasively for the creation of Arab self-government and administration in Iraq. She was also one of the first to advocate for Faisal to be appointed as king of Iraq. Faisal's appointment would duly come, but only after a series of San Remo Conference-provoked nationalist disturbances, the extent of which Bell had predicted. In the meantime, the costs incurred by the British government owing to its late-wartime military occupation of Iraq, which after April of 1920 became officially mandatory, had begun to be prohibitive.

Charged with managing Britain's mandate in Iraq, Sir Percy Cox was a veteran practitioner of British diplomacy in the Middle East. Sent to the Gulf by the government of India as chief political officer, Major-General Cox became Britain's pre-eminent voice in the Gulf and Mesopotamia during the war.[38] Based first in Basra and then later at Baghdad, he conducted the triangular imperial relationship of Britain, Mesopotamia and the Ottoman Empire. Of great moment in this relationship was the siege of British-held Kut al-Amara. This had begun in December 1915 after General Charles Townshend's Mesopotamian campaign had stalled with a defeat by Ottoman forces at Ctesiphon. The campaign would prove to be a catastrophic disaster for the British. Some 23,000 British and Indian troops died at Kut, and afterwards thousands more suffered the same fate while being force-marched by the Ottomans into captivity in Anatolia. Ultimately, in February of 1917, Kut was re-taken in a successful relief operation by British and Indian troops and Mesopotamia fell under wartime British control.[39]

Throughout this period Cox had worked closely with the powerful Arab sheikh Ibn Saud, convincing him ultimately not to place his wartime support behind the Ottomans. Part of the manner in which this delicate piece of diplomacy had been carried out was to offer the Arab leader a substantial monthly subsidy of £5,000 to ensure his loyalty to the British. Meanwhile, Saud's main rival, Sharif Hussein, was also being courted by the British. Cox became indispensable to British diplomacy in the region during this period, a fact demonstrated by his appointment as Britain's first ambassador to Tehran in September of 1918, just as the First World War drew to a close. His major piece of work in the time immediately following his move to Iran was to negotiate the Anglo-Persian Agreement, which gave the British exclusive access to the fast-developing Iranian oilfields centred on Masjed Soleiman, the site where oil had first been discovered back in 1908.

Six years later, in 1914, Churchill as first lord of the Admiralty had negotiated for the British government the purchase of a 51 per cent share (at a cost of £2.2 million) in the London-based Anglo-Persian Oil Company (APOC) as a key component of the country's naval policy.[40] As he told the House of Commons in June of that year, less than two months prior to the outbreak of the war: 'What we want now, is a proved proposition, a going concern, an immediate supply, and a definite prospect with potentialities of development over which we can ourselves preside. These we find in Persia'.[41] Supported overwhelmingly by parliamentarians, the Anglo-Persian Agreement was issued by the foreign secretary Lord Curzon in August of 1919, which had the immediate effect of solidifying Britain's key stake in Iranian oil production. The agreement would be denounced as monopolistic by other countries – especially by Britain's main oil-rival in the region, the US – and it would also prove unpopular with many in Iran. But to both Cox and Curzon it represented a singular diplomatic achievement that stood to reinforce Britain's geopolitical pre-eminence in the region. Not only that, but, Curzon stated emphatically, it gave

Iran the 'best chance for recuperation for a century'. What were the British to do, Curzon continued rhetorically in a statement made to the British Cabinet, simply allow the country 'to rot into picturesque decay'?[42] In exchange for a controlling interest in APOC Britain guaranteed it would respect Iranian independence, initiate tariff reform, engender extensive railway building, and supply weapons and munitions for Iran's defence.

Cox's key role in the Anglo-Persian Agreement had put him at the centre of diplomatic events in the Middle East. Consequently, following his attendance at the Paris Peace Conference and a brief return to India, he was transferred back to Baghdad in the autumn of 1920. He was sent there to exert a calming hand in Iraq after a popular uprising had broken out earlier that year. The Iraqi Revolt, which had come in response to the decision by the San Remo Conference to make official Britain's League of Nations mandate over Iraq, had cost the civil commissioner Arnold Wilson his job. It would fall therefore to the steady hand of Cox to right the listing ship of Iraqi governance, or so it was assumed in London. It was a task, as Cox announced in Arabic to the reception committee upon his arrival in Baghdad in October, to which he much looked forward. He was there, he stated firmly, so that the mandate might yield an Arab government that would work for an as yet undetermined length of time before achieving Iraqi independence. As recorded by his chief adviser Gertrude Bell, who was present in Baghdad to witness Cox's arrival, 'His words were interrupted by expressions of assent and agreement on the part of his audience'. As Bell continued in a letter written to her father, Sir Hugh Bell, 'It is quite impossible to tell you the relief and comfort it is to serve under somebody in whose judgement one has complete confidence. To the extraordinarily difficult task which lies before him he brings a single-eyed desire to act in the interests of the people of the country'.[43]

The Iraqi Revolt, the aftermath of which Cox had been sent out to Baghdad to assuage, had begun in May of 1920 with a series of street protests and mass meetings. These initial events had been mainly peaceful, if impassioned, and had included a formal presentation made to Commissioner Wilson by a group of representative Iraqis of a plan for national independence to be achieved incrementally. Wilson, however, had rejected the plan outright as being impractical and hurried. In response to its summary rejection, unarmed mass protests had broken out, which turned steadily into widespread armed revolt. The reaction by Wilson, and under him General Sir Aylmer Haldane as commander-in-chief in Iraq, would be both swift and unduly harsh. In the end the British would put into the field over 100,000 men to quell the rebellion. This high number of troops was reinforced at the war secretary Winston Churchill's request by the equivalent of an infantry division brought in from Iran as well as by the deployment of two squadrons of the Royal Air Force. The Iraqi nationalist rebels were similar in number to the British and Indian troops, but their weaponry and equipment were far inferior and their casualties would approach a level ten times that of the British. By the time the revolt was brought under control in October of 1920 the British had lost 1,000 men, with up to 1,800 wounded. But the Iraqis had suffered much more grievously, with somewhere between 6,000 and 10,000 men killed, along with a similar number wounded.[44]

As the revolt had raged throughout much of 1920 so had Churchill's frustration risen over the high cost being paid by the British in blood and money under their mandate in Iraq, as well as the soaring number of casualties amongst the country's beleaguered people. As secretary of state for war and air he had responded to the crisis in Iraq, as he believed himself obliged to do, by authorizing the deployment of additional troops and by sending in air support. But having done so Churchill wished now to end the strong-armed and expensive British military presence in Iraq as soon as possible. The thin tax-collection regime that the British had imposed upon the country stood in stark contrast, he angrily told Haldane, to 'the waste of force and of money which is going on in Mesopotamia'. Haldane was determined equally to maintain strict military control in Iraq, however, which he argued was necessary because the Arab population of the country would respect the British mandate only if a 'strong hand' was used against them.[45] Whatever Churchill may have made of the racist tenor of Haldane's reply is unknown. Politically, however, as he wrote to the chancellor of the Exchequer, Austen Chamberlain, 'I am determined to save you millions in this field'. Churchill's goal was to reduce the figure from its current annual level of £20 million down to £7 million. To achieve this significant reduction he wished to prioritize air defence over the deployment of ground troops as a much more sustainable and economical means of ensuring Iraq's security in the future.[46]

No one, it might be surmised, could have been more pleased to hear of Churchill's intentions in this regard than Bell. Throughout most of this tension-wracked period of time in Iraq she had been living in her central Baghdad house, growing in despair over the rampant violence taking place all around her. She had become increasingly frustrated, too, by the fact that the British government through the India Office could not seem to grasp that continuing along the path of exercising its present form of quasi-military rule in Iraq was a recipe for disaster. Finally, however, the replacement of the unsteady Wilson by Cox in October of 1920 as the revolt petered out offered a path towards political reform and widespread peace. Earlier, in January of that year, Bell had written again to Edwin Montagu, the secretary of state for India, to voice her concerns as well as to offer her prescriptions for the future good governance of Iraq. *Al-Khatun* ('the Lady'), as she was called by the Arabs, could some-times write discursively and at great length in her correspondence with officials. In this particular letter to Montagu, Bell had written plainly and persuasively – as well as at length – about the means to make meaningful political progress in Iraq. As she explained to him, the British must not 'ask them [the Iraqi people] what exactly it is that they want. By far the greater number don't know and are merely bewildered by being asked . . . Therefore, don't ask; these two words should be written in letters of fire. What we should do . . . is to say: 'This is what the great government ordains for you'.

To be sure, these words of Bell's are both prescriptive and patronizing. As fundamentally sympathetic as Bell was to Arab nationalist aspirations, she shared nonetheless with all of her British colleagues a pronounced authoritarianism. Still, Bell's long experience in the Middle East, together with an undoubted receptivity to the state-building hopes of most politicized Arabs, meant that her authoritarianism was leavened by an enlightened view of the Arabs' capacity to rule themselves successfully in a modern manner in the near future. Remember, she counselled Montagu, 'and here I differ from most of my colleagues' – writing in January of 1920 when presumably she would have been thinking mainly of Wilson – 'in ordaining we must be guided by a sympathy, almost superhuman, with the ambitions, yes, and even with the pretensions which are agitating our world to-day, shaking it to bits, you might say – to little bits'.[47]

Bell's January 1920 letter to Montagu was but a prelude, however, to the 156-page-long document that she delivered later to the India Office and which would be published in December of that year. Entitled the *Review of the Civil Administration of Mesopotamia*, originally the task of its research and writing had been assigned to Arnold Wilson, who in turn had passed it on to the much more able Bell.[48] In it she would lay out in fine detail the recent constitutional and legal history of Iraq. Bell provided also what she believed to be the cardinal principles that should underlie British policy prescriptions for the long-term success of Iraqi governance, both under Britain's immediate mandatory purview and once the country had achieved true independence.

By the time that Bell's *Review* was presented to Parliament in late 1920, Lloyd George's government would be well on the way to altering its approach to Iraq's future. The publication of the *Review* caused no less than 'a fandango' at Westminster, as Bell later commented ruefully, mainly because of the novelty of it having been authored by a woman. But regardless of the gender of its writer, the *Review* was well received and would act as a key piece in the British government's change of course by offering an expert evaluation of the current state of the Iraqi polity. Bell's *Review* marked a clear point of departure for the final iteration of British rule over the country, laying bare the political necessity for Britain to work towards transitioning from mandatory control to Iraqi self-determination and independence. Indeed, Bell's commitment was for Iraq to achieve 'apparent sovereignty *immediately*', as she had stressed earlier in her letter to Montagu, 'with a view to allowing it to develop into real sovereignty as quickly as I can teach the Arabs to make it do'.[49] Therefore, as the end of 1920 approached, the stage was set for the British government to reconsider fundamentally the nature of its prevailing policy in Iraq as a means to revising its whole post-war position in the Middle East. 'What a difficult world', Bell would later write (and without recognition that the British were in part the authors of this world), 'the war has bequeathed to us!'[50] Although Churchill did not know it yet, the task of trying to make sense of the Middle East's part in that world was about to fall to him. His days as secretary of state for war and air were numbered, and a move to the Colonial Office – and the ministerial responsibility to make British policy for the Middle East – now awaited him.

3

CHURCHILL AT THE COLONIAL OFFICE
TOWARDS THE CAIRO CONFERENCE

As secretary of state for war, Winston Churchill would spend the last weeks of 1920 in the throes of dealing with a trio of complex files, the most pressing of which remained the severe unrest in Mesopotamia. The first of these files concerned the attempt by the British government, along with certain of its recent wartime allies, to resist the advance of the revolutionary Bolshevik Red Army as it bid to consolidate a still-tentative rule over the unruly vastness of the former Russian Empire. For Churchill, such resistance had become mainly diplomatic and rhetorical but of no less importance than when the British had deployed military force against the Reds two years earlier. 'My view', he stated emphatically in a speech given to a group of Oxford University students on 18 November, 'has been that all the harm and misery in Russia have arisen out of the wickedness and folly of the Bolshevists ... The policy I will always advocate is the overthrow and destruction of that criminal regime'.[1]

The civil war in what, in 1922, would become the Soviet Union had preoccupied Churchill for much of his post-war political life, but to this at that moment in late 1920 could be added the similar turmoil of the Irish War of Independence. A conflict of much violence meted out by both sides, the war in Ireland would continue until late 1921 before being brought to an end through a negotiated peace in which Churchill played a crucial role. But until that future date the ferocity with which the republican Irish fought for their independence against a British government determined to deny it to them was to engross Churchill for much of his ministerial time.[2] 'Quit murdering and start arguing' was his cryptic if censorious advice to Sinn Fein, the political arm of the Irish revolutionaries. If such were to occur, he promised them, 'I shall not be behindhand in doing my utmost to secure a good settlement'. The Anglo-Irish Treaty of December of 1921 would be the result.

Then there was Mesopotamia, or Iraq as it had begun to be called. Though the Ottoman Empire had been defeated soundly by the Allies two years earlier, Britain itself had not yet achieved a formal bilateral settlement with the new successor state of Turkey. For Churchill, this key wartime victory needed to be tessellated properly with Britain's post-war diplomacy so that its position in the former Ottoman territory of Mesopotamia could be made secure. Hence his impatience to reach an agreement with Turkey that would go some distance in removing the need for Britain's continued and expensive military occupation of Iraq, as well as its expenditures elsewhere in the hitherto Ottoman-controlled Middle East. Such 'thankless deserts', he would complain bitterly to the prime minister David Lloyd George, needed to be governed better, more cheaply, and with greater local independence than they were at present if Britain were to come out from under an increasingly heavy post-war colonial financial burden. Just that year, for example, the cost to the British taxpayer of governing Iraq, Palestine and Arabia would reach almost £40 million, the equivalent today of close to £1 billion. Fully half this amount had been expended on Iraq alone in order to suppress the protracted rebellion that had divided the country for most of the year. Indeed, as Churchill complained to Lloyd George, 'there is

something very sinister to my mind in this Mesopotamian entangle-
ment coming as it does when Ireland is so great a menace'.

In the last weeks before Christmas 1920 Churchill continued in a
state of high vexation over all three of these geopolitical problems.
Indeed, he had begun to question his ability to solve any of them while
remaining at the War Office. Complicating the picture for Churchill
was that his stand on Turkey and by extension on Iraq was one with
which Lloyd George disagreed. The prime minister was strongly anti-
Turk, as was the majority of the Cabinet. Churchill, on the other hand,
had developed a greater sense of pragmatism concerning Turkey than
had his colleagues. He had come to believe that an agreement with
Britain's former enemy might well prevent Turkish-induced trouble
from occurring in Iraq, which had been a chronic fear during the revolt
of 1920.

More positively, Churchill held also that it was possible to foresee
the new state of Turkey employing some of its useful former Ottoman
diplomatic habits. As he told the Cabinet, it might 'recreate that
Turkish barrier to Russian ambitions which has always been of
utmost importance to us'.[3] Still, he was not yet so far into his post-
Dardanelles political regeneration that he could afford to lose the
key support of the prime minister. The failed Allied attack on the
Ottoman-held Dardanelles Straits in 1915 had been initiated by
Churchill during his time as first lord of the Admiralty. And its
disastrous outcome as part of the broader Gallipoli campaign had
been blamed mainly on him. As a consequence, he had resigned from
Cabinet and it was not until 1917 that he was able to reassert himself
politically thanks to the support of Lloyd George. Churchill wished
to maintain such political favour, and therefore on 23 December he
wrote to the prime minister lamenting that they were 'drifting apart
on foreign policy ... new interests' might need to be explored, he
continued, to forestall a break between them as the two leading
members of the coalition government.[4] Meanwhile, unbeknownst to

Churchill, Lloyd George himself had come to a similar conclusion: he too had begun to wonder if his dissatisfied minister might not be better placed in a new portfolio, namely that of the Colonial Office.

As the year 1920 drew to a close, with the prospect of a Cabinet reshuffle hanging in the air, Churchill decided to slip out of London to enjoy a few days of relaxation in the country at Port Lympne, the luxurious Kent mansion owned by Sir Philip Sassoon. A prominent member of both the Sassoon and Rothschild banking dynasties, an MP, and a necessarily discreet homosexual, Sir Philip had purchased the striking Cape Dutch-style house in 1913.[5] Located near Ashford, Port Lympne overlooked Romney Marsh and beyond it the English Channel. Although in the words of Sassoon's recent biographer Damian Collins Port Lympne would eventually become a 'sybaritic mansion', in its 1920s heyday it served mainly as a country house weekend retreat for Sassoon's many friends in government and high society. As one of their privileged number Churchill would greet the New Year at Port Lympne in the company of a select group of ministers including Lloyd George himself, as well as the Irish secretary Sir Hamar Greenwood, an expatriate Canadian. Along with the expected frivolity of the season in which both he and the equally sociable Lloyd George readily engaged, Churchill's stay at Port Lympne provided him with the perfect opportunity to speak directly to the prime minister about his future role in Cabinet.

Thus it was that on 1 January 1921 Churchill asked for a new Cabinet appointment and Lloyd George offered him one. It was indeed to be the Colonial Office for Churchill in succession to Alfred Milner, 1st Viscount Milner, the long-time stalwart of empire whose many years of service were by then winding down. As much as Churchill had begun to anticipate the possibility of leaving behind the War Office and going to the Colonial Office, he did not say yes straightaway to the prime minister's tempting offer.[6] Churchill's acceptance of it, he told Lloyd George, would hinge upon the prime minister's willingness to allow for a restructuring and enlargement of the Colonial Office by creating within it a new and dedicated 'Middle East Department'. His interest in colonial affairs, had been deepened by the time that he had spent as under-secretary during the earl of Elgin's tenure at the Colonial Office from 1905 until 1908. He also recognized that the territories to which he would be expected to give close direction were supervised by London in a rather haphazard manner.[7] It was his recognition of this point especially that gave him pause as he mulled over the prime minister's offer during the first few days of January, before agreeing to it.

In the weeks that followed, Churchill readied himself in various ways for this new venture. Still, as much as he was determined to make a success of it, he feared that it might 'break' him.[8] But before all else Churchill was keen to get away and enjoy a brief holiday in France, in the welcome company of his wife Clementine, for what they both agreed was a necessary break. It would be their first holiday together since the end of the war over two years earlier. Just prior to departing London on 10 January, however, Churchill had a pressing order of business to take care of. He wished to conduct an interview with T.E. Lawrence in hopes of persuading him to become his special Arab adviser at the Colonial Office.

By January of 1921 Lawrence was probably the most famous Englishman in the world. His fame had exploded two years earlier in 1919 as a result of the 'lantern slide' images of 'Lawrence of Arabia' that had flickered across the screen of the Royal Opera House in Covent Garden, and then later at the much more capacious Royal Albert Hall. The show, entitled 'With Allenby in Palestine and Lawrence in Arabia', was two hours in length and with its inclusion of a number of film segments and live musical accompaniment it had proven to be enormously popular. All told, this multimedia depiction of the Arab Revolt was thought to have drawn an attendance of some 1 million people during that year in London alone. Produced by the energetic American producer Lowell Thomas, the revolt was presented as a heroic endeavour undertaken by the Arabs with the critical assistance of Lawrence and the British.[9] As the enemy, the Ottomans were portrayed as the villains of the piece, standing in the way of Arab national liberation.

Having gone to the Middle East during the First World War intending to come back with a 'hero' to market in both Britain and America, Thomas had found his man in the adventurous Lawrence. He fit Thomas's bill perfectly – at least initially – and Lawrence would emerge quickly as the star of a show that had begun its run with top billing given to Lord Allenby. But the stentorian Allenby would prove to be no match for the charismatic Lawrence in the world of budding screen stardom. Dressed in the flowing white robes of an Arab sheikh, Lawrence appeared to have been plucked from Central Casting's version of the *Arabian Nights*. Soon enough however, the so-called 'Uncrowned King of Arabia' – as he had been breathlessly dubbed by *Strand Magazine* in the spring of 1920 – would grow tired of the ephemeral nature of fame. Indeed, by the time Churchill invited him for an interview at the beginning of 1921, Lawrence was living as a semi-recluse near Westminster Abbey, just a short walk from Parliament Square. There, in a Barton Street flat provided for his use by the well-known architect Sir Herbert Baker, he had begun to write *Seven Pillars of Wisdom*. When published in 1926 it would reinforce Lawrence's fame.

A few years earlier, immediately after the war, Lawrence had first met Churchill upon his arrival home from Damascus to plead the Arabs' case in front of the War Cabinet's Eastern Committee. Like most others, Churchill had admired the younger man. At that time Churchill was serving as minister of munitions, the post given to him by Lloyd George during the summer of 1917 which had resurrected his political career after the damage inflicted upon it by the Dardanelles. A short time later, in January of 1919, Lloyd George had completed a Cabinet reshuffle in which he moved Churchill to the War Office. The Paris Peace Conference allowed Churchill and

Lawrence to become better acquainted still. Churchill, in his Cabinet role, and Lawrence, as principal adviser to Prince Faisal – his 'virtual shadow', in the words of Faisal's biographer – would cross paths on a number of occasions in Paris.[10] As the acknowledged leader of the Hashemite Arabs and at that moment at the head of the embattled Arab government of the semi-independent Syria, Faisal would form one half of a formidable, though ultimately unsuccessful, diplomatic tandem with Lawrence during the conference. Churchill was by now not a little in awe of the diminutive Lawrence, who had won the complete trust of Faisal. Moreover, Lawrence had remained utterly uncowed by the large British delegation at Paris, most of whom were intent on rejecting what both he and Faisal hoped to achieve by way of Arab independence. Indeed, as Churchill would later effusively remark about Lawrence, he was 'a dweller upon mountain tops where the air is cold, crisp and rarefied, and where the view on clear days commands all the Kingdoms of the world and the glory of them'.[11]

After agreeing to take over at the Colonial Office (and before leaving for his holiday in France) Churchill was determined to interview Lawrence about whether he might be willing to join him as his special adviser on Arab affairs. He assumed that such a move would bring immediate credibility to his approaching ministerial office. But he understood too that it might well court criticism from those, such as the foreign secretary Lord Curzon, who took a less accepting view of the political accommodations owed to restive colonial peoples. Having earlier declined a meeting, Lawrence had agreed to see Churchill on 8 January. That day – a Saturday morning – Lawrence walked the short distance from his Westminster flat to the War Office, which remained Churchill's ministerial home until the following month.[12]

The War Office building was a place crammed full of British imperial memories, the embodiment in steel and stone of the British imperial ideal.[13] For Churchill, as a cradle imperialist, the War Office, the Admiralty – where he had been a decade earlier as first lord – and now the Colonial Office were natural places to be.

For Lawrence, on the other hand, as an Oxford scholar and desert archaeologist turned unorthodox military officer, intelligence operative and guerilla leader, the War Office with its attendant bureaucracy was less of a natural fit. Conversely, the Colonial Office presented him with the apparent possibility of redressing the failure at Paris of not having secured Arab independence. As Lawrence wrote a short time later to the elderly former desert traveller and anti-imperialist Wilfrid Scawen Blunt: 'Winston is a new and very keen mind on the Middle East business, & I hope will take it the right way. It's a very great chance given me'.[14] Lawrence indeed was hoping very much for a second chance in his thwarted advocacy of the Arab cause. Upon his return from Paris in the summer of 1919, and with his hopes for Arab independence crushed, he had slipped into the slough of despond. As his mother recounted, so depressed was Lawrence during this time that in their Oxford home he would sit 'the entire morning between breakfast and lunch in the same position, without moving, and with the same expression on his face'. But despite telling a friend at the beginning of January that he had 'given up politics', here he was, just a few days later, with a fresh opportunity to overturn the abiding disappointment of two years earlier. Accordingly, by the time Lawrence had departed his meeting with Churchill at the War Office he had agreed in principle to come on board. In securing the services of 'Lawrence of Arabia', Churchill's nascent Middle East Department had got off to a rousing start. Still, not everyone was sure that Lawrence was the right man for the job. A short time later, on 14 February, for example, and just as Churchill was about to assume office, his personal private secretary Eddie Marsh raised a flag of caution that Lawrence might be ill-suited to such service. As Marsh wrote to his chief: 'Are you sure that Col. Lawrence would come? ... He is not the kind of man to fit easily into any official machine ... and I see trouble ahead if he is allowed too free a hand'.[15]

But Churchill was confident in his choice and departed for France with Clementine. On 10 January they left London by train for Nice, where the next fortnight would be spent together in the convivial company of a group of wealthy and influential friends. En route to the Riviera they stopped first in Paris, where Churchill had a conversation with Alexandre Millerand, by now the country's president. Of surpassing concern to both men was the continuing turmoil in the Middle East, which had continued to exert a strong bearing on Anglo-French relations, especially over the issue of the future of Syria. Meanwhile, of a much different kind of importance to Churchill while in Paris was the opportunity to exhibit some of his recently completed paintings. By this point his six-year-long amateur painting interest – which had begun in 1915 during the darkest days of his post-Dardanelles political banishment – had yielded fruit: this would be the first official exhibition of his artwork, held at the small and fashionable Galerie Druet under the pseudonym of 'Charles Morin'. Churchill was delighted eventually to learn that six of his canvases had sold.[16]

Arriving in Nice on the 12th, the Churchills settled into their hotel and soon established a steady routine: games of tennis for Clementine – who was considerably more athletic than her often sedentary husband – and much painting for Winston. The clear light of the Riviera proved a boon to his brush strokes and the next two weeks would fly by in a highly enjoyable respite from the usual rigours of life at the War Office. Included too was a round of socializing with friends and colleagues such as Sir Ernest Cassel and Max Aitken, 1st Baron Beaverbrook. Both of these men had come to be an important part of Churchill's close personal circle: Cassel indispensable to the health of Churchill's financial affairs, and Beaverbrook certainly by this time, if not indispensable politically, a ubiquitous presence in Churchill's life.[17]

At the end of January Churchill's sunny southern reverie came to an end and he returned to London. Clementine, in the meantime, stayed on in France but removed to nearby Saint-Jean-Cap-Ferrat to enjoy more tennis-playing and to extend her break from supervising the children at home. Their fifth and youngest child, a girl named

Marigold, had been born just two years earlier.[18] The holiday had done its job though, because once back in London and into political harness Churchill would finish his tenure as secretary of state for war in keen anticipation of moving across Whitehall to his new appointment at the Colonial Office.

The position of colonial secretary which Churchill now occupied was not among Britain's Great Offices of State. But since the end of the First World War the territorial and demographic size of the British Empire had never been more extensive, so the job of colonial secretary certainly ranked not far beneath them in prevailing importance.[19] In its second and modern iteration, dating from 1854, the Colonial Office had grown significantly in reach, even though the incremental way in which the empire itself had expanded meant that not all of its constituent territories fell under the office's control. India was an obvious exception: it had been under the direction of the East India Company until the middle of the nineteenth century and thereafter under that of the Crown. There were other anomalies too, one of which was Egypt. Much later, beginning in 1925, and in a similar manner, separate secretariats would be created for the dominions, such as Canada and Australia. But in Churchill's day, both when he had first served at the Colonial Office as under-secretary sixteen years earlier, and now as he moved into the top job, these departmental anomalies remained disruptive to the smooth running of the ministry: he regarded as problematic, for example, Foreign Office control of Egypt. From the outset therefore he was determined to grasp the nettle of such anomalies, especially in relation to the form that Middle East governance might take in the future. Symbolic of Churchill's reforming instincts in this regard is the fact that his private secretary during his time at the Colonial Office would be Ralph Dolignon Furse. Later regarded as the 'father of the modern Colonial Service', Furse would be instrumental in putting in place a series of reforms in the late 1920s that did much to shape the service's membership and ethos for a generation. His centrality to the service would be made permanent when he was installed as its director of recruitment in 1930, a position held until his retirement in 1948.[20]

In the protracted lead-up to receiving the seals of office later in February, Churchill had immediately begun to plan the restructuring of the Colonial Office by putting together the new Middle East Department. The prime minister's permission to do so had made it clear that he expected Churchill to accomplish much in his new Cabinet post. And the new colonial secretary would waste no time in placing his imprint upon affairs. To others, both within the government and outside it, especially in the popular press, Churchill's exalted status – just then he was effectively heading up *three* ministries: war, air and the colonies – was proof that he had become too prominent a figure at Westminster. The *Manchester Guardian*, for example, decried the 'sweeping powers' Churchill had been accorded by Lloyd George. While this sort of criticism might have been expected from the political left, even *The Times* wondered whether an apparently autocratic Churchill would continue to rule over all these ministries, as well as Britain's colonial territories, in a despotic style.[21]

If press criticism mattered little to Churchill, resistance from within the government itself, on the other hand, was potentially a source of much greater difficulty. In particular, the chief source of such internal criticism was to be found in the august personage of Lord Curzon at the Foreign Office. By 1921, Curzon's star had begun to dip towards the political horizon. Early on, during his celebrated Oxford undergraduate days in the 1880s, Curzon had been seen as a coming politician of unmistakeable promise and a likely candidate for prime minister. But since his ignominious resignation as viceroy of India in 1905, the long-expected prize of the top office had eluded his grasp. Still, he remained a powerful political figure. Appointed foreign secretary by Lloyd George in the autumn of 1919 Curzon would remain in post until 1924, only to die the following year. To Churchill,

Curzon had been a rival since the days of the First World War. Moreover, Curzon had remained someone for whom 'gratitude and resentment', as one criticism ran, were equal responses to an over-bearing manner, patrician birth and an Eton and Oxford education. If Curzon's peers at Balliol could not resist poking fun at him for being a 'superior person', then later others could not do so either.[22] Clementine, for example, referred to him simply as the 'All Highest'.[23] Still, he had risen high indeed, had fallen and risen again, and in 1921, though his star was on the wane, Curzon, as foreign secretary, remained formidable. He also regarded himself – not without reason – to be an expert on the affairs of the Near and Middle East.[24]

Churchill's remit over the 'Middle East' – the term itself was a newish one, American in origin and not yet in common usage in Britain, denoting essentially the states or regions of Egypt, Mesopotamia, Persia, Palestine, Syria and Saudi Arabia – meant that his ministerial authority would necessarily clash with that of others, especially Curzon's as foreign secretary. The Foreign Office's control over Egyptian affairs as well as those of the Hejaz meant that these two areas stood outside Churchill's grand plan for the new Middle East Department. A special Cabinet committee on the question, chaired by Sir James Masterton-Smith, under-secretary at the Ministry of Labour (he would become permanent under-secretary of state for the colonies later in 1921), had been created by Lloyd George, and went on to recommend that the putative Middle East Department's scope be limited to Mesopotamia, Palestine, Arabia and Aden. This decision would reduce in size Churchill's original – more robust – plan, but the department remained large enough still to impinge upon the authority of the Foreign Office, as well as that of the India Office, the secretariat for British Crown rule in India. Accordingly, Churchill had begun already to try and smooth the terminally choppy waters of inter-ministry competition by writing to Curzon on 8 January. Had the foreign secretary, he queried, 'any advice that you may be willing to give me and also the aid – indispensable at so many points – of the Foreign Office'?[25] Curzon was not easily mollified in this regard however, and would complain shortly about having suffered 'a reverse at Churchill's hands' because of the scope of the Middle East Department. Later, he objected even more strongly in a letter to his wife that the new colonial secretary wanted 'to grab everything in his new department and to be some sort of Asiatic Foreign Secretary'.[26]

In the meantime, at the nearby India Office its secretary Edwin Montagu was likewise vexed by the prospect of the pushy Churchill impinging on his own administrative territory.[27] Despite the fact that Montagu's personal relations with Churchill were much friendlier than those between Churchill and Curzon, Montagu recoiled none-theless at what he took to be an example of typical Churchillian over-reach. Montagu had deep roots at the India Office, having served as its under-secretary during the four years leading up to the war. Then, in 1917, Lloyd George had made him Indian secretary, a role that would make him responsible for the Montagu–Chelmsford Reforms leading to the passage of the Government of India Act in 1919. One of the first British Jews to hold a place in Cabinet, Montagu's anti-Zionist views clashed with the converse position held just as firmly by his cousin Sir Herbert Samuel, who would be appointed the following year as Britain's first high commissioner to Palestine.

Just a short time before finally taking office as colonial secretary, Churchill spent the weekend with Lloyd George at the new prime ministerial retreat of Chequers Court, a sixteenth-century manor house in Buckinghamshire located some 40 miles north-west of central London.[28] 'You would like to see this place', Churchill wrote excitedly to Clementine, who remained on holiday in France. 'Perhaps you will some day!' Churchill's jaunty mood that weekend was not simply a reflection of his enjoyment of the manifest comforts of Chequers, but also owed something also to the fact that his termi-nally stretched finances had been eased recently by an unexpected windfall. 'We must try to live within our income', he had written plaintively if unconvincingly to his wife on 27 January, unaware that just a day earlier his bachelor first cousin, Lord Herbert Vane-Tempest, had been killed in a railway accident in Wales.[29] Now, Vane-Tempest's considerable wealth – the probate value of his estate would ultimately be about £56,000 (an amount worth approximately £2.5 million today) – was coming Churchill's way as his only surviving male heir.

By the time that most of these initial departmental machinations and prime ministerial discussions had run their course, Churchill was ready to take over at the Colonial Office. Leaving behind the War and Air ministries meant walking away from the bracing military tension of the Russian and Irish files, at least for the time being. But his personal engagement could not have been higher. Indeed, 13 February 1921 – the day that at last he would receive the seals of office as colonial secretary – was a red-letter day for Churchill. The next morning he began his tenure at the Colonial Office, settling once again into the familiar surroundings that he had come to know sixteen years earlier.

Churchill's discussions with Lloyd George at Chequers over that early February weekend had revolved mainly around his increasingly solid plan to fashion a permanent resolution of the complicated British geopolitical position in the Middle East. As Churchill understood it, his main task at the Colonial Office – at least initially – was to fashion, and then to see implemented, a comprehensive framework integrating the three great pieces of British regional policy: the McMahon–Hussein correspondence; the Sykes–Picot Agreement; and the Balfour Declaration. He envisaged that these three policies could be made to work in concert. However, this was not the way in which they had come to be viewed by many of his Cabinet colleagues, nor by the public. Churchill wished to eliminate the discordancy and disaggregation of these separate policies and replace them with a prevailing unity that would solve for the British state the expensive and turbulent geopolitics of the Middle East. Accordingly, both at Chequers and during the early weeks that followed as colonial secretary, Churchill concentrated on working towards this unity through sustained conversation with his officials and the relentless writing of policy memoranda.

The first of these three British Middle East policies put under review by Churchill was the one that had been undertaken in 1915 by the British high commissioner to Egypt, Sir Henry McMahon, in correspondence with Sharif Hussein. The promise of some form of national independence made to the Arabs should they fight on the British side had been overturned by events since the end of the war. To Churchill, however, this state of affairs needed to be resolved through a renewed effort to move the Arabs towards that original goal. And it could be achieved, he believed, if his prescription for the new Middle East Department's remit was applied to the situation in the near future. In the words of the historian Warren Dockter, for Churchill, Britain's support for Arab independence 'was a debt of honour to pay to the Hashemite family for their support during the war'.[30]

Second on the list for Churchill was to examine afresh the implications of the Sykes–Picot Agreement. Sykes may have been a man 'clearly marked out for service in the East', as Churchill had put it, but to others, such as Lawrence, he had been untrustworthy and dilettantish. Lawrence's particular animus owed itself mainly to the fact that the Arab independence for which he had so keenly fought appeared to have counted as not much more than a pipe-dream to Sykes. 'Complete independence means ... [p]overty and chaos', Sykes had remarked about Arab aspirations for freedom. 'Let him [Lawrence] consider this as he hopes for the people he is fighting for'.[31]

As colonial secretary, Churchill aimed to come to terms with Sykes–Picot by ensuring that its provisions and implications were settled finally under his watch. To do so meant adopting a firm but conciliatory view of France's abiding mandate over Syria and

Lebanon. This point had been discussed thoroughly by Churchill and President Millerand of France in Paris in early January when Churchill had been en route to Nice. Equally however, and necessarily vital to an Anglo-French entente in the Middle East, was Britain's (and to be sure Lawrence's own) influence over the Arabs, specifically over Faisal himself. Since Faisal's removal as king of Syria by the French the previous summer, Millerand had complained to Churchill that both Faisal and his supporters had been conspiring against the occupying French to bring about his potential restoration to the Syrian throne. During their recent meeting in Paris Millerand had stressed to Churchill that such actions had to cease, a view which was shared by Curzon at the Foreign Office. As the foreign secretary had bluntly put it, he 'preferred to quarrel with the Arabs rather than with France'.[32] On this point Churchill required no convincing, however, because he had begun to develop alternative plans for Faisal that would see him prevented from having any future as monarch in Syria. In so doing, France would be given a free hand in Syria in exchange for a similar form of autonomy for Britain in Mesopotamia, Palestine and Transjordan.

The third plank of Churchill's developing Middle East policy focused on the Balfour Declaration. Churchill's own moderate Zionist sympathies had been emboldened by the declaration's public commitment by Britain to create a Jewish national homeland in Palestine. Despite his sometimes sharp criticism of Zionist activism, Churchill was in favour of establishing a new Jewish polity in the Holy Land. His clearest public statement had come two years earlier in the *Illustrated Sunday Herald* of 25 January 1919, in which he had criticized the so-called Jewish character of Marxist theory and thereby that of Russian Bolshevism. Of the 'diabolical purpose' of Lenin himself – who was of course not Jewish – he would say only that 'All tyrants are the enemies of the human race' and that 'All tyrannies should be overthrown'. But Zionism itself, wrote Churchill, was an 'inspiring movement' and a proper outlet for 'National Jews' who showed no sympathy towards Russian Bolshevism and whose loyalty to their respective countries was to be praised. The Jews, he lauded, 'are the most remarkable race that has ever appeared in the world'. He predicted a 'Jewish State', 'which would from every point of view be beneficial', and reflect 'the truest interests of the British Empire'.

Years later, in 1956, and after his second tenure as prime minister had come to an end, Churchill would explain to the US president Dwight D. Eisenhower that 'I am, of course, a Zionist, and have been ever since the Balfour Declaration'.[33] But in Churchill's mind his endorsement of Zionism – both then and earlier – had never made him anything less than sympathetic towards Arab nationalist aspirations. After all, as he had once written about the British Empire in an unsent letter to Lloyd George, 'we are the greatest Mohammedan power in the world'. At the time that Churchill wrote these words the enormous Muslim population of British India was uppermost in his mind. But the point remains nonetheless. Arab–Jewish tension, disaffection, even hatred, were not necessarily more intractable or unresolvable, Churchill believed firmly if perhaps unrealistically, than once had been the emnity between Boer and Briton in South Africa, or between the French and English in Canada. Ultimately of course, the division between Hindu and Muslim would confound everyone, Indian and Briton alike. Still, if communal feuding in other parts of the British Empire could be defused over time, then so too, Churchill believed, could it be within Palestine.

Despite Churchill's seemingly fulsome endorsement of Zionism quoted above, his views did not mean that he was against Palestine's resident Arab population. And he certainly did not undervalue President Millerand's view that ever since 1917 Zionism had been 'disturbing' the entire Arab world.[34] But to Churchill, Arab–Jewish relations could be made to harmonize. They could reach political equipoise if a settlement was negotiated in the right way and by the right people. In the first place, he believed, the raw material existed sociologically between Jews and Arabs, in the form of their shared

Semitic ethnicity, to achieve comity. In the language of Lloyd George's Baptist chapel upbringing, the 'sons of Isaac' and the 'sons of Ishmael' should be able to achieve peaceful co-existence in the modern world. In the councils of the remade Colonial Office both sides of the argument would have their champions, especially in the form of the strongly pro-Arab Lawrence and the equally stalwart Zionist Colonel Richard Meinertzhagen, who would be Churchill's adviser on military affairs in the Middle East. Despite the obvious tensions and apparent contradictions of these undertakings, Churchill took the position that they might yet come to yield a rational and comprehensive settlement of all that had been stirred mightily in the Middle East by the impact of the First World War and the defeat of the Ottoman Empire.

Settling down to work at the Colonial Office in mid-February, Churchill worked quickly to firm up his new team of Middle East Department advisers as well as to assign them the tasks that he intended to see carried out. Moreover, critically, he decided also that he should visit in person the lands over which his newly acquired authority as colonial secretary would now run. Earlier as war secretary he had thought that he ought probably to visit the highly restive and militarily expensive Mesopotamia. As his new Cabinet appointment approached, however, he had decided that not only should he switch destinations to Egypt, but that its capital Cairo would make for an ideal location to hold a conference on the future governance of the Middle East. It would be both the right occasion and, since Egypt's own future would not be under discussion, the correct location, to make public just how his vision of a recast British policy in the region might be realized. However, as Churchill wrote to Lord Allenby in Cairo at the end of February, he was not unaware of the controversial reputation that he had gained in Egypt. Since 1919 Churchill had adopted a critical stance towards the country's emergent nationalism. It might not therefore be wise for him to go there. 'I am anxious that my presence should not be a cause of embarrassment to you or local disorder', he wrote to Lord Allenby. Churchill then went on to suggest that it might be better if the proposed conference were to be held in Jerusalem. He advised Allenby to discuss the matter with Sir Herbert Samuel, 'if you think it necessary. Keep me informed. I am entirely in your hands'.

Since first being offered the Colonial Office by Lloyd George at the beginning of 1921 Churchill had worked remarkably quickly. Even for him the pace while transitioning to his new ministry had been breakneck. Persuading Lawrence to join him had been a key achievement. To Churchill, Lawrence's close relationship with Faisal would need to function as the necessary hinge-point if his plan for reform in the Middle East was going to work. As far as Churchill was concerned Faisal had absolutely no future in Syria. The French mandate there meant effectively that the country had become a dead letter for him. This position is exactly what had been discussed with Millerand in Paris, and it had been communicated to Lloyd George also. To Churchill, Iraq alone remained a place where Faisal's legitimate kingly aspirations might be satisfied and Arab expectations for a state of their own be met. Moreover, if Faisal could be placed on the Iraqi throne and the country given some measure of independence according to the agreements made at San Remo the year before, then Britain could begin to scale back its military commitments in the country significantly and reduce its massive annual level of spending. As much as Churchill might have wished to see the Hashemite Arabs come to realize a form of post-war independence, equally did he desire to economize Britain's £20 million fiscal commitment in Iraq. If this economizing course of action was not achievable, he had warned Lloyd George in January, then simple fiscal pressure would win the day and the British would be 'forced by expense of the garrisons to evacuate the territories ... gained in war'.[35]

The crux of the emerging plan was to be the enthronement of Faisal in Iraq, and the best – indeed, probably the only – person able to persuade him of the logic of what Churchill had in mind was Lawrence. Despite Lawrence's abiding sense of post-Paris failure, he had never really ceased advocating for the Arabs. In the autumn of 1920, for example, he had penned articles for a variety of London newspapers in which he continued to press for Arab independence. In the pages of both *The Times* and the *Observer* he had sung Faisal's praises as an Arab leader of 'prophetic fire', as well as one who was both 'honest and tactful'. The deteriorating and expensive situation in Iraq Lawrence laid mainly at the feet of the ineffective civil admin-istration of Arnold Wilson, made worse by the harsh military command of General Haldane.[36] Their failure in this regard, Lawrence concluded, meant that the time had come for a fundamental change in Iraqi local governance. As his close colleague Major Hubert Young had been told earlier, the longstanding 'Indianizing' policy needed to be reversed.[37] Accordingly, the country had to be taken away from India Office control, he maintained, and placed on the track of British mandatory rule leading eventually to independence under Faisal as king.

But if Churchill and Lawrence had started down the path towards Faisal's enthronement as king of Iraq they were merely joining others already headed in the same direction. Lord Curzon was one of the most notable in this regard. The foreign secretary believed similarly that a cardinal change needed to be achieved in Iraqi governance to make the country a success, and that meant Faisal becoming its king.[38] In anticipation of this growing possibility, Faisal had already departed the Hejaz – where he had been living since his hurried deposition from the Syrian throne in July – for London in November of 1920. Upon his arrival the next month he had resided briefly at Claridge's Hotel before removing to the more private confines of a townhouse in nearby Berkeley Square. In this new location he had entertained guests such as Lawrence, conducted interviews, and let it generally be known that he was willing to fall in line with the fast-consolidating British plan of placing him on the throne of Iraq.

The plan to enthrone Faisal – and soon also to enthrone his brother Abdullah in Transjordan – would begin now to be spoken of in certain British government circles as comprising the 'Sherifian Solution'. As such, it was seen as a means by which to cut the Gordian knot of problems plaguing the post-war Middle East and put in place strong national leadership from which reforming government might emanate. Unsurprisingly given Churchill's characteristic verbal dexterity, he seems to have coined the term himself, and together with Lawrence began immediately to work out what such a plan might mean in practice.[39] Having 'got Lawrence to put on a bridle and collar', in January Churchill had instructed him immediately to query Faisal about his receptivity to the idea of being made king of Iraq.[40] Curzon would ask an emissary to pose exactly the same question to Faisal, which he had initially declined to answer on the grounds that his father, Sharif Hussein, believed that Abdullah should be placed on the Iraqi throne, not him. Faisal added, however, that he doubted the success of such an idea. Later, Faisal would be invited to the West Sussex estate of Shillinglee, owned by Lord Winterton, a Conservative MP who a short time later became under-secretary of state at the India Office. Winterton was a friend of Faisal's from the Arab Revolt, during which he had fought for the Arab Northern Army. Over a weekend in January 1921 Winterton had acted as Curzon's agent in continuing to press the idea on Faisal of accepting the Iraqi throne. It was a task also taken up by Lawrence: he too had been invited to spend the weekend at Shillinglee as a house-guest. By Sunday, it seems that working together Lawrence and the others had achieved their mission; Faisal now 'agreed to become king of Iraq'.[41] It was only a matter of time therefore until the Sherifian Solution would come to form the centre-piece of Churchill's plan for renewed British policymaking in the Middle East.

Working on the burgeoning Sherifian Solution were a clutch of advisers who enlarged the Middle East Department's staff complement by giving it breadth, depth and ballast beyond that provided by the dominant Churchill–Lawrence axis. The first of these additional officials was John Evelyn Shuckburgh, appointed as departmental secretary by Churchill. An Old Etonian, Shuckburgh had served for many years at the India Office before being drafted by Churchill into his Middle East Department staff. He was sympathetic towards Arab nationalism and would remain in the department for a decade, embodying 'the traditional concept of the public servant. Hardworking, experienced and responsible'.[42]

Churchill's other main appointment to the Middle East Department was Hubert Young. Like Shuckburgh, he was a strong proponent of the Arab cause, later penning a memoir entitled *The Independent Arab*. A career artilleryman, Young had become a British political officer in Mesopotamia during the First World War, during which time he had befriended Lawrence. He would go on to win the Distinguished Service Order near the close of the Syrian campaign in September of 1918 during which his inveterate diplomacy earned him the nickname *Makik* ('Shuttle') from the Bedouin.[43] After the war, Young joined the Foreign Office's Eastern Committee from which he had transferred to the Colonial Office at Churchill's behest to become assistant secretary.

In staffing the new Middle East Department, Churchill did a thorough job of creating a professional, progressive and balanced unit of policymakers. Clearly, the considered position of its membership tipped the scale towards the pro-Arab side. But, as we have seen, Meinertzhagen – who had acted as a key member of Allenby's intelligence staff during the Palestine campaign – was strongly Zionist in a manner that offered Churchill a persuasive voice to counter the pro-Arab stance of his other main staff members. To Churchill, his own Zionism would never mean that he conceived of the Jewish–Arab question to be an either/or proposition, however. Additionally, he remained convinced that the Colonial Office's Middle East Department was exactly the right place for planning the future governance of Iraq, as well as elsewhere in the region. Consequently, he advocated removing the India Office from its continuing supervisory role, and reducing too the role of the Foreign Office.

As much as a fully staffed Middle East Department would bring more voices to the Sherifian Solution, for Churchill Lawrence remained its key figure. It was on him that Churchill relied most heavily to solve the Middle Eastern puzzle.[44] This reliance was not misplaced. To Faisal, Lawrence was entirely dependable. 'He takes up the challenge and does not tire or easily lose', as he described him admiringly. 'He was also truthful in his promises, a matter that made the Arabs trust him. He lived with them and did not patronise them. That is why they loved him'. Accordingly, Churchill's ear was cocked permanently in the direction of Lawrence, especially in relation to Faisal's willingness to accept the Iraqi throne. Churchill's 'virgin mind' on the entire subject of the Middle East, as he once put it in conversation with a staff member, thus remained ready to be led in the direction advocated by Lawrence.[45]

In addition to the core members of the department, Churchill also consulted other experts. One of the most important of these was Sir Arthur Hirtzel, deputy under-secretary of state at the India Office. Churchill had tried to hire Hirtzel for service in the Colonial Office, but he had declined. But Churchill directed a series of probing questions to him nonetheless in an attempt to increase his breadth of knowledge across all constituent issues pertaining to the Arabs and Arabia. These questions ranged from determining 'a uniform system of spelling and pronouncing Arab names'; to asking for 'a *large* map of Arabia and Mesopotamia'; to 'whether it would be right or possible to form a Mohammedan Guard of Indian volunteers for the protection of the holy places'. Of greater importance still was the relationship between the members of the Hashemite royal household, as well as its diplomatic relations with the competing Arab dynasty located in central and eastern Arabia and headed by Sharif Hussein's chief regional rival, Ibn Saud. Would Ibn Saud be 'offended', Churchill asked Hirtzel, 'if a son of King Hussein is made ruler over Mesopotamia, or will he not care?' Further he queried, 'What are the principal doctrinal and ritualistic differences involved between the Shia, the Sunni, and the Shabi [Wahhabist] Mohammedans?'[46]

Churchill's curiosity and growing perspicacity to these ends were almost boundless, but he would continue to lodge his greatest trust over the cardinal Hussein–Faisal question in the judgement of Lawrence. And by as early as mid-January Lawrence had told his new chief that Faisal – having received fresh assurances of support from his father – had become a willing party to the Sherifian Solution. 'The advantage of his taking this new ground of discussion', wrote Lawrence, 'is that all questions of pledges and promises, fulfilled or broken, are set aside. You begin a new discussion on the actual positions today and the best way of doing something constructive with them. It's so much more useful than splitting hairs. Feisal can help very much towards a rapid settlement of these countries, if he wants to: and if we can only get them working like a team they will be a surprising big thing in two or three years'.[47]

As a prologue to the Cairo Conference, Lawrence could not have articulated its aims any more clearly than he did here. Churchill was in the business of Arab state-building and Lawrence's assessment that the situation demanded a fresh start was a useful one. It was not to be a break, he believed, in the sense of having a totally clean slate upon which to work, but in the sense that the situation was new and had progressed to the point of all-party congruence. Accordingly, Churchill moved quickly in February towards forming a definite plan and a set agenda for Cairo that would hold the potential to remake the Middle East along the lines he intended. In so doing he believed that a clear demonstration could be made of the benign power of the British Empire to lay the groundwork for a new Arab state in Iraq – and perhaps other countries beyond – with the potential to become the 'big thing' in the region that Lawrence had predicted.

By the beginning of February 1921 therefore, before Churchill had even taken the seals of office, his Middle East Department was hard at work. Churchill had managed to finesse objections to its creation, as well as criticisms of his alleged penchant for empire-building and, undaunted, pressed ahead with his plans. In the process the Sherifian Solution had moved to the heart of the proposed agenda for Cairo. Lawrence was invested deeply in this new vision for Middle East governance. His formal appointment to the Colonial Office – made official on 18 February – brought with it an annual salary of £1,600, a large sum and £600 more than what Lawrence had asked for.[48] But Churchill was pleased to reward Lawrence royally in this way. Suddenly finding himself flush, Lawrence would use some of his new salary to fund a journey to the Middle East by Eric Kennington, the sculptor and official war artist he had enlisted to make chalk portraits of the principal figures of the Arab Revolt for use as illustrations in *Seven Pillars of Wisdom*. Originally, before signing on for service at the Colonial Office, Lawrence had planned to accompany Kennington to the Middle East at his own expense. Now he would not be able to do so as planned, but the two men would meet up there later nonetheless.

From mid-February onwards Lawrence had been engaged fully in drawing up the Churchill-envisioned agenda for the Cairo Conference. He, John Shuckburgh and Hubert Young sat together in a corner of the Colonial Office picking apart the various issues at hand. 'Talk of leaving things to the man on the spot', Lawrence wrote of this exciting period leading up to the start of the conference: 'we left nothing'. Indeed, like most diplomatic summits, the principal figures involved at Cairo prepared for the event in such a way as to maximize the possibility of achieving their goals. In anticipation of Cairo, Lawrence and Young operated as a two-headed sounding board for Churchill, fielding the questions that might come his way in the Egyptian capital, mooting answers and pointing out potential pitfalls and likely points of friction. 'You must take risks', Lawrence advised Churchill firmly, 'make a native king in Iraq, and hand over defence to the RAF instead of the Army'.[49] On the latter point Churchill was convinced already of its potential efficacy and economy, both by Lawrence's experience of the effective use of air power during the Arab Revolt and by the professional opinion of Air Marshal Sir Hugh Trenchard, chief of the Air Staff. Everything that the British wished to achieve in the Middle East, Lawrence believed, was possible, given that the main policymakers at the Colonial Office had now reached essential agreement over the future course Iraq should take.

In the pale winter light of a London February, Lawrence, Young and Shuckburgh – the so-called 'department council' – proceeded to tick off the main points on their fast-developing list. They were making 'great progress ... on the Agenda for the conference', Shuckburgh informed Churchill's trusted lieutenant, Eddie Marsh, on 25 February: the totality of the colonial secretary's plan for Cairo was rounding into form. Young remained resolute that the 'Sherifian family' be made to see the necessity of the 'mandatory principle'. Several weeks earlier he had emphasized the point in a letter to Wyndham Deedes, the British civil secretary in Jerusalem: 'I want a Sherifian ruler for Mesopotamia, and I want another for Trans-Jordania ... We need no longer consider the French. They have done the dirty on us [in Syria], and we must now go our own way'.[50]

Meanwhile, as Churchill's designated Arab adviser, Lawrence remained in the lead during these heady planning days in advance of the event. In addition to working with his colleagues in the Middle East Department, Lawrence continued to meet regularly with Faisal to keep him abreast of preparations for Cairo. If all went according to plan at the conference, it was implied to Faisal, then he would indeed become king of Iraq. The agenda that Lawrence and his colleagues were developing contained a series of points. All of them, he believed, offered a form of redress to Faisal and the Arabs for the resounding blow that their expectations for independence had suffered two years earlier at Paris. Rarely in politics is a second chance possible. But in February of 1921 that is exactly what was being anticipated by Lawrence to come at Cairo.

In the meantime, accompanying Faisal during his stay in the West End of London was not only a serious effort at diplomacy for Lawrence; it was proving also to be a good deal of fun for both of them. Lunches were had with eminent writers such as E.M. Forster and Siegfried Sassoon, both of whom appealed to Faisal's literary sensibilities, and there were also weekends in the country, such as the one spent at the duke of Devonshire's palatial Chatsworth House in Derbyshire.[51] Faisal himself was feeling just as confident as Lawrence about his prospects in Iraq. Indeed, as his biographer notes, Faisal understood one of the outcomes of the Iraqi Revolt of 1920 to have been propelling forward his candidacy for the country's throne. As his representative in London, Colonel Gabriel Haddad, put it: 'Faisal had decided to take a keen interest in the throne of Mesopotamia, which would make up for the loss of his one in Damascus'. In fact, Faisal had contributed some £40,000 of his personal fortune to support the Iraqi Revolt. This action was not known to the British but it speaks to Faisal's own part in the quest to become king of Iraq that transcended even the keenly held desire of Churchill and Lawrence to engineer such an outcome. As Faisal's close aide Rustam Haidar diarized at the time about his chief: 'he was partial to Iraq, saying that he had tried the Syrians and does not want to work with them any further'.[52]

Meanwhile, with the conference growing ever closer, Churchill sought to conclude final arrangements with Sir Percy Cox, the high commissioner in Baghdad. Indeed, from the moment that he had taken over at the Colonial Office Churchill was committed to having a face-to-face encounter with those, like Cox, who operated in the field. 'The questions at issue cannot be settled by interchange of telegrams', Churchill had told him firmly. He made clear to Cox also the expected range and scope of what the conference was intended to accomplish. As the key British 'man-on-the-spot' in the Middle East,

Cox would be relied upon by Churchill to act as one of his chief counsellors at Cairo. Churchill ran through the Middle East Department's agenda with him, which included putting in place a new ruler for Iraq; deciding on the future course and size of the British garrison there; determining how long it would take to reduce the size of the current over-large British troop deployment in the country; budgeting the amount of money that would be required by a reduced, but nevertheless ongoing, mandatory British commitment in Iraq; and, finally, mapping 'the extent of territory to be held and administered' throughout the region. These points, Churchill informed Cox, would form the basis of the conference's deliberations.

In spelling out to Cox the direction in which he wished to take the conference, Churchill wasted no time in attempting to orchestrate the means by which to achieve it. Reducing the size and cost of the British troop commitment in Iraq, the first item on the list, would serve, in Churchill's view, to achieve significant economies in the Treasury's multi-million-pound level of expenditure as well as to push the country towards greater independence. A singular impediment to this outcome, however, was the degree to which there remained some agents of the British government who wished to maintain as draconian a military grip on Iraq as they believed was warranted by the restiveness of the prevailing political situation. Chief among them was the British commander-in-chief in Iraq, General Sir Aylmer Haldane. A cousin of Richard Haldane, who had been secretary of state for war in Sir Henry Campbell-Bannerman's Liberal Cabinet while Churchill was under-secretary of state at the Colonial Office, General Haldane had his own personal history with Churchill, beginning with their joint service as part of the Malakand Field Force in India back in 1898. Now, over twenty years later, Churchill and Haldane would find themselves thrown together again.

As preparations for the conference drew to a close, Churchill planned to leave for Cairo on 1 March. On 16 February, Lawrence met with

Faisal for the final time before setting off for Egypt himself two weeks later. Both men were confident that at Cairo a great success lay in store. But before leaving Lawrence made plain to Faisal that as Churchill's Arab adviser the nature of their own relationship would now necessarily have to change. Faisal understood. Lawrence recounted their meeting in a note to Churchill written shortly after it had taken place: '[I] explained to him that ... [t]his would necessarily alter our relations, and particularly would prevent his asking me certain questions: but the appointment had not changed my opinions'. He added that Faisal had responded pithily, 'that he would like to lose all his friends in the same way'. Lawrence continued that he had told Faisal that the upcoming conference at Cairo was going to be 'between the Secretary of State and his British lieutenants, in which the politics, constitution, and finances of the Arabic areas in Western Asia would come up for discussion in whole or part'. Lawrence stressed to Churchill that he had made it clear to Faisal that the conference would be 'of direct interest to his race, and especially to his family, and I thought present signs justified his being reasonably hopeful of a settlement satisfactory to all parties. I mentioned specially the Mesopotamian, and Trans-Jordan questions'.[53]

Lawrence's final point concerning Transjordan contained two elements which Churchill had just begun to contemplate seriously. The first of these was to ensure that the future of Transjordan be settled by denying the Zionists' aspiration to include it within the existing territory of Britain's Palestine mandate. It was Churchill's considered position that instead a separate state of Transjordan must be created and necessarily put under Arab administration. So doing would merely be a reflection of the fact that its current population was almost wholly Arab and had been so for millennia. In ensuring that Transjordan remained Arab, Churchill believed that Britain could fulfil the promise made in the McMahon–Hussein correspondence, as well as adhere to the recommendations of the Sykes–Picot Agreement. Unsurprisingly, Chaim Weizmann proved unwilling to accept Churchill's staunchness on this point. The Zionist leader believed – and had emphasized as much to his followers – that Churchill had 'a low opinion of the Arab generally', which he thought might preclude the establishment of an Arab Transjordan.[54] But Churchill refused to back down on his plan for Transjordan, and that had put an end to the matter. In making the comment about Churchill's view of the Arabs, Weizmann was wide of the mark. It is true that under Lawrence's influence Churchill had indeed developed an unflattering view of the so-called 'town' Arab; that is, Palestinian Arabs who did not fit the glamourous public image given to the Bedouin 'desert' Arabs, especially through the active lens of Lowell Thomas as the chief sponsor of the Lawrence of Arabia legend.[55] But that shared prejudice did not prevent Churchill from believing in the compellingly Arab nature of the putative Transjordanian state. Ultimately, Churchill would make plain in a speech given later in March at Jerusalem what he believed to constitute Britain's full intent in issuing the Balfour Declaration and its corresponding vision for the future of Palestine. 'Our promise was a double one', he stated, made to both Jews and Arabs.

Accordingly, and as a complement to placing Faisal on the throne of Iraq, Churchill's intention was to ensure that his elder brother Abdullah would accede to the throne in Transjordan and in so doing confirm the infant state's essential Arab character. Double king-making had presented itself to Churchill as part of the Sherifian Solution as the only viable option for success, especially since Abdullah had decided during the previous November to take up residence at Maan in southern Transjordan as a possible prelude to acting against the French in Syria. Lawrence's relationship with Abdullah from the moment they had first met in October of 1916 in Jeddah had been less than trustworthy, and he remained dubious about the extent of Abdullah's aptitude for leadership. Consequently, Lawrence suggested to Churchill that he and Abdullah should meet in Jerusalem once the conference in Cairo had concluded. In late

February, on the cusp of leaving for Egypt, Lawrence was reminded that in advance of joining the Middle East Department Churchill had promised him 'direct access to himself on every point, and a free hand, subject to his discretion. This was better than any condition, because I wanted the best settlement of the Middle East possible'.[56] Very soon, for both Lawrence and Churchill, making kings of Faisal and Abdullah would be to achieve just such a 'best settlement'.

4

'EVERYBODY MIDDLE EAST IS HERE'
TEN DAYS IN CAIRO, ACT I

On the evening of 1 March, as planned, Churchill departed London for Cairo. He would go via Marseille, stopping briefly to pick up Clementine who had concluded her extended holiday in the south of France. Churchill's beloved mother Jennie, a long-time presence in London high society, had married for the third time a few years earlier and was living in a townhouse in Berkeley Square, close to where Faisal then resided. She wrote a note of farewell to the elder of her two sons: '*bon voyage* – & a speedy return. Give my love to Clemmie – I hope you will find her none the worse for her 'prowesses' [her tennis games]. I will look after the children & give you news of them. They are great darlings & do you both credit!'[1] As it turned out, this note was the penultimate one written to Churchill by his mother. A few months later, in June, Jennie Porch – as she had become after her final marriage – died at the age of sixty-seven following complications from a broken ankle that had turned gangrenous. Heartbroken by the loss of a mother who had been his champion always, Churchill was buoyed nonetheless by his memories of her love and charisma as well as by what he would later write was 'her eternal youth of spirit'.[2]

Once the Churchills had reunited at Marseille on 2 March, they sailed immediately for Egypt. This was the first time that Clementine had accompanied Churchill abroad on official business. Perhaps it was the exciting prospect of a Mediterranean and North African journey that had prompted her to write to Churchill just a week earlier about her anticipation of 'living in blissful contemplation' and of a 'smooth and carefree future'. For his part, after being without her for some five weeks, he wrote to say that 'I am so looking forward to seeing your dear face again'.[3] The next six days spent crossing the Mediterranean Sea on board the *Sphinx*, an aptly named French steamship, would be enjoyable.[4] The passage also gave Churchill the opportunity to approve the final agenda for the Cairo Conference that had been created over the preceding weeks by his Middle East Department staff members, Lawrence, Shuckburgh and Young.[5] On 8 March the ship reached Alexandria, where Churchill asked to be taken to nearby Aboukir Bay. The site held special historical appeal to him as a former first lord of the Admiralty owing to the decisive victory won there in 1798 by Admiral Horatio Nelson and his fifteen captains, the 'Band of Brothers', over the Napoleonic fleet. It was a triumph that would change the course of the French revolutionary regime and help to solidify Britain's growing command of the seas during the following century.

In Alexandria, the Churchills spent two nights at the sumptuous Savoy Palace Hotel. According to an admiring local newspaper, it could 'compare most advantageously with those in Cairo and Upper Egypt', which was high praise indeed considering that the heart of the tourist zone lay to the south. The Churchills and their entourage, including 'one maid and three male servants', departed for the Egyptian capital on the 10th.[6] The party also included Churchill's recently assigned bodyguard from Special Branch, Detective Inspector Walter Thompson, a strapping former Metropolitan police constable. He too boarded the luxurious train which had been put at Churchill's disposal by Fuad I, the Sultan of Egypt, for the 100-mile journey south to Cairo.[7] Thompson's burly presence was a welcome one: in anticipation of Churchill's arrival a large number of Cairenes gathered to denounce him owing to his public opposition to the demands made by anti-occupation Egyptian nationalists. Indeed, placard-waving protesters had already greeted him in Alexandria – 'Down with Churchill', they had shouted – and his train had been pelted with stones.[8]

Churchill was well aware that his reputation preceded him in the country. So too were others. In fact, not long before Churchill departed London, Curzon had written him to say that holding the conference in Cairo would prove to be a mistake. Churchill's well-known anti-independence views, the foreign secretary stated, meant that he should expect public demonstrations which would serve to exacerbate the strong anti-British sentiment present already in the country. Moreover, in Curzon's view, by going to Egypt Churchill once again would be 'stepping boldly' onto Foreign Office territory and in general empire-building at other ministers' expense. Churchill had reacted angrily to the advice, interpreting it as little more than yet another swipe by the foreign secretary, although Curzon's point of view was shared by Lord Allenby in Cairo. He too had been concerned about the potential for mass protests against Churchill, a phenomenon that he had been dealing with himself for the better part of two years, ever since his appointment as high commissioner back in March of 1919.[9] In the event however, upon arriving in Cairo, Churchill decided to disembark from the train up the line at a suburban stop. By so doing he avoided the angry crowd that had been waiting for him at the main terminus of Central Station. After leaving the train, Churchill, Clementine and the rest of the party proceeded to make their way unmolested to the site chosen to hold the conference, the opulent riverside Semiramis Hotel.

Located along the Nile in the heart of modern Cairo and named after the legendary Assyrian queen, the Semiramis was the most luxurious hotel in the city, if not the most famous. That particular designation belonged to Shepheard's Hotel, which was located nearby and dated from the mid-nineteenth century, and had long been the unofficial headquarters of the expatriate British community in the city. Opening much later in 1907, the Semiramis was to be the last in a string of hotels built by the well-known expatriate Swiss hotelier, Franz Josef Bucher.

Having settled in Cairo, Bucher began to build luxury hotels, a process which culminated in the Semiramis. Commencing in 1906, its construction would be a substantial project lasting for over a year. The hotel rose along the Nile next to the Khedive Ismail (now the Qasr el-Nil) Bridge, which then was the sole river crossing from Cairo to the pyramids at nearby Giza. Bucher employed some 1,300 people in the construction of the hotel. Upon its grand opening in February of 1907 the four-storey baroque-style structure with its blinding snow-white facade became an immediate architectural icon located in the most exclusive part of the city. The Semiramis Hotel's original 112 rooms and suites were finely appointed in the French Empire style, except for the brass bedsteads, which had been imported from England. Red-carpeted staircases, elaborate chandeliers, and life-size ebony statues dominated the hotel's interior. Meanwhile, its roof was made flat, perfect for the garden designed to be reminiscent, it was said, of the hanging gardens of ancient Babylon. Occupying a prominent location in Garden City, the Semiramis was the first major hotel in Cairo to be built alongside the river. The Semiramis had as its near neighbours the British high commissioner's Residence, the British Army's Qasr el-Nil barracks, Ismailia (now Tahrir) Square and the American University in Cairo.

In 1910, a few years after the Semiramis opened, it was sold to Charles Buehler, another Swiss hotelier who owned a number of properties elsewhere in Egypt. The Semiramis would become Buehler's crown jewel, one of the key hotels at the heart of Egypt's famed annual November-to-April 'Winter Season'. During this six-month period thousands of wealthy Europeans and Americans flocked to the country on holiday to take in its plethora of ancient historic sites, bask in its glorious desert sunshine, and relax sybaritically in its well-appointed hotels.[10] As Rudyard Kipling remarked following his own Winter Season visit to the Semiramis in 1913: 'The Swiss are the only people who have taken the trouble to master the art of hotel-keeping. Consequently, in the things that really matter – beds, baths, and victuals – they control Egypt'.[11] Eventually, Buehler expanded the popular Semiramis's number of rooms and reinforced its reputation for unparalleled luxury. In choosing to hold the Cairo Conference where he did, Churchill acted completely in character for someone who relished the best of creature comforts. Still, given the heightened political atmosphere prevailing in Cairo, personal security remained an important concern. But that requirement too had been met. 'We are lodged in the Semiramis Hotel', Churchill informed the Colonial Office's secretariat, 'which Lord Allenby considered the only one suitable from the point of view of the public order'.[12]

In 1921 Cairo's population was around 1 million people, making it the largest city in Africa. Just two years earlier in 1919 the almost forty-year-long British occupation of Egypt had reached an inflection point when a nationalist-inspired uprising had jolted the occupiers severely. In response, the British had begun to negotiate with nationalist leaders to end what they maintained had always been their temporary presence in the country. Originally, the British occupation had been precipitated by the Khedivial regime's deep financial crisis of the 1870s, which a conflicted William Gladstone as Liberal prime minister had attempted to solve by forcibly seizing control of the Egyptian state in 1882.[13] For most of the next generation administrative power in what formally remained Ottoman Egypt would be exercised by the British under the commanding figure of Evelyn Baring (later Earl Cromer).[14] As agent and consul-general, Cromer became Britain's all-powerful proconsul even as Egyptian nationalism began its concurrent and inexorable rise.

The advent of the First World War and with it the enemy status of the Ottomans prompted the British to extend a formal protectorate over Egypt, which had the effect of freezing the country constitutionally for the next four years. But the end of the war brought about a renewed drive for indigenous control of Egypt's future, especially by the nationalist Wafd Party, led by its determined and charismatic leader Saad Zaghloul. Having been exiled to Malta by the British in the spring of 1919, Zaghloul's absence occasioned widespread nationalist disturbances during which hundreds of Egyptians, as well as a small number of Europeans, had been killed, alongside much destruction of property. In the midst of what would grow into the Egyptian Revolution, the Lloyd George government, as we have seen, had sent Allenby to Egypt as high commissioner in March in an attempt to quell the violence and lead the way forward to a constitutional and hopefully irenic settlement. Allenby's appointment would be supplemented by the arrival of the Colonial Secretary, Lord Milner, in December of that same year to undertake a commission of inquiry into the prevailing political situation in Egypt and to offer recommendations for staged reformist action. Milner's report would be eventually delivered to the British Parliament in February of 1921, on the eve of the Cairo Conference and just before Churchill's official move to the Colonial Office. Milner's main recommendations were to end the protectorate and to introduce the constitutional reforms necessary to bring about Egyptian independence. His position in this regard was one shared broadly by Allenby.[15] Churchill, however, dissented sharply from their view, a stance that had earned him the opposition of the high commissioner in Cairo as well as from any and all Egyptian nationalists.

In contrast to Churchill's arrival in the Egyptian capital on 10 March, Lawrence had slipped into Cairo on the same day without raising a ripple. He had left London on 2 March as well, travelling with a few other Middle East Department colleagues, including Hubert Young.

They took the same route as Churchill, via Marseille and Alexandria, and arrived in Cairo eight days later. Lawrence, naturally, was keenly anticipatory of the conference. Still, he remained mildly disappointed that he had to give up the planned tour to visit many of his old wartime haunts in the region in the company of his artist friend, Eric Kennington. In a letter to the writer and poet Robert Graves he wrote that the trip with Kennington was something that he had been 'keen as mustard' to do. Still, the alternative to that trip having gone 'fut (or phut?)', Lawrence continued jocularly to Graves, was to get down to work turning the Sherifian Solution into concrete action at Cairo, while at the same time seeing to Kennington's artistic success in the service of *Seven Pillars of Wisdom*. To that end, he added, 'as an official I'll be able to help him even more than ever'.[16]

The day after Churchill and Lawrence's arrival in Cairo, Gertrude Bell, along with nine of her colleagues from Iraq, including Sir Percy Cox, rolled into the city's Central Station. Having departed Baghdad on 22 February they had travelled over 1,000 miles by train and ship to reach the Egyptian capital. Although reluctant initially to attend the conference, once she arrived in Cairo Bell was glad to be part of it. Considering that Lord Cromer had once written admiringly of Bell that she knew 'more about the Arabs and Arabia than almost any other living Englishman or woman', it was well that she had got over her reluctance and had agreed to attend. Even better was the fact that waiting for Bell and the Iraq party to arrive at the station had been the 'picturesque' Lawrence, as Bell had referred to him once in Paris during the Peace Conference when he had insisted on wearing Arab dress to one of the sessions. 'I was glad to see him!', she wrote home enthusiastically after-wards in Cairo. From the railway station Bell and Lawrence proceeded immediately to the Semiramis, where the two old friends (he usually called her 'Gerty') ensconced themselves in her room for 'an hour's talk' prefatory to the official start of the conference the following morning.[17]

By March of 1921 Bell and Lawrence had not seen one other for some two years. During this time Lawrence's celebrity had mushroomed internationally, especially in Britain and North America. 'Backing into the limelight' is how his growing ambivalence about such celebrity would later be aptly described.[18] Their friendship – as well as their mild rivalry – had endured however, and Bell proceeded to take him to task for his earlier campaign in the London press during which he had strongly criticized the nature of Britain's civil policy in Iraq, especially during the recent uprising. It is 'far worse than we have been told', as Lawrence had expressed it in the *Sunday Times* in March of 1920, 'our administration more bloody and inefficient than the public knows'.[19] Meanwhile, while Bell chided Lawrence for his pointed newspaper commentary, Lord Allenby, living just minutes away from the Semiramis at the British Residency and 'up to [his] neck in politics', was readying himself likewise for the opening session of the conference. Indeed, he had been anticipating a number of 'visitors next month', as he had written to his elderly mother in late February. 'Mr. Winston Churchill comes out, to confer with officers from Mesopotamia and Palestine', he wrote to her on 24 February. 'He & others will stay at a hotel in Cairo'. They were there now, he continued in a subsequent letter to his mother Catherine, so all was in order for the conference to begin.[20]

By the standards of most diplomatic conferences of the time the gathering at Cairo was relatively small, comprising just thirty-nine delegates in total. Still, 'Everybody Middle East is here', Lawrence wrote home grandly to his mother.[21] They represented half a dozen different British and colonial diplomatic missions, departments and ministries.[22] Someone dubbed the participants the 'forty thieves', which drew an immediate chuckle from Churchill.[23] Of the main actors, Churchill – by virtue of his position as colonial secretary, but also because of his alpha personality – would set the tone of the proceedings, as well as its timetable. Never an early riser, Churchill opened the conference on 12 March, a Saturday, at 10:30 a.m. in the hotel's spacious ballroom, an elaborately decorated space located on the hotel's main floor. A notice containing the time and location of the opening session had been distributed to each delegate's room the previous evening by the conference secretary, R.D. Badcock, a Colonial Office staff member who had come out from London for the occasion. After that initial late start, on the days that followed proceedings would commence at 9:00 a.m. and carry on until late afternoon. All told almost fifty committee meetings would take place in the span of little more than a week, which made the business-end of the Cairo Conference a rather hard-working affair.[24] Its main series of meetings would continue to occupy the hotel's ballroom, complemented by the Restaurant Français, the dining room, and the drawing room where the conference participants, along with a necessarily restricted number of Winter Season guests, took their meals, relaxed with a drink and socialized. Security at the Semiramis remained tight throughout the conference. Although Thompson the detective accompanied Churchill everywhere he went, the colonial secretary could be rather blasé about his personal safety, even in a place such as Egypt where politically motivated murder had become a regular occurrence over the preceding half-dozen years.[25]

On Friday evening, 11 March, after finishing her hour-long conversation with Lawrence, Bell had gone to the Churchills' suite to meet them both and to have an introductory chat with the colonial secretary. He was not there, however, having departed earlier for a meeting with Sir Percy Cox. But Bell was charmed by Clementine nonetheless. Bell 'had a long talk' with Mrs Churchill, as she would inform her stepmother, Lady Florence Bell, in a letter.[26] Still, it had been her husband with whom Bell had most wished to confer on the eve of the conference. Bell had met Churchill once before, years earlier while travelling in Sicily, and knew him only slightly. The meeting that evening was her first with Clementine.[27]

Bell had arrived in Cairo with some deep misgivings about Churchill, as well as with his political superior back in London, Lloyd George. Her reaction to their handling of the continuing violent and chaotic state of affairs in Ireland was especially critical. Indeed, it had recently drawn from Bell a harsh assessment of both men. To her father, Sir Hugh Bell, she had written in January that 'As for state-craft, I really think that you might search our history from end to end without finding poorer masters of it than Lloyd George and Winston Churchill. But why did we put them where they are? It's our fault'. At Bell's invitation her father had decided to come out from England to Cairo for a holiday and so soon enough they would be able to discuss this point in person, as well as many others. She had labelled Churchill and Lloyd George 'rogues' in another letter written to her father just days later, both men engaged always in what she derided as political 'hanky panky'. However, in the several weeks that elapsed between making these strong denunciations of Churchill and her arrival in Cairo, Bell's views had begun to moderate substantially. Gradually, she came to recognize more fully the creative and useful parameters inherent in the colonial secretary's proposed Sherifian Solution. Her understanding of Churchill's plans in this regard was helped along significantly too by the fact that Lawrence had regular access to him and would use it to reassure Bell about the direction in which the Sherifian Solution was intended to go. In this way Bell's misgivings about the colonial secretary were fairly quickly allayed. In fact, very soon after arriving in Cairo she began to refer to Churchill as both 'admirable' and 'masterly', which was rather a long way from the 'rogue' that she had called him just a short while earlier.[28] In any event, by the first morning of the conference the initial introductions had been made and business could begin.

In addition to meeting with Sir Percy Cox shortly after his arrival, Churchill had made a point also of conferring directly with Allenby at the British Residency. Following their first meeting the two men then stepped out into its spacious back garden, which ran as a greensward down to the banks of the Nile. The building itself was impressively columned and complemented by a large garden capable of holding hundreds of guests, as had occurred, for example, the previous year, when Allenby hosted an enormous throng of some 2,500 people who had gathered to celebrate the Sultan's birthday. From their first meeting on the evening of his arrival in Cairo on the 10th, for the duration of the conference Churchill would enjoy the tropical greenery of Allenby's garden along with the arresting view it provided of the Nile. Part of his enjoyment came in seeing the marabou stork that was living permanently in the garden. It was something of a pet to the high commissioner and as such the massive bird had taken to following him around as he strolled through the garden, guarding him in a distinctly jealous manner against any human or animal intrusions.[29]

Presiding at the Cairo Conference came easily to Churchill. He did so over both the plenary and combined committee meetings and, as Bell would later observe with approval, 'the small political committees into which we broke up'.[30] At the first session of the conference on the morning of 12 March, Churchill laid out to those assembled the format and parameters of the days to follow. The thirty-four delegates represented the British, Mesopotamian, Persian Gulf, Aden and Somaliland Missions. (The five-person Palestine Mission, headed by Sir Herbert Samuel, would not arrive until mid-week.) Included in this number were a handful of delegates designated simply as consultative members, including a couple of Lawrence's old comrades from the Arab Revolt, Pierce Joyce, who served as adviser to Jafar al-Askari, Iraq's minister of defence, and Colonel Kinahan Cornwallis, Egypt's minister of finance. Churchill insisted that complete confidentiality be kept by the delegates about the nature and extent of their discussions. 'The Secretary of State wishes to emphasize', his memorandum to them in this regard read, 'the necessity of absolute secrecy in the affairs of this Conference ... he hopes that even fragmentary information of secret and official matters will not leak out'.[31]

The public's estimation and knowledge of the Cairo Conference's work was of significant importance to Churchill, especially in his own Scottish constituency of Dundee. Indeed, he had written to its Liberal Association president, Sir George Ritchie, in late February in an attempt to explain to him that both creating the Middle East Department and convening the Cairo Conference were in the service of Britain's serious and long-term interests in the region. Churchill stated emphatically, in an unusually long letter for him, that the press had got it wrong in suggesting that 'my object in undertaking the charge of this department will be to build up a costly and vainglorious Middle Eastern Empire at the expense of the British taxpayer. My object is exactly the opposite'.[32]

Given Churchill's lingering reputation for self-promotion, the British press had trained an especially sceptical eye on the creation of the Middle East Department, as well as on the conference itself. *The Times*, for instance, referred to the Cairo Conference as being little more than Churchill's 'Durbar', a pointed reference to the elaborate spectacle that had been staged in Delhi by the then viceroy Lord Curzon in 1903 to mark the previous year's coronation of the King-Emperor Edward VII. Similarly the *Daily Herald* mocked Churchill for being an 'amateur Alexander', swanning about Egypt in the manner of a latter-day conqueror.[33] In the same vein, Curzon remarked cuttingly that Churchill would 'be under an irresistible temptation to proclaim himself King in Babylon'.[34] While accusing anyone of politically motivated theatricality was rich coming from a seasoned practitioner of the art such as the former viceroy, there was a modicum of truth to the various charges made – all diplomatic summits comprise a form of political theatre. But Churchill, Lawrence and the rest of the Middle East Department had worked hard to ensure that unlike some grand diplomatic meetings this one would be both brief in duration and focused on producing tangible and implementable results.

Lawrence entered the Semiramis ballroom as the conference began on that Saturday morning in March attired in a lounge suit and not, as sometimes was the case, in Arab dress topped by the distinctive *keffiyeh* cotton headscarf. Bell – the sole women delegate invited to attend the conference – joined him, along with Allenby (as an ex officio observer), Cox, Young, Trenchard and Haldane. Others present included Sir Geoffrey Archer, the governor of British Somaliland, who had arrived in Cairo transporting two frisky lion cubs destined for their new home at the London Zoo, as well as Sir Geoffrey Salmond, air officer commanding, Middle East.

There were two other noteworthy delegates in the room who had come along with Bell and Cox from Baghdad and who were representative of a small contingent of leading Iraqi ministers in office since the previous year. The first was Jafar al-Askari, Iraq's defence minister, who had been a close colleague of both Faisal and Lawrence during the Arab Revolt.[35] The second was Sir Sassoon Eskell, the minister of finance, a Jewish patrician from Baghdad. Eskell was admired and trusted greatly by Bell. 'The man I do love,' she had gushed earlier, 'is Sasun Eff. [Effendi] and he is by far the ablest man in the [Iraqi National] Council. A little rigid, he takes the point of view of the constitutional lawyer and doesn't make quite enough allowance for the primitive conditions of Iraq, but he is genuine and disinterested to the core. He has not only real ability but also wide experience and I feel touched and almost ashamed by the humility with which he seeks – and is guided by – my advice.'[36] Moreover, Eskell represented the 80,000 Jews who resided in Baghdad, a number that comprised almost half the city's population.

In inviting Jafar and Eskell to attend the conference, of which – noted Bell – they had been 'much gratified', Sir Percy Cox had made a 'master stroke', she believed. She would add that having the two Iraqis there 'will give the Conference a feeling of the reality of the Arab government. After all, it's their fate which is to be decided so why shouldn't they take a hand'. Bell was much less enamoured, however, at the presence in Cairo of Arnold Wilson as a consultative member in his new capacity as managing director of the Anglo-Persian Oil Company. Tall and heavily built, with a dark moustache and an abrasively forthright manner, Wilson was hard to miss. But given their recent animosity over the Iraqi Revolt Bell had nonetheless tried to do just that. As she reported matter-of-factly to her stepmother: 'We had a cordial meeting but I've not seen him to talk to and don't much want to'.[37]

One of the first pieces of business attended to by Churchill on the opening day of the conference was to create its two main committees, one political and the other military and financial. He would chair the first committee himself, while designating General Sir Walter Congreve, who in 1919 had been named as Allenby's successor as general officer commanding in Egypt and Palestine, to chair the second. Congreve had travelled back to Egypt from London on board the same ship as Churchill, which had afforded them both plenty of time to discuss the conference agenda and to propose a committee structure. The timetable of the conference was decidedly tight and its implementation closely controlled by the colonial secretary. For the benefit of the assembled delegates that morning the conference agenda was gone through point by point. Churchill emphasized that by the end of their ten days together it was hoped that they would achieve a comprehensive regional settlement reflective of the collective vision and scope of the Colonial Office's Middle East Department.[38]

While the reduction of British expenditures in Iraq remained of singular importance to Churchill, he was equally strong in his commitment to achieve a diplomatic breakthrough that would consolidate Britain's continuing paramountcy in the region while also propelling decisive future state-building. Implicit in his prioritizing of Britain's strategic position was a recognition that a certain degree of local nationalism was a necessary – even a welcome – lubricant in finding the right calibration for turning the imperial wheel. Some historians have pushed the financial point too hard, contending that Churchill was acting merely as the Cabinet monetarist in Cairo, working only to achieve economies in Treasury spending before all else.[39] However, such an interpretation does not fully enough take into consideration

Churchill's genuine commitment to finding and crafting a lasting and fair settlement in the Middle East, first in Iraq and then in Palestine, as well as between Arabs and Jews.

Churchill was no mere political instrumentalist. He was guided by a set of gradualist, if paternalist, constitutional ideals through which he believed the territories of the post-Ottoman Middle East could both develop politically and thrive economically. In order to accomplish these two ends the British imperial state needed to step back, which Churchill was quite willing to see happen. But only if what would then stand in its place spoke of real constitutional progress reflective of the interests of all parties, both local and metropolitan. If Churchill had wished simply to cut expenditures and run from the region, for example, he never would have brought in Lawrence as his closest adviser. After all, since 1917 Lawrence had emerged as the single most important and influential ally the Arabs possessed in the Western world. No less committed to the same ends (in Iraq, at least) of a just and lasting constitutional and fiscal arrangement were Cox and Bell. As the latter pointedly remarked, 'if we retain the mandate we must spend the money on it which it demands'. The fact that Lawrence and Churchill were of a common mind over Iraq – especially about the necessity of confirming Faisal as its new king – meant that as far as Bell was concerned the experts who knew the country best were being heard and their advice followed. As she described the situation at Cairo to her close friend, the military governor of Baghdad, Lieutenant-Colonel Frank Balfour: 'Not the least favourable circumstance was that Sir Percy and I, coming out with a definite programme, found when we came to open our packets that it coincided exactly with that which the S[ecretary] of S[tate] had brought with him'.

Favourable indeed: once Churchill had finished informing the assembled delegates on that first morning as to the committee structure and its due remit, and they had 'opened their packets', he turned his attention directly to the question of what constituted the primary part of the Sherifian Solution: the projected enthronement in Iraq of Prince Faisal. Even though neither the Middle East Department nor Cox had ever envisaged anyone other than Faisal as Iraq's future king, within the country itself competition for such an august appointment did exist.[40] Indeed, there were a number of candidates who merited attention, if not serious consideration, especially if it were not to appear later that Faisal had simply been enthroned by the British. To almost everyone at the conference, the fact that Iraq's future lay in becoming a monarchical state was assumed. Consequently, the only prominent dissenting voice in this regard belonged to Harry St John Bridger Philby, a mercurial British government official who had been one of Cox's advisers in Baghdad before becoming minister of internal security. Philby had come to favour – secretly, at first – the Hashemite dynasty's chief regional rival, Ibn Saud, as a more suitable candidate for the Iraqi throne than Faisal, if a king were needed at all. Indeed, Philby had already begun to advocate for an Iraqi republic. He had taken up this position mainly because he believed that the Arabs had been betrayed by both wartime and post-war Great Power diplomatic machinations. He was both an abiding anti-Zionist as well as a promoter of the House of Saud, which he believed to be the only hope for true Arab independence and unity. Eventually, Philby's radical position on this issue would drive him out of British service altogether; in the late 1920s, not long before converting to Islam, he would become a special adviser to Ibn Saud himself.[41]

In chairing the conference's opening meeting of the duly constituted Political Committee, Churchill put before its membership a list of the half-dozen names of those besides Faisal who had been deemed suitable for consideration as candidates for the Iraqi throne. The members of the Political Committee on that first day of meetings were Lawrence, Cox, Young and Bell, with Badcock acting as secretary. The names Churchill bruited for their consideration were Ibn Saud; the aga khan, leader of the Shia Ismailis; Khazal bin Jabir, a prominent Persian sheikh and an ally of the Anglo-Persian Oil

Company; Sehzade Mehmed Burhaneddin, a Turkish prince; Talib al-Naqib, the Iraqi Minister of the Interior; and the elderly Abd al-Rahman al-Gillani, the *naqib*, or Islamic leader, of Baghdad.[42]

Of the six candidates, the only two who posed a significant challenge to Faisal's expected endorsement as king were Talib and the *naqib*. Talib's political power base in the southern Iraqi city of Basra was strong, and as an Iraqi acutely sensitive to the country's Shia minority he was opposed to Faisal's candidacy on both ethno-tribal (Hashemite) and religious grounds (Faisal was Sunni). Meanwhile, the *naqib* maintained a significant political following in Baghdad. Both Cox and Bell were highly wary of both men, however, most especially of Talib, and had made a point of not including him in their delegation at Cairo. In response to having been left out of the Iraqi delegation Talib had been 'deeply chagrined', Bell would write home later, and one might reasonably assume angry. In Baghdad politics especially, Talib was a political force to be reckoned with, and not long before Bell's departure for Cairo he had attempted to win her over to supporting his keenly held claim to the Iraqi throne. 'Amid potations of whiskey', Bell recounted afterwards, the insalubrious and formerly exiled government minister had 'whispered in my ear in (more and more) increasingly maudlin tones that he had always regarded me as his sister, always followed my advice and now saw in me his sole support and stay'. Throughout that hazy evening in Baghdad Bell had done her best to 'murmur colourless expressions of friendship', she confessed, but had not altered her position that despite a measure of personal popularity Talib would be a disaster if made Iraq's king: he was divisive and had exhibited no attributes of statesmanship. At the conference Bell bluntly delivered this same judgement, recording later that Talib's hopes for the kingship were 'doomed to disappointment', to which she added tartly: 'it's a disappointment that would be confined to himself'.[43]

The Political Committee's initial deliberations ran into the afternoon of 12 March and, although the outcome was never really in doubt, the various candidates were each given their proper due. To be sure, Churchill and his Middle East Department staff maintained their support for Faisal as the only viable candidate, in their view the only man who had the necessary leadership skills, the gravitas and the reputation to make the proposed kingdom work. Cox and Bell, however, were present at Cairo to do more than merely bend to Churchill's will. Bell had asked for and received from Lawrence a full briefing of the content of the Sherifian Solution during their earlier private meeting in her hotel room. Only then would she agree that the Middle East Department was indeed well poised to work for an acceptable and progressive form of Iraqi independence.

Meanwhile, Cox had been the first person to speak in committee to the issue of who should be Iraq's king and he gave a forthright and comprehensive explanation as to why Faisal was the right candidate for enthronement in Iraq. Certainly Cox and Bell were the two committee members, along with the pair of Iraqi ministers, who knew the country best. To all of them, Faisal offered the best hope of effective monarchical leadership in Iraqi state-building. Cox and Bell as local experts provided a strong and necessary endorsement of the Sherifian Solution's potential to furnish Iraq with a form of government that would work to the country's long-term advantage.

As the Political Committee's opening session continued into Saturday afternoon, Cox's initial support of Faisal was to be buttressed by both Lawrence and Bell. For Lawrence especially, not only was Faisal clearly superior as a potential king to the other named candidates, but he was also a much better option than his brother, Abdullah. Although never really coming close to acquiring the Iraqi throne and not on the list of candidates under consideration at Cairo, the possibility of Abdullah doing so remained live. The reason for this possibility stemmed from the potential objections of his father Sharif Hussein. Simply put, Hussein preferred Abdullah in Iraq while keeping open the possibility of Faisal's restoration in Syria. Lawrence would make clear to the committee however that in his view Abdullah was the wrong man for Iraq. Faisal, Lawrence believed – unlike

Abdullah – was 'an active and inspiring personality' who could 'pull together the scattered elements' of the country.[44] He had been loyal to the British during the war, Lawrence continued, as well as being honourable and cultured.

As much as the committee heard Faisal praised in this way, back in London the man himself would give no indication in his correspondence of the time that he thought the Iraqi throne was simply his for the taking. Though a willing participant in the British plan to forward the cause of Arab unity and state-building, he did not consider his prospective elevation to Iraq's throne to be automatic. The French might have locked up control over Syria for the time being but it might not be lost forever, Faisal believed. In the meantime, all of Iraq, the Hejaz and Transjordan might well become the engine of a renewed British-backed Arab comity that had the potential to become an irresistible force for the advent of nation-state-style modernity in the Middle East. Ultimately, King Hussein accepted the logic of this argument, as did Prince Zeid, Faisal's younger brother. In a note Faisal had written to him on the eve of the Cairo Conference he had put it this way: 'Reaching Damascus and beyond will be now much easier after the [new] government is formed in Baghdad'.[45]

By the time the Political Committee's first session ended in the late afternoon on the 12th, the Middle East Department's case for Faisal to become king of Iraq had been made convincingly. Indeed, Churchill chose to reinforce the point to its members – in the words of the recording secretary – that the Sherifian Solution had 'enabled His Majesty's Government to bring pressure to bear on one Arab sphere in order to attain their own ends in another'. Cox was confident that upon Faisal's introduction to the people of Iraq through the National Council he would be strongly endorsed. As Bell well knew, however, engendering such unity would be a monumentally difficult task as 'all shades of opinion' needed to be represented if success were to be had.[46]

As the first day's proceedings wrapped up, the Political Committee had served notice – if such had ever been required – that the monarchical future of Iraq would form the core of the Cairo Conference. For Churchill, his commitment to reaching a sustainable Iraqi political settlement under the future kingship of Faisal had been given unmistakeable affirmation by the deliberations undertaken on that opening day.[47] And now that the defining inaugural session had concluded, and the languid late-afternoon hours were upon them, both he and the other delegates readied themselves for a drinks reception to be hosted that evening by Lord and Lady Allenby at the British Residency.

By March of 1921, and after two years in post, the Allenbys were well-ensconced in Cairo. Latterly childless – their only son, Michael, had been killed aged just nineteen while fighting on the Western Front in 1917 – they formed an accomplished ambassadorial team. As a career soldier, however, Lord Allenby had not taken naturally to diplomacy. Indeed, as Bell would remark archly later, 'Much as I like him I think we need in Egypt a better diplomat than he'.[48] Still, thus far his handling of the ongoing constitutional crisis in Egypt had been measured and sure-handed, if occasionally blunt. In fact, Churchill was of the opinion that Allenby's approach to the Egyptian nationalists had not been blunt enough. His dissent would harden considerably the following year, when the Allenby Declaration would make clear the high commissioner's commitment to seeing Egypt gain real, if gradual, independence from the British.[49] But for now, as the sun set on a warm late-winter day in Cairo, such concerns were put away and replaced by the convivial sound of glasses of wine and tumblers of gin and tonic clinking along the banks of the Nile.

Almost all of the thirty-four delegates then in attendance at the conference were at the reception hosted by Lord and Lady Allenby on that first evening. Though Lawrence's previous experience as a diplomat at the Paris Peace Conference had familiarized him with the high style of many such British government events, the affluence and glamour of the Semiramis Hotel had taken him aback.[50] 'Here we live in a marble & bronze hotel, very expensive & luxurious', Lawrence informed his mother; 'horrible place: makes me Bolshevik'.[51] As was his wont, Lawrence could gild the lily from time to time but clearly the level of comfort experienced thus far in Cairo was a world away from what had defined his ascetic existence in the desert during the Arab Revolt. Drinks at the British Residency would have been yet another example of the blandishments of diplomatic life, although Lawrence does not say so in his letters of the time. Nor does he mention the particular moment of excitement that evening occasioned by the appearance of Sir Geoffrey Archer, the governor of British Somaliland, who arrived at the reception with his two playful lion cubs in tow. Young, adventurous and with varied interests that accorded well with his official position in Africa (he was for example an accomplished ornithologist), Archer's reputation also as a stellar colonial governor preceded him. Recently he had managed to bring an end to the protracted twenty-two-year resistance to British rule in Somaliland that had been carried out by Mohammed Abdullah Hassan, known to the British at the time as the 'Mad Mullah'.

In bringing along the irresistible cubs to the Residency that evening Archer set the cat among the pigeons. Indeed, Lord Allenby's own recounting of what the cubs – 'about as big as retriever dogs' – did next cannot be bettered. 'They broke loose', he explained in a letter to his mother, 'and went full gallop for my Marabou stork. He fled for his life. They nearly got him; but Archer and his black servant raced after them, and just stopped them in time.'[52] The 'enchanting baby lions', as a smitten Bell later described them, thus had made for a lighthearted conclusion to the first day of the conference. They had provided a welcome distraction from the serious business of state-making in the Middle East that had got underway that morning and which would continue apace for the balance of the week and well beyond.[53]

'WE HAVE DONE A LOT OF WORK'
TEN DAYS IN CAIRO, ACT II

The reception hosted by the Allenbys at the British Residency at the conclusion of the opening day of the Cairo Conference was its first social highlight. From the moment that Sir Geoffrey Archer's pair of young lions scampered across the garden in pursuit of Lord Allenby's terrified pet stork they would become an amusing focal point for conference delegates.

On Sunday, 13 March, following the garden reception and a small dinner party that Churchill hosted afterwards back at the Semiramis, the delegates convened for their second day of deliberations. They did so now according to various committee assignments. For Lawrence, this 'odd conference', as he had whimsically called it to the sceptical anti-imperialist Wilfrid Scawen Blunt just prior to departing London for Cairo, was heading already in the direction that he had hoped it would. He had added to Blunt: 'I'll either get my way or resign – or even do both things!'[1] The scope for Lawrence to act accordingly remained in place but neither outcome was very likely considering the way in which the Political Committee had concluded its first round of talks a day earlier. Those discussions had seen Lawrence 'binding himself to the Arab, or rather Hashemite, cause', as his stance would later be described, and in so doing solidifying his reputation as a man of action turned practitioner of diplomacy.[2] As much as Churchill admired Lawrence for his legendary exploits on the battlefield, what he required from him just then was diplomatic acumen. And on that first day of the conference Lawrence had delivered.

Once again, at the Political Committee's Sunday meeting, its membership was comprised of Churchill, Cox, Young, Lawrence and Bell. Considering that this small five-person committee was at the centre of events in Cairo, it is to Churchill's credit as chair that he included in its deliberations Bell, the only woman delegate at the conference. Lawrence had remarked in the past – although with a hint of chauvinistic admiration – that Bell 'was not very like a woman'. Indeed, Bell herself had observed of the less than satisfactory state of her domestic affairs in Iraq that 'what I really want is a wife to look after my household and my clothes. I quite understand why men out here marry anyone who turns up'. But even though Bell's Oxford education, archaeological pursuits, inveterate travel and government service – even her long-time habit of cigarette smoking – were at that time typically male preserves, her femininity was otherwise clearly reflected in her taste for fashionable, expensive clothes and elaborate hats. 'Pay whatever you have to, my dear', she had directed her American missionary friend in Baghdad, Dorothy Van Ess, to do for her while shopping in Bombay: 'I must have clothes'.[3] Bell had twice been disappointed deeply in love, both men having died, so her fiercely lived independence, though mediated ultimately through an unconventional persona, might easily have been otherwise.[4]

During the interval since the previous day's meeting Churchill had drafted a telegram to send to Lloyd George in which he planned to inform him that the matter of Faisal's selection as the future king of 'Irak' – in committee that day Badcock had recorded the first official (phonetic) use of the new name for Mesopotamia – had been decided. 'I think we shall reach unanimous conclusions among all authorities', Churchill wrote in the draft, 'that Feisal offers hope of best and cheapest solution'.[5] That morning he put the draft before the Political Committee for wordsmithing. Cox, in particular, asked for changes in tone that would alter the telegram to make it less pronounced in declaring unalloyed British support for Faisal's selection. Churchill and the other members agreed with this suggestion and Churchill told them that he would take the draft telegram to the Military Committee for its approval before then sending it off to London.

Once this piece of business had been completed the Political Committee turned its attention to the various other matters that were at hand. One of the most important was the proposed timetable for Faisal's arrival in Baghdad as the presumptive king of Iraq. Sometime during Ramadan, which would fall from 8 May to 8 June that year, was preferred. There was much speculation too as to what kind of local reception might be expected. Bell commented that she was confident Faisal would be welcomed by most Iraqis with great acclaim, although the likelihood remained nonetheless that a certain amount of opposition would come from Sayyid Talib and his many and vocal supporters. Lawrence reiterated Churchill's point from a day earlier about maintaining strict confidentiality. Faisal himself, he said, should be enjoined to say absolutely nothing of what he might well have surmised by then was being decided about his fate at Cairo.

The next day, 14 March, the Political Committee met for a third time. For this meeting Churchill called for the participation again of the two Iraqi ministers, Jafar al-Askari and Sassoon Eskell, to solicit from them a national perspective as to who might be best suited to occupy the country's throne. At the meeting both Iraqi ministers chose to endorse Faisal as the candidate greatly preferable to any of the others under consideration. Jafar Pasha, as he was called in a nod to his long-time Ottoman service, deemed it essential that, in order to maximize the country's expected goodwill, Faisal should arrive in Iraq as soon as possible. It was recommended therefore that he come to Baghdad as early as 18 April, before Ramadan. Eskell then expressed concern that some of the other candidates – namely the ageing *naqib* of Baghdad, Abd al-Rahman, as well as Talib al-Naqib – would likely employ extensive propaganda against Faisal and resist any attempt made by him to elicit their support. Still, as a veteran of Iraqi politics, Eskell was not overly pessimistic about this prospect, commenting that both the *naqib* and Talib would probably choose to resign their posts in the existing Iraqi government, but if they did so it should not be seen as a major cause for concern.

As for the candidacy of Ibn Saud, Jafar and Eskell's jointly held position was that as a prospective candidate for the throne of Iraq he was totally unacceptable. Both Iraqi ministers were strongly of the view that Ibn Saud simply 'could not be considered', as he was seen by too many people in Iraq as posing a fundamental existential threat to the future of the country. He had no popular standing in Iraq, they maintained, nor could it be expected that any would develop.[6] For Churchill, hearing the two Iraqi delegates express firmly in committee that neither the *naqib* nor Talib were suitable candidates to lead Iraq was a most welcome vindication of the Middle East Department's choice of Faisal as its candidate. As he would cryptically inform Lloyd George a few days later: 'Talib who is acutely intriguing for job is a man of bad character and untrustworthy. Nakib is tottering on the brink of grave. That Sherifian system offers far better prospects than these we have no doubt whatever'.[7]

In parallel with the meetings held by the Political Committee, the Military Committee had also begun to meet on the first afternoon of the conference, 12 March. Chaired by General Congreve, its membership was substantially larger than its political counterpart, numbering fourteen delegates plus a secretary. The size of the Military Committee was reflective of the many service chiefs present at the Cairo Conference and of the central place that reductions in the cost of Britain's military commitments would play in its deliberations. The quid pro quo for reducing the British Army's presence in Iraq was to increase that of the Royal Air Force, but also to undertake the creation of a full-fledged 'Arab Army', which was expected eventually to supersede that of the British. As Iraq's minister of defence, Jafar Pasha took the lead in proposing the establishment of the new Arab Army in committee on the 12th, at which time a dedicated subcommittee was formed to discuss the proposed scheme more fully.[8] Both the general Military Committee and the five-man subcommittee participated in by Jafar continued to meet over the next few days. Afterwards, it would report to the combined meetings of the Political and Military Committees that Churchill commenced chairing on the afternoon of 13 March and would meet each day until the 19th.

Jafar Pasha's full participation in the conference had come about as a natural extension of his Baghdadi birth, his ministerial appointment and his long-time military service. Initially, that service had come through a period as an officer in the Ottoman Army, the latter part of which saw him stationed at Aleppo in northern Syria. Once war broke out in 1914 Jafar had fought against the Allies at the Dardanelles, after which he had been awarded the German Iron Cross and was promoted to general. Subsequent fighting in Libya at the head of the pro-Ottoman, clan-based Senussi forces had led to his capture by the British at the Battle of Agagia in February of 1916, followed by a term of imprisonment in Cairo. Later that year, after the Arab Revolt in the Hejaz had broken out, he would decide that his sympathies lay ultimately with the cause of Arab nationalism. Subsequently, once freed from prison, Jafar threw his support behind the Hashemite dynasty in its surging resistance to Ottoman rule. Later, after Sharif Hussein had become convinced of his unimpeachable loyalty, Jafar was invited by Faisal to take a leading role in the fight, and together with Lawrence he would act as a key commander of Arab forces for the balance of the war. Present at Damascus for the city's liberation in October of 1918, afterwards Jafar was appointed military governor in Syria and then inspector-general of the army. Following the downfall of Faisal's short-lived Syrian regime in the summer of 1920, Jafar made his way home to Iraq and to the opportunities that awaited him there. Once resettled in Baghdad he quickly became an advocate of Faisal's prospective kingship of the country, as well as a member of the fledgling Iraqi National Council in anticipation of Iraq's expected independence.[9] Physically large – 'colossally fat', according to the razor-thin Bell's pithy description – and with a ready laugh, the convivial Jafar had a reputation for jolliness and proved to be a popular figure with the other delegates at the conference.[10]

On Tuesday, 15 March, the Political Committee met for the fourth time. Having dealt effectively with the question of Faisal becoming Iraq's king, the committee then gave over most of the session's remaining time to discussing in detail the complicated case of Kurdistan. Direct Ottoman rule there had commenced in 1831 and lasted until the Turks were defeated by the Allies in 1918. Afterwards the Kurds, like Mesopotamia itself, came under British mandatory control.

At the time of the Cairo Conference in 1921 the Iraqi Kurds – numbering about 5 million – continued to occupy their historic homelands that were strung across a mainly mountainous region in the northern part of the country. Significant populations of Kurds were to be found also in neighbouring Turkey and Iran. Altogether these areas were known as Greater Kurdistan. The Kurds, like many other imperialized peoples in Europe and elsewhere, had begun to aspire to the political promise of Western-style nationalism in the late nineteenth century. This desire would be demonstrated by the creation of the Society for the Rise of Kurdistan in 1918. Shortly thereafter, at the Paris Peace Conference, a public commitment was made to support the creation of an independent Kurdistan, which was reflected in the provisions of the constituent Treaty of Sèvres. However, the rise of a strongly competitive post-war Turkish nationalism, and the resulting Turkish War of Independence begun in protest to the treaty after it was signed in August of 1920, had left the

1. Winston Churchill in 1920, looking typically bullish and well into his post-Dardanelles political rehabilitation as Secretary of State for War and Air.

2. Lord Allenby in 1920, not long out of his First World War general's uniform and into his civil role as Britain's High Commissioner for Egypt.

3. Sassoon Eskell, a leading member of Baghdad's large Jewish community, pictured here in a photo from 1909, was a key figure in the Iraq Government and a favourite of Gertrude Bell's.

4. The ultimate man-on-the-spot for the British in the Middle East, Sir Percy Cox – pictured here in 1918 – would be appointed Britain's Acting Minister at Tehran that year prior to transferring a short time later to Baghdad as High Commissioner.

5. T.E. Lawrence in 1917, alone in the desert – as was his wont – during a lull in the Arab Revolt.

6. Gertrude Bell, as she appeared in 1921, on the eve of the Cairo Conference and at the height of her influence upon events in Iraq.

7. From the rooftop of the Semiramis Hotel in the 1920s, an unobstructed view across the Nile to the Pyramids at nearby Giza.

8. Cairo: medieval and modern. The Citadel, dating from the era of Saladin's sultancy in the twelfth century, fronted by a caravan of 1920s automobiles similar to those used to transport Conference delegates to the Pyramids.

9. The Cairo cityscape in the 1920s, facing southeast from the roof of
the Semiramis Hotel, with the Mokattam Hills in the distance.

10. Cairo Conference delegates – the so-called 'forty thieves' – at the Semiramis Hotel in March 1921: present at the creation of the modern Middle East.

11. Shortly after this photo was taken at Giza Churchill would slip from his camel. 'How are the mighty fallen', his wife Clementine remarked wryly.

12. Here, in a 1920 photo of the well-appointed dining room at the Semiramis Hotel, Churchill would host a grand dinner to mark the end of the Cairo Conference.

13. The three chief founders of the new state of Transjordan – Churchill, Lawrence and Abdullah – walk determinedly through the grounds of Government House, Jerusalem, in March 1921.

14. A pensive Prince Faisal in 1919, in anticipation of his brief and ill-fated Syrian kingship to come the following year.

15. Dressed as usual in military uniform, Jafar al-Askari was an important presence at the Cairo Conference, and would be indispensable to Faisal's new Iraqi state.

16. Gertrude Bell relaxing with King Faisal and a group of government officials on a picnic near Baghdad in 1922. She was determined to do all that she could to see him succeed as King of Iraq.

17. The supreme Arab dynast, Ibn Saud, in Mesopotamia with Sir Percy Cox and Gertrude Bell in 1916.

18. 'Ned' Lawrence and 'Gerty' Bell at Cairo in 1921. Though rivalrous colleagues, they mirrored one another in the constancy of their aspirations to see Arab statehood achieved.

19. Churchill with Jerusalem's Anglican bishop, Rennie MacInness, in March 1921. They admired one another but differed sharply over the future course to be taken by Palestine.

20. Britain's first High Commissioner for Palestine, Sir Herbert Samuel was a committed Zionist. But like Churchill, he wanted to see a pluralist state succeed. Here they are together at the ground-breaking for the Hebrew University of Jerusalem in March 1921.

21. The Cairo Conference was one of the few times that Clementine would ever accompany her husband on state business. She had a highly enjoyable time in Egypt and, as pictured here at Government House in Jerusalem, so too in Palestine.

colonized Kurds in a continuing position of semi-statelessness. Pointedly, this position of vulnerability included those Kurds living in Mandatory Iraq.[11]

In the meeting room at the Semiramis where the Political Committee gathered for its session on the morning of 15 March, the best-informed members on the question of the future of the Kurds in Iraq were the Baghdad governmental duo of Sir Percy Cox and Gertrude Bell. Also considered to be an expert on the Kurds was the lesser-known figure of Major Edward Noel. The composition of the committee's membership that day remained the same as it had been earlier in the week, except for the addition of Noel, who was included in the conference delegates as a consultative member but was alone among their number in being listed without any kind of govern-mental, ministerial or service attachment.[12] A career military officer, after completing his training at the Royal Military Academy in Woolwich Noel had been commissioned as an artilleryman before transferring to the Indian Army in 1908. A few years later he would transition into British service in Persia during the First World War. Known by some as the man who had performed the remarkable feat of cycling from England to India twice in consecutive years, 1909 and 1910, Noel was a shadowy figure whose later wartime and post-war work had come mainly as a British spy.[13] He was awarded the Distinguished Service Order in 1919, the same year that he served on active special duty in Kurdistan. Noel's inclusion in the confer-ence and as a guest of the Political Committee for its meeting on the 15th was of a piece with Cox and Bell's considered position that the Kurdish population ought to be retained within Iraq rather than permitting it to form an independent state.

On the complicated issue of the Kurds, however, Churchill had arrived at the conference believing that independence was in their best interests as a people. He held also that Kurdish independence would reduce the potential for the British Empire to become embroiled in any additional and unnecessary regional geopolitical entanglements, especially with the resurgent Turks. His position therefore – and he staked it out at the beginning of the meeting – was that 'Kurdistan' should be allowed to form itself as a political entity outside the future borders of an independent Iraq. Churchill noted too, as a matter of fairness, that 'British policy was giving very great support to the Arab cause and that it could not overlook the rights of the Kurdish minority'. Moreover, Churchill continued, Kurdish autonomy was vital because he feared that in future an Arab-ruled Iraq would not properly take into account the minority position of the Kurds. He forecast that the result of such a stance would lead very likely to an endless cycle of sub-national acrimony, not to mention prohibitive financial cost. The Kurds would either be 'ignored' on the one hand, or 'oppressed' on the other, as he put it, and therefore left with no option but resorting to violence to gain their independence.

Churchill's position on the Kurds was one that had been shaped closely by the advice received from the Middle East Department. Both Hubert Young and Lawrence held the view that the Kurds should be allowed to attain post-Ottoman independence free from future Arab control. Accordingly, that day in session they too advocated for the creation of a Kurdish state. For the immediate future, they stressed, such independence would need to come under the supervision of the British high commissioner and not under the control of the Iraqi government. As Lawrence spoke, however, Bell's temper flashed as he explained his objections to seeing the Kurds fall under Iraqi rule. In reply to Churchill's question in this regard Lawrence had stated flatly that 'it was his opinion that the Kurds should not be placed under an Arab Government'.[14] In hearing Lawrence's words, Bell rounded on him immediately, lashing out as if he had turned traitor, calling him a 'little imp', and doing her utmost to cause him embarrassment and to undercut his position. Her attack seems to have worked: in its aftermath Lawrence's 'ears and face turned red', it was said, and he was not much heard from again for the balance of the meeting.

As Bell's heated reaction demonstrates, Churchill's comments followed by those of Young and especially Lawrence had been alarming both to her and to the likeminded Cox. Consequently, as soon as it was their turn to address the committee they chose to criticize strongly the position that had been taken so robustly by Churchill and his two departmental advisers. To Cox, it was inconceivable, he stated emphatically, that the main Kurdish districts of Kirkuk, Sulaymaniyah and Mosul should be hived off from a newly constituted Iraqi state. All three of them, he insisted, were integral to the country and of signal importance to its economy, in particular the potential for commercial oil production that existed at Mosul. After Cox had finished speaking Bell then weighed in strongly, bolstering Cox's position by arguing that the Kurds' future in Iraq was vital to the country's success and must be made to work. Indeed, she stressed too 'that Mosul should be included' within the country's future redrawn borders. In a bid to stall for time she added that in any case the moment remained premature to decide the Kurds' fate. Bell suggested therefore that the question should not be settled at Cairo but rather be delayed for at least six months so that the Kurds themselves might be able to declare their preference between independence and Iraqi rule through a process of public consultation. She was sure that by then, once the new regime had been put in place, the Kurds would show themselves to be 'anxious to join the Iraq Government'.[15]

In adopting an uncompromising stance against the creation of an independent Kurdistan, Cox and Bell had opened up one of the only significant policy differences at the conference that would exist between themselves and the Middle East Department. Indeed, the ultimate fate of the Kurds would remain an unanswered question at Cairo. In pushing for them to be included within Iraq, Cox and Bell had shown themselves to be supremely supportive of the Arab cause, regardless of what it might mean for other formerly subject peoples of the Ottoman Empire. On this front, however, Bell herself was no less than consistent. She was opposed equally to Zionist aspirations in

Palestine and believed that British enforcement of the Balfour
Declaration meant certain disaster for the Arabs: 'Our iniquitous
policy of making it a home for the Jews', she had called it in a complaint
made earlier to her father. She had told him also that the Balfour
policy was costing the British government a great deal of money in
the form of troop commitments needed to garrison Palestine, money
that would be better spent in Iraq where the call on its use was much
more urgent. But, she concluded with a sharply anti-Semitic retort,
'The Jews can buy silence on the subject of expenditure'.[16]

At this point in the Political Committee's proceedings the furtive
figure of Major Edward Noel stepped into the icy atmosphere of the
dispute over the Kurds. In choosing to intervene, Noel suggested that
what British policy in the region actually required was the establishment of a Kurdish 'buffer state', as he called it, to keep the Turks at
bay while at the same time providing a useful 'counter-balance [to]
any strong anti-British movement which might occur in Mesopotamia'.
For Noel, the issue was one mainly of regional geopolitics as opposed
to national self-determination. For him, it was vital that the British
move to blunt any attempt by Turkey to inflame residual Ottoman
feeling within the country, which might have the effect of making it
more difficult for the British to exert mandatory supervision in Iraq
than it had proved to be already. Finally, as the session drew to a close
and with the discomfort of the testy exchanges over the Kurds
lingering, Churchill chose to invoke the example of the governor-
general of South Africa's position in respect of the Union of South
Africa and Rhodesia. This position, he said, was analogous to what
was being suggested for Iraq and 'Kurdistan'. Altogether however, as
the meeting ended Churchill found himself out-pointed by Cox and
Bell on the Kurdish question.[17] Consequently, he chose to defer to
their expert on-the-spot opinion and acquiesce on the question of
Kurdish independence by concurring with their view that the Kurds'
best future lay under eventual Arab control. Yes, Churchill agreed,
theoretically the Kurds should be able to choose their own national

destiny according to what Bell had suggested earlier. But effectively the die had been cast for Iraqi Kurds to remain under Arab rule in perpetuity. Indeed, Churchill's pre-Conference views on the Kurds were to prove remarkably prescient. The decision to refrain from moving to create a Kurdish state at Cairo would have a long and controversial afterlife in Middle East affairs that has lasted – with horrific consequences for the Kurdish population – down to our own day.[18]

As the daily meetings continued apace, so too did the opportunities for conference delegates to enjoy the many attractions of Cairo and its environs. For Churchill himself, such opportunities meant especially the pleasure of packing up his box of brushes and paints and motoring off to various sites in and around the city to capture them on canvas. Clementine, meanwhile, spent a good deal of time shopping, accompanied occasionally by Bell, whose wardrobe remained a constant preoccupation.[19] For his part, Lawrence, having met up with the recently arrived Eric Kennington, accompanied him to the British Residency so that he could commence work on painting Lord Allenby's portrait for inclusion in *Seven Pillars of Wisdom*. 'I have had a portrait done in pastel ... for a book which Lawrence is writing', Allenby wrote to his mother on 18 March. 'I think the likeness good. I am also', he continued, 'sitting for a Zionist sculptor, for a bust of me which they are going to put up in Beersheba. It will be 2½ times life size, in white stone, on a column. So far he has not quite finished the clay model; but it looks quite like me'.[20]

Allenby's sculptor, Abraham Melnikov, had come to Cairo from his adopted home in Jerusalem just a few days earlier in advance of Sir Herbert Samuel, the recently appointed British high commissioner for Palestine. Samuel, born in 1870 in Liverpool, had been educated at Balliol College, Oxford before later entering politics and winning a seat for the Liberals in the 1902 Cleveland by-election. Appointed in 1909 as chancellor of the Duchy of Lancaster, he was the first practising Jew (Benjamin Disraeli, the two-time nineteenth-century Conservative prime minister, had converted to Christianity in his youth) to sit at the Cabinet table. Subsequent appointments, including that of home secretary – both during and then well after the First World War – came on either side of the five years he spent in Jerusalem as high commissioner. Samuel had taken up the appointment during the previous summer, so he had been less than a year in post before coming over to Cairo to participate in the conference.[21] He, along with the four other members of the Palestine Mission, arrived in Cairo on the 16th in anticipation of the first meeting of the combined Palestine Political and Military Committee, which was set to convene under Churchill's chairmanship the next morning.

The Palestine Political and Military Committee duly met on that Thursday morning, 17 March, and contained a membership of fifteen. Most of the leading figures at the conference were in attendance. Alongside Churchill and Samuel sat General Congreve and Air Marshal Trenchard. The other members of the Palestine Mission – Sir Geoffrey Salmond, Major General Frederick Peake, Major F.R. Somerset and Sir Wyndham Deedes – attended also, as did Bell, Lawrence and Young. For the preceding five days of the conference the committee's discussions had revolved essentially around Iraq. On this day, however, the attention of the committee's delegates would shift mainly to Palestine. Churchill opened the meeting by stating that the task before the committee was to discuss British mandatory rule in Palestine under its main 'two aspects', as he termed them. The first of these, he said, was Palestine's relationship to Iraq, as well as to Arabia more broadly. The second was its internal development, especially with reference to the Zionist question.

In London, prior to the conference, the Middle East Department had drafted a report in which it had made plain its view that the territory of Transjordan – or 'Trans-Jordania' as British nomenclature denoted the country at the time – should be demarcated cartographically from Palestine. Until that time, a capacious understanding of the traditional boundaries of Palestine had prevailed amongst the British. Churchill asked Young to read aloud this report, after which Samuel stated that he agreed with the idea that Transjordan required to be governed along different lines than Palestine, 'partly owing to the question of Zionism' and its potentially negative impact on the local Arab population. He was equally clear in stating, however, that Transjordan should not be regarded as constituting a putative Arab state. Rather, it should be seen as a constituent part of the larger British mandate over the traditional territory of Palestine.[22] Accordingly, 'the main question of the moment', Samuel contended, was how to deal with the issue of Prince Abdullah's current presence in Amman, the Transjordanian capital, and what his potential permanent residency there might portend for the future of Transjordan and Palestine. At this point in the discussion one supposes that a muffled sigh might have been heard coming from Lawrence. Envisaging Abdullah in any kind of leadership role had posed a problem for him always. But here at Cairo force of circumstance would mean a necessary alteration of view. Indeed, Lawrence had come to the conclusion already that, to make the Sherifian Solution work across the region, Abdullah's cooperation and elevation were going to be indispensable.

Abdullah's encampment at Amman spoke of his abiding belief that irrespective of the violent actions undertaken by the French against Faisal during the previous summer, his brother remained the rightful king of Syria. Accordingly, Abdullah's own understanding of Transjordan was that it continued to be part of that broader Syrian kingdom. Once the Hashemite claim to the throne in Damascus had been duly restored – which he believed to be inevitable – then Transjordan's own future in turn could become settled and secure. In holding fast to this position, however, Abdullah would find himself essentially to be at the head of a viable army of one. By the time of the Cairo Conference it was clear to almost everyone that neither the British nor Faisal himself were going to defy France's insistence that Syria's future lay under its control. Indeed, if Iraq's future as a British mandate with Faisal as its king was going to be accepted by France, however grudgingly, then its mandatory claim to Syria would have to be respected in turn by the British. Accordingly, during the very next week in London, in a meeting at the Foreign Office, Lord Curzon would make Britain's accommodating position over Syria abundantly clear to the French ambassador Charles de Beaupoil. In return for the British having chosen not to oppose France's unseating of Faisal in Damascus in 1920, Curzon stated, the French should now allow the British a free hand in re-seating him themselves in Baghdad in 1921.[23]

For Lawrence, as well as for Churchill, Young, Cox and Bell, Transjordan's future as an Arab state under British supervision was the only possible way forward to balance all of the competing interests in the region, notwithstanding the strong objections that this stance would elicit from the Zionists. Samuel, in addressing the committee, was keenly aware of the British position in this regard. He did not, therefore, oppose it strongly because he recognized that the future of Palestine as a (predominantly) Jewish homeland rested on an equivalent commitment by Britain to support an Arab Transjordan. Later, Samuel would come to object overtly to this position. But as far as the British government was concerned, it was one that needed to be accepted by the Zionists as a necessary compromise to make the totality of the pledges contained within the Balfour Declaration work for both Jews and Arabs. Samuel, therefore, was keen to ensure that 'no anti-French campaign should emanate from Trans-Jordania', which would have the effect of causing France to oppose Britain's plans elsewhere in the region, most especially in Palestine.

At this heightened point in the meeting Lawrence weighed in with his view that an Arab state under Abdullah might very well act as a safety valve in the region: pressure to check anti-Zionism in Transjordan could be brought to bear on a ruler whose position was dependent upon British support. Samuel responded that he feared Arab raids across the border into Palestine would continue nonetheless. But Lawrence countered, stating that these raids 'could best be solved by a good system of government east of the Jordan'. He added that if Abdullah 'proved that he could behave' – in Lawrence's mind no proper presumption about that could be made – the situation might be managed effectively to the benefit of both parties.

Of course, the question of Abdullah's potential 'behaviour' begged the follow up query – which was voiced by Major Somerset, the British representative in Transjordan – as to what could be done to expel Abdullah from the country should he not ultimately be selected to be its king (or 'emir', as his status would be initially). Herein lay the rub, and Churchill knew it, which is why he spoke up quickly to make plain the idea that Abdullah's selection would be based on a clear and beneficial mutuality. A British-backed government in Transjordan with Abdullah at its head, he believed, would support a broader regional solution that allowed for the continued aggrandizement of the Hashemite dynasty. Yes, Churchill commented, 'miscreants from Palestine would always be able to find refuge in Trans-Jordania', and therefore be the cause of potential upset. But a stable Sherifian government in Transjordan, one that was not actively anti-French nor demonstrably anti-Zionist, should be able to succeed. In addition, if a guarantee could be elicited from Ibn Saud not to oppose Abdullah's appointment in Transjordan or interfere with it afterwards, then installing him there would make the situation that much more secure.

From the British perspective the likelihood of Abdullah's willingness to accede to the Transjordan throne and secure its future as an Arab state appeared both necessary and assured. Nevertheless, not everyone in the room that day was convinced by the prevailing Sherifian logic of the colonial secretary and his coterie of advisers from the Middle East Department. Dissenters to the plan did exist and they made known their objections. Most notably, Wyndham Deedes, Sir Herbert Samuel's civil secretary in Palestine, objected strongly to Abdullah's designation as Transjordan's king-in-waiting. Deedes argued to the contrary, stating bluntly that Abdullah was completely unsuited to serve as the future ruler of the country as he had never before held a position of serious political responsibility. Deedes acknowledged also, however, that the presence currently of Abdullah in Amman had become an impossible problem to solve diplomatically. Regrettably therefore, in the civil secretary's view, the British had no option but to regard 'his appointment as a *fait accompli*'.

Following Deedes's comments, General Congreve proceeded to offer an overview of what might be required militarily in Transjordan, both to keep the peace and to restrain Abdullah should he wish in future to launch some sort of irredentist move against Syria. Here Lawrence spoke up again, agreeing with Congreve and confirming altogether that 'the whole situation largely depended upon the military position'. Churchill then followed suit, instructing Congreve to convene a military subcommittee for Palestine. He was to report back to the larger committee with its findings on the size of the garrison required in order to secure Transjordan, 'bearing in mind', Churchill reminded him, 'the support which could be given by the Air Force'.[24] Following these instructions to Congreve, the meeting was adjourned in anticipation of the subcommittee's recommendations, which would be shared at a second gathering of the full Palestine Political and Military Committee to come.

By the afternoon of 17 March and the conclusion of the first meeting on the future of Palestine, the unofficial half-way mark of the conference had been reached. As usual, Churchill would steal away at almost any opportunity to paint, and occasionally to sightsee. He did so again that day after the morning meeting had terminated, as he and Clementine slipped off to visit the ancient Cairo Citadel along with the nearby 'City of the Dead', an enormous centuries-old Islamic necropolis established mainly for the local poor. Gertrude Bell, meanwhile, availed herself of the same kinds of sightseeing opportunities in the company of her father, Sir Hugh, who had arrived recently in Cairo from Aden. 'I can't tell you how pleased I am', Bell wrote to her stepmother Lady Florence in reference to her father's visit. 'I only hope now that the Conference will drag on so that we may have more time together'. Sir Hugh had arrived just a day earlier and immediately father and daughter began to take in as much of the fabled city as Gertrude's conference schedule would allow.[25]

During that same afternoon of the 17th, while Churchill toured Cairo with his wife and Bell entertained her father, Lawrence attended the meeting of the newly constituted Palestine Military Sub-Committee. Eight delegates had been chosen for it, including Congreve as chairman, along with General Percy Radcliffe and Air Vice-Marshal Salmond. They proceeded on the assumption that Abdullah would be appointed emir of Transjordan in the manner discussed earlier that morning. It would be necessary for Transjordan to remain in friendly relations with the British government, and the committee agreed that a battalion of infantry, two squadrons of cavalry and a section of artillery should be put in place to secure Abdullah's presumptive position. Stationed at Amman, these forces 'would not be passive but active', it was agreed, and 'strong enough to quell any element of the population that might be unfriendly to the Government'. In addition to these land forces, Salmond proposed that a series of aerodromes be constructed at Amman, Irbid and Kerak. These were to form part of a comprehensive structure of air defence for Transjordan that if properly integrated with existing land forces would be able to make possible a substantial reduction in the size of the British imperial garrison, or even to see it 'completely withdrawn in the near future'.[26]

With the subcommittee's work complete, beginning the next morning the combined Palestine Political and Military Committee convened for a second time. Churchill chaired the meeting with a view to achieving a provisional political settlement over Transjordan while ensuring that the necessary military muscle to maintain it would be supplied at not too great a cost to the British Treasury. He proceeded to read aloud the report produced by the subcommittee the previous afternoon, which had been transcribed – like many of the reports at the Cairo Conference – by a member of Allenby's

British Residency staff.[27] General Radcliffe offered his support immediately for the recommendations contained in the report, while Sir Herbert Samuel 'called attention' to the possibility of the withdrawal of troops coming at some later date. He objected strongly to this possibility, stating that complete withdrawal should not be countenanced but rather a phased reduction of troops only. Samuel explained that a full withdrawal in favour of an Arab force was much too risky a move to contemplate. Indeed, he warned that it would be a 'fatal error' that could lead to anti-French and anti-Palestine movements gaining their head in the country. He then proceeded to link explicitly the full British garrison in Palestine (which included Transjordan, he noted) to Britain's broader strategic position in the Middle East. 'It was', Samuel stated, 'not merely intended to maintain order in that country, but should be regarded as an Imperial reserve and as a protection for the Suez Canal'. Churchill, whose view of the British Empire would remain Egypt-centric always, agreed readily with him on this point, adding that 'our forces in Egypt and Palestine should support each other reciprocally'. Still, he made it clear to all those in the room that the central principle of a reduction in military expenditures remained in place nonetheless. This principle, Churchill said, applied to all of Britain's areas of responsibility throughout the Middle East.[28]

By meeting's end on that afternoon of 18 March the main business of the Cairo Conference was beginning to draw to a close. The central question of its proceedings – that of Faisal's future accession to the Iraqi throne – had been settled. 'This procedure', Churchill wrote to the prime minister afterwards, 'which was devised by Cox, Miss Bell and Lawrence carries with it the unanimous support of all authorities here'.[29] Similarly, the future of Transjordan appeared to have been settled too. Meanwhile however, the question of the size of British military expenditures in the region continued to be discussed in earnest in committee, as did the concomitant plan for an Arab Army.[30] At both the level of the main Military Committee as well as that of a constituent subcommittee, which would meet for the first time on the 19th, a new 'National Army' for Iraq remained on the table for discussion.

Chaired by Sir Percy Cox, the subcommittee included General Edmund Ironside, General Officer Commanding, Forces in Persia, as well as Jafar Pasha, the scheme's primary author. The subcommittee considered that the establishment of an Iraqi army was 'a matter of vital importance'. As a means to establish both its legitimacy and desirability, Jafar insisted that the same rate of pay be offered to those men recruited into it as pertained for those serving currently in the British garrison. The proposed number of men to comprise Iraq's new National Army was set at 5,000. They were to be recruited within a year of the agreement being struck. Significantly, the costs associated with the National Army were to fall upon the Iraqi government. Indeed, these were exactly the kind of economizing recommendations that were music to Churchill's ears. Earlier, on the 14th at a combined meeting of the Political and Military Committee, Churchill had stated that the working budget of £30 million for the British garrisons in Iraq and Palestine must be reduced. The approach to do so would be three-pronged, he continued. First, a reduction in the number of British troops from approximately 25,000 to 15,000 to yield an immediate savings of some £4 million with a longer-term reduction closer to £10 million. Second would come the raising of Arab (and Kurdish) troops in precisely the fashion to be laid out shortly in committee by Jafar. Third, troop reductions on the scale advocated by Churchill would then be offset by the expanded air defence scheme under the design of the air chiefs Trenchard and Salmond. Altogether, the plan appeared both seamless and achievable, which is exactly the message that Churchill had conveyed to the prime minister in his recently sent telegram.

Indeed, the scheme for 'the control of Mesopotamia' that had been developed by the Royal Air Force was taken up fully by the delegates during these latter days of the conference. Baghdad (using the base located nearby at Fallujah), Basra and Mosul were proposed as the main locations for housing up to twelve RAF squadrons, to be accompanied by armoured car companies that would provide ground-based protection for the airplanes.[31] To both Churchill and Lawrence the potential of the RAF to reduce British troop commitments, as well as to widen the scope of supervisory capability, would go a long way in solving the defence problem. The recent use of aeroplanes by the British in Somaliland to defeat the 'Mad Mullah' – along with the earlier example of their highly effective deployment against Ottoman forces during the Arab Revolt – offered a compelling demonstration of what could be accomplished through the use of airpower as a supplement to, or even in place of, ground troops. Indeed, the resultant idea of regularized colonial air policing had arrived to stay, although its use in the future would often prove to be baleful.[32]

As the Cairo Conference drew ever closer to its end, other important questions remained unresolved, however. One of the most pressing was that of providing subsidies to those Arab rulers, such as Ibn Saud, whose regional aspirations were strongly competitive, especially regarding the Hashemites. Born in Riyadh in 1875, Ibn Saud was emir of Nejd, having reconquered it in 1902 in the name of the 300-year-old dynastic House of Saud. Just a few months after the Cairo Conference wrapped up he would become Sultan of Nejd, and then king a few years later. Ultimately, in 1932, Ibn Saud would become the first king of what was by then being called Saudi Arabia. All told, he was an epic Arab dynast, with two-dozen wives who bore him as many as seventy children, including forty-five sons.[33]

Lawrence held a strongly positive view on the question of giving subsidies to Arab rulers. He pointed out on 18 March, for example, during the second meeting devoted to the topic by the Political Committee, 'that it was essential that we subsidise Ibn Saud sufficiently' as 'he possessed very great power to do us harm'. From his experience in the Arab Revolt, Lawrence knew the truth of this kind of reality more than most of his contemporaries. Lawrence's sole allegiance had been always to the Hashemites and now, in his view, the only way to ensure that Ibn Saud would be kept clear of potentially threatening the Sherifian Solution was to pay him off. To this end, two days earlier Churchill had instructed that a subcommittee on subsidies be formed, whose membership was to include Cox, Lawrence, Colonel Kinahan Cornwallis and Major T.E. Scott, the resident and General Officer Commanding at Aden.

After convening on the 18th, the subcommittee recommended that the amount being paid currently in subsidies to 'obtain certain political results' should rise two and a half times from a total of £96,000 to a level of £248,000 per year. Fully £200,000 of this recommended amount was to be given to just two men. Ibn Saud should be paid £100,000 (Cox had lobbied for still more, £120,000), an increase of £40,000 over the current amount, and the other £100,000 should be sent to his arch-nemesis and the key to the Sherifian Solution, Sharif Hussein. In exchange for the subsidy Hussein was to ensure that no anti-French propaganda would emanate from the Hejaz. As well, he was not to allow the Islamic holy places of Mecca and Medina to become sites from which jihad could be launched. Rounding out the subsidies, a much smaller amount was to be set aside for Fahad Bey, a leading Bedouin chief who was known to Lawrence from the Arab Revolt. In exchange for £12,000 annually Fahad was to keep his territory open for the establishment of a small number of RAF airfields. Finally, there was Muhammad ibn Ali al-Idrisi, the emir of Asir, a small kingdom in what later would become south-western Saudi Arabia. He had rebelled against the Ottomans as far back as 1910 and had supported the Allies throughout the First World War. Accordingly, he was to be subsidized at the same annual rate as Fahad, £12,000 per annum.

Ibn Saud, however, remained the key to Britain's ability to work unhindered both with the Iraqis and with the Palestinians, as well as with the other Arabs in the region. Moreover, the British needed him to keep a tight rein on his own extremist Wahhabist sectarians, who wanted no cooperation with Westerners nor with their Muslim co-religionists whose fidelity to Islam they did not accept. Ibn Saud is 'the greatest factor in Arabian politics', the subcommittee observed, and although 'His relations with us have been uniformly friendly ... From his central position he can invade South-West Mesopotamia, Koweit, [and the] Hedjaz'. Accordingly, the 'skilful use of our subsidy, which is probably now as large as the total revenues of his Government from other sources' was to ensure that no action would be taken by him against the three territories named above. In short, the subsidy was made to purchase regional peace and as far as the subcommittee was concerned it would be money well spent.[34]

At the termination of all conference meetings on Saturday the 19th, most of the committees had finished their work, although that of the Palestine sub-committee would be transferred to Jerusalem, the agreed site of its planned conclusion.[35] In addition to the major decisions taken at Cairo concerning Faisal, Transjordan and the reaching of economies in military spending, the delegates had also turned their attention to other persistent issues. The presence, for example, of a large number of post-war refugees in Iraq, which included some 14,000 Armenians, as well as hundreds of Russians and Assyrians, was of prevailing importance. The Armenian population in Iraq – based mainly in Basra – had grown out of an historic community that dated from the early seventeenth century. The arrival of thousands of Armenians fleeing the genocide carried out by the Ottomans during the First World War had driven up their number. The conference concluded that the best option available for the infant Iraqi state was to send these refugees to various ports along the Black Sea where they would be given, it was assumed, some measure of sanctuary. Bell in particular weighed in on the refugees' fate, taking the view that 'if a number of destitute persons were thrown on the country it was probable that they would fail to obtain employment, and would therefore only be a source of crime'.[36] As blunt as her words sound, at that time in the early twentieth century there did not exist international refugee agencies of the type that would later come into existence, nor did the British wish to enlarge the scope of their already strained relations with the Turks by forcing the issue of the Armenians' fate. In the end, however, most of the refugee Armenians would remain where they were in Iraq. Finally, as to the more practical tasks taken up by the conference, came the decision to ensure the consolidation of air and automobile routes between Palestine and Iraq. In so doing it was believed that certain elements of geopolitical and economic unity might emerge out of the Sherifian regional ideal.[37]

Altogether, by their second weekend in Cairo, it was clear to the leading participants at the conference that they had good reason to be well pleased with what had been achieved and therefore with where matters stood in planning for the future of the Middle East. Churchill especially was in the vanguard of this contented band of delegates as the conference wound down, but so too were Lawrence and Bell. In a letter to his mother on 20 March, for example, Lawrence described the many events of the conference, including that he was happy to have seen Allenby 'several times'. He was 'very fit', Lawrence informed her, adding that he was especially pleased about Kennington's portrait of Allenby.[38]

In the meantime, Bell too was pleased with the way the meetings had gone, having predicted at the outset that 'this is going to be a nice conference – it's immensely interesting'.[39] Now, with the conference on the verge of ending, she would write even more enthusiastically to a friend that 'It has been wonderful. We covered more work in a fortnight than has ever before been got through in a year'.[40] She was supremely gratified to have had the two Iraqi ministers in attendance. Indeed, she had spent much of the rail and boat journey from Baghdad to Cairo two weeks earlier in conversation with both of them, as well as in translating from Arabic into English Jafar's report on the proposed Arab Army. In addition, Bell had spent much time happily 'reading Arabic' with Sassoon Eskell.[41] The attendance at the conference of the two Iraqi ministers – an Arab and a Jew – in her view had supplied it with a necessary national, as well as a symbolically ethnic, component. Moreover, given how both of them had been consulted closely in committee – especially Jafar – their presence at Cairo had not been an exercise in mere tokenism. Allenby too, even though he was not involved directly in the sessions, was well pleased with the way in which the conference had proceeded. Still, he would voice the opinion that as far as Egyptian security was concerned a high number of British ground troops should remain in place, at least for the time being.[42] Not the least of Allenby's reasons for his satisfaction with the conference – tied as it was to the question of British troop deployment – was that there had been very little nationalist protest in the streets of Cairo during its ten-day run. Indeed, as he reported to his mother, there had been only 'one slight demonstration, by a few hundred rude students', who had chanted anti-Churchill slogans loudly outside the Semiramis Hotel.[43]

As the conference drew to a close, on Sunday morning, 20 March, Churchill and a small number of delegates departed the hotel by automobile convoy for nearby Giza. He was determined to ensure that their time in Egypt would include some memorable sightseeing. Their first stop was the old Mena House Hotel, one of the first European-style hotels in the country. They were greeted there by the sheikh of Mena, resplendent in gold-coloured robes and mounted on horseback, after which they toured the manicured and verdant gardens and grounds of the hotel.[44] The group was then introduced to a herd of camels brought in for the occasion so that a short ride could be taken to view the pyramid complex and the Sphinx. After that, they undertook a longer journey by camel overland to the ruins of the storied ancient city of Memphis, located at Saqqara about 12 miles south of Giza, where they enjoyed a picnic lunch and viewed the surrounding sites.

After taking in the pyramids and the Sphinx, the group remounted their camels and rode southwards to Saqqara. Camels are notoriously ill-tempered beasts, odorous in the extreme and possessed of an elephant-like memory. The one-humped dromedary, or Arabian camel, is suited perfectly for life and travel in the desert. Its walking pace is about 3 miles per hour – although they are capable of surprising and ungainly bursts of speed during which they can reach up to 40 miles per hour at the gallop – so the journey took a few hours to complete. En route Churchill endured an uncomfortable moment when his camel's saddle loosened, causing him to slide off its back and land with a thump in the sand. 'How are the mighty fallen', quipped Clementine.[45] Though uninjured, except for his pride and a slightly grazed hand, restoring his physical equilibrium along with his ministerial dignity took him a few minutes to achieve.[46]

Continuing on apace, the conference party arrived at Saqqara in the early afternoon, had lunch, and then relaxed briefly before being shown around its ancient ruins. Memphis, founded by King Menes around 3,000 BC, had served as the capital of ancient Egypt's Old Kingdom. It was a place subsumed by history, from the melding of Egypt's Old and New Kingdoms, to Alexander the Great's crowning there as pharaoh in the fourth century BC, to the creation of the Rosetta Stone some 200 years later. The Necropolis, the ancient burial ground for Memphis located at Saqqara and featuring the famous Step Pyramid of Djoser, was toured by some members of the group. Churchill, however, perhaps tired out by his eventful morning on camelback, decided to skip the tour. Instead, he opted to pursue his favourite hobby and reached for his easel, brushes and paints. Towards the late afternoon most of the group set off on the return journey to the Mena House. Lawrence and Churchill, however, lingered behind for a time before mounting their camels together again and riding back to Giza at speed. Later, in November of 1922 when his government advisory days had come to an end, Lawrence would remind Churchill of this evocative shared experience in the desert: 'do you remember your camel-trotting at Giza, when you wore out all your escort, except myself, & I'm not a fair competitor at that!'[47]

The next day, 21 March, Churchill gave an elegant culminating dinner at the Semiramis. The morning had begun with a formal conference group photograph taken in front of the hotel. This photo would become well-known in almost the same way as the one taken the day before at Giza. In it, Churchill can be seen seated in the middle of the front row at the centre of the assembled delegates who rise in several serried ranks behind him. He is flanked on either side by a pair of British high commissioners, Sir Percy Cox on his left and Sir Herbert Samuel on his right. Alongside them in the front row sit generals Congreve, Haldane, Ironside and Radcliffe. Directly behind Cox stands Lawrence, wearing a lounge suit and with his fingers knotted tightly together. On one side of him is the figure of Jafar Pasha, bulging rather noticeably in his military uniform and sporting an Ottoman-issue helmet, and on the other Air Vice-Marshal Salmond. Nearby stands the patrician Sir Sassoon Eskell, bewhiskered and sporting his customary tarboosh. Then comes Gertrude Bell, as usual attired in a long coat trimmed with a fur collar and wearing a wide-brimmed flowered hat. Next to her is the imposing figure of Sir Geoffrey Archer. Arnold Wilson can be located near the top right corner of the photo, standing as far away from Bell as possible. Finally, in front of them all and towards the left of the photo are the two lion cubs with their unnamed Somali handler. Altogether in its organized presentation and confident air the photograph is one that sums up neatly the diplomatic work of the previous ten days. It is demonstrative too of the manner in which highly important decisions of the sort taken at the Cairo Conference occurred in the last significant era of British imperial power and within the context of post-First World War conference culture.

Later that evening came Churchill's gala dinner. The Semiramis was known for the quality of its French cuisine and the delegates were treated to the best that the hotel had to offer.[48] Decorated grandly, the ballroom was full to overflowing with all the delegates, together with a number of their spouses and other guests.[49] Sir Percy had brought his wife Louisa, Lady Cox, to Cairo, and Bell's father, Sir Hugh, was in attendance also. It was a 'great dinner', Allenby wrote afterwards to his mother, punctuated by the giving of a number of toasts and speeches. Churchill himself naturally gave a speech, and so too did Sir Herbert Samuel and Allenby. Sir Walter Congreve and Sir Geoffrey Salmond then offered brief remarks, which rounded out the formal addresses. In addition to the quality of its cuisine, the Semiramis was known too for its concerts and dancing, and these also formed part of the evening. Altogether the dinner was a great success. Still, for Allenby at least, as immensely enjoyable and festive as that summative evening at the Semiramis turned out to be, he was hoping soon for 'a little rest from big dinners and such functions', as he wearily put it in a letter home.

But there would be a few more such events to come. The next morning, Allenby accompanied Churchill to the Abdin Palace for an interview with the sultan. Built in the 1860s by Khedive Ismail, the palace was sumptuous and finished throughout with a surfeit of gold. It was located not far from the Semiramis; later that year the sultan would add to it a verdant hanging garden. Fuad, who had become sultan of Egypt in 1917, would cause Allenby great frustration in 1922 at the cessation of the formal British protectorate over Egypt and the promulgation of the eponymously named Allenby Declaration. In the period following the declaration, and as the renamed King Fuad I of Egypt, he would make a practice out of peremptorily dissolving parliament and otherwise abusing his constitutionally constrained powers. Allenby would find these actions to be both exasperating and compromising of his plan for the proper application of the new Egyptian constitution. However, at that moment, in March of 1921, Fuad welcomed both Churchill and Allenby warmly to the palace for what would be an extended one-and-a-half-hour visit during which time, Allenby wrote home, 'they had a real heart to heart talk, I am glad to say. Each was much impressed by the other; and Churchill accepted my view that the Sultan is a sound man, worthy of our confidence and support'.

The positive view of Fuad expressed at that moment by Allenby would change soon enough. But later that day he returned to the Palace along with Churchill and accompanied by over a hundred others drawn from both the Cairo Conference as well as from the Egyptian government. The Sultan had invited them all for a 'big banquet'. It would be big indeed, Allenby recorded, 'magnificently done, as are all his entertainments'. Sultan Fuad's sumptuous dinner that evening marked the last major event of the conference. If the previous evening's dinner at the Semiramis had signalled its end formally, the Sultan's banquet at the Abdin Palace acted as a spectacular addendum to the conference's ten days of deliberations. It remained now only for an intimate dinner party at the British Residency on the evening of 23 March to bring the Cairo Conference firmly to an end. Writing again to his mother, Allenby would describe this valedictory dinner as 'rather distinguished'. Joining him was Churchill and Samuel as well as the governor of Somaliland, Sir Geoffrey Archer, and Major T.E. Scott of Aden.[50] At the dinner's end Churchill and Samuel, together with their wives and assistants, along with Lawrence, Young and a handful of others, boarded a special midnight train to begin the journey to Jerusalem. It was to be in the Holy City, therefore, that the Cairo Conference would truly conclude.

All the major participants at the conference had good reason to be pleased late on that evening of 23 March 1921 as Churchill's private train pulled out of Cairo's Central Station. Bound initially for Ismailia, located on the west bank of the Suez Canal, the train would cross into Sinai before reaching Gaza en route to Jerusalem. For Churchill and the Middle East Department, the Cairo Conference had gone mainly to plan and therefore had been a success. If, as Young believed, the

War Office had hoped 'to scuttle from both Palestine and Mesopotamia', the success of the conference meant a different outcome was at hand.[51] Faisal would become king of Iraq while his rivals for the throne had been either passed over or effectively controlled. Meanwhile, his regional dynastic competitors had been dealt with similarly through the provision of financial subsidies. In addition, Iraq's territorial boundaries and its internal demographic composition were beginning to take administrative shape. British government expenditures in Iraq and Palestine would be reduced significantly in line with Churchill's view 'that everything that happens in the Middle East is secondary to the reduction of expense'.[52] Even though Churchill was not an economizing instrumentalist, there is no doubt that he believed in the close relationship between growing colonial independence and declining imperial expense. For him, together they made for a properly tessellated combination.

For Lawrence however, just as for Churchill, his work was not nearly over yet. The same can be said too of Cox and Bell. The questions taken up and the decisions made by the conference's many specialized meetings needed now to be operationalized within the turbulent world of Arab–Zionist inter-communal politics. Moreover, the situation would be exacerbated by France's continuing paramountcy in Syria, leading presently to formal mandatory power. In the meantime, Lawrence wrote wearily home to report that 'We have done a lot of work, which is almost finished'.[53] But in a certain way his most important work was about to begin. Jerusalem and Transjordan awaited, in what would be his and Churchill's concerted attempt to position Abdullah successfully under the Cairo Conference's Sherifian umbrella. Meanwhile, Bell too girded herself for what lay ahead in Iraq. 'When we get our Amir [Faisal] out he will need a great deal of help and guidance', she wrote to her old friend Frank Balfour on her own journey back to Baghdad.

And so the Cairo Conference had come to an end amidst much optimism and confidence, but with an element of trepidation too for what the future held in store for the complicated geopolitics of the Middle East. Bell bid an emotional goodbye to her father after having spent a 'wonderful week' with him, knowing that she must return to Iraq and remain there for a long time to come.[54] Meanwhile, Sir Hugh would ride on the special midnight train with the Churchill party, accompanying them as far as Suez before taking ship for home and a return to his business interests that, worryingly, as he had just revealed to Gertrude, had begun recently to falter.[55] The ten days of the Cairo Conference may have been over, but the work to implement its broad-based plan for post-war state-building and governance in the Middle East had just begun.

6

NOT QUITE FINISHED AT CAIRO
ON TO JERUSALEM

As Churchill's special train pulled out of Cairo's Central Station just before midnight on 23 March he may well have reclined, lit one of his ubiquitous Cuban cigars, and anticipated a postscript to the Cairo Conference that would see him take up residence in Jerusalem for the week to follow. Lawrence climbed aboard the same train and shared a bunk with Churchill's temporary aide-de-camp, Wing Commander Maxwell Coote, on the almost 500-mile overnight passage to the Holy City. Earlier that day Lawrence had sent a message to Faisal in London informing him of where matters stood regarding his prospective enthronement as king of Iraq, as well as the next steps to be taken. 'Things have gone exactly as hoped', he wrote. 'Please start at once for Mecca by the quickest possible route ... I will meet you on the way and explain details. Say only that you are going [to see] your father and on no account put anything in the press'.[1]

On the train that evening a festive mood prevailed, as it had done for the last couple of days since the end of the conference's working sessions. 'We're a very happy family', Lawrence had written to his mother earlier from the Semiramis Hotel.[2] On the train also, along with Sir Hugh Bell and the Samuels, were the visiting worthies Lord and Lady Reading who had been at the British Residency for the previous couple of days as guests of the Allenbys. 'I took him [Lord Reading] to the Pyramids', Lord Allenby wrote home, 'and Mabel took Lady R – who is rather an invalid – to the Cairo bazaars'. Reading, like Sir Herbert Samuel, was a prominent Jewish figure in British society and government who had just completed a term of almost eight years as lord chief justice of England, the first of his faith to hold the position. Just then he was on his way to India to take up the appointment of viceroy, another first for a British Jew.

In the early hours of the 24th – having bid farewell to the Readings and Sir Hugh at Ismailia – the rest of the Churchill party crossed the Suez Canal by barge and then changed trains for the rest of the journey. Their first stop would come at Gaza, located just beyond the border between Egypt and Palestine, which had been the scene of some extremely fierce fighting during the First World War. Allenby's ultimate victory there in November of 1917 had triggered that autumn's successful Palestine campaign and the capture of Jerusalem.

Churchill's nationalist-stirring arrival two weeks earlier in Egypt would be given a small reprise as his train pulled into Gaza. The city had been rebuilt considerably after it had been levelled by Allenby's Egyptian Expeditionary Force just over three years earlier, but it bore still the hard evidence of recent warfare.[3] Gaza's population was small, perhaps 15,000, of which only a handful were Jews. The train arrived about 8 o'clock in the morning, after which Churchill, Samuel and Lawrence took a brief tour of the city. Its residents had been made aware of the great man's arrival however, and many of them had gathered in the streets to greet him. But unlike the denunciations that Churchill had received earlier in Alexandria, in Gaza he would be met mainly by 'Cheers for the Minister!' and 'Cheers for Great Britain!' The shouts were in Arabic, which neither Churchill nor Samuel understood. Still, Lawrence, being perfectly fluent in the language, could hear amidst the din a smattering of voices shouting, 'Down with the Jews!' and 'Cut their throats!' This knowledge he elected to keep to himself.[4] The reaction to Churchill's brief stop in Gaza would be mostly positive. But as much as the decisions made about the future of Iraq and Transjordan in Cairo might be lauded by Arabs, passing through Gaza was a reminder of the extremely thorny thicket of Arab–Jewish politics that he was about to enter in Jerusalem.

Leaving Gaza later that day, their train arrived in Jerusalem by mid-evening. The date coincided with Maundy Thursday, the eve of the holiest day of the year for Christians, not that the largely unreligious Churchill had ever paid close attention to the celebration of Easter. One might have thought that Lawrence, on the other hand – having grown up in the strongly Anglican evangelical parish church of St Aldate's in Oxford – may well have taken note. In any event, the Churchills would be staying as Sir Herbert and Lady Samuel's guests at Government House. Opened in 1910 while under Ottoman rule and called the Augusta Victoria building, it was located on the southern face of the Mount of Olives and possessed a commanding view of the Old City. During the First World War the Augusta Victoria had been used by the Ottomans as a military headquarters and hospital. In December of 1917, following Allenby's taking of the city, he made it his headquarters. Beginning in 1920 when Samuel arrived as British high commissioner it had been converted into Government House. The most striking feature of the complex was its 200-foot-high bell-tower, while its most convenient was full-service electricity, which had made it the first set of connected buildings in the country to be modernized in this way.

To the Churchills however, electricity or no, after the hedonistic comforts they had enjoyed at some of Egypt's best hotels Jerusalem's Government House presented itself as a rather cold and uninviting Teutonic-style pile. Nonetheless, for Churchill there was much work to be done over the coming days. For Clementine on the other hand, the holiday would continue, beginning with attendance at an Anglican

Good Friday service the next morning. For members of the Church of England living in or visiting Jerusalem during this time, their spiritual home was to be found usually at St George's Cathedral. It had opened a generation earlier in 1899, succeeding Christ Church, which until then had been the seat of the Anglican bishop in Jerusalem. Dating from 1849, Christ Church was located in the Old City near the Jaffa Gate and directly across from the Citadel where Allenby had read out his proclamation on 11 December 1917, marking the advent of British control over Palestine. Together with St George's, Christ Church offered a substantial Anglican presence in the Holy City, made that much more pronounced by the strong public profile maintained by the Anglican bishop in Jerusalem since 1914, Rennie MacInnes.

Having come from a long line of parliamentarians and generals and educated at Harrow School and Trinity College, Cambridge, Bishop MacInnes was completely at ease with British establishment society. In the lead-up to the victory of the Egyptian Expeditionary Force (EEF) at Jerusalem, Allenby had kept in close touch with him, and the bishop was a tireless worker on behalf of all those, regardless of their religious affiliation, who called Jerusalem home. During the war MacInnes had been forced to live elsewhere – mainly in Cairo – but the success of the EEF's Palestine campaign had made his return to the city greatly anticipated, by himself, as well as by many of its residents. During his temporary stay in Cairo MacInnes had corresponded regularly with Allenby, mainly about when it might be safe to return and take up residence again at St George's. Allenby had kept MacInnes apprised of his progress, writing to him, for example, in late November 1917, that 'I am not yet in occupation of Jerusalem ... though my troops are not many miles distant'. Later, after Allenby had won control of the city, MacInnes asked him whether he might be allowed to fly over Jerusalem to observe the state of its post-war condition. Allenby had declined this request – 'aeroplanes are ill adapted to carry Bishops' he wrote, presumably with a smile – but the request itself was a measure of the determination of the man to return to Jerusalem and shepherd his erstwhile flock. Very soon thereafter however, in January of 1918, Allenby had informed MacInnes that 'I hope soon to welcome you in Palestine', which indeed he was able to do the next month. 'I am glad to say', as Allenby wrote to him on 13 February, 'that I think there is no reason why you should not come to Jerusalem. I hope, therefore, that you will do so as soon as convenient to you; and I am sorry to have kept you away so long'.[5]

Bishop MacInnes's dedicated work in Egypt and the Sudan during his wartime exile had made him a widely known and well-respected figure in the Middle East. In Jerusalem especially, his reputation for humanitarianism and ecumenism was strong. He had developed also a determined objection to the claims made by Zionists to expand the number of Jewish immigrants to Palestine. And he did not hesitate to say so. In November of 1919, for example, his uncompromising views on the subject of Zionism – 'It is Political and not Religious' – were headlined in the *New York Times*. Worldwide publicity for his anti-Zionist stance was the result.[6] Indeed, Allenby too would remain highly circumspect about whether the British should be pursuing a policy of permitting high levels of Jewish immigration into Palestine against the clear wishes of its historically preponderant Arab population.[7] Allenby's departure for Egypt in order to become high commissioner in March of 1919 had ended his direct association with MacInnes, but he continued to sympathize with the bishop's stance against Britain's policy of creating a Jewish homeland in Palestine in defiance of the objections of the vast majority of its residents.

In passing through Gaza en route to Jerusalem, as we have seen, Churchill had found himself in the midst of many of those who would increasingly give voice to these same objections, although he was not readily cognizant of the fact owing to his lack of Arabic. Clarity for Churchill in this regard, however, would soon come. Given his commitment to implementing the Balfour Declaration, Churchill did not agree with MacInnes on the issue. But their opposing positions would have no discernible impact on the two men as they stood side by side at a ceremony on the afternoon of 26 March, held within the hushed confines of the city's British Military Cemetery (later renamed the Jerusalem War Cemetery along what would become called 'Churchill Boulevard'). The two were in attendance to pay tribute to fallen British Tommies, as well as to soldiers from the other allied countries whose lives had been lost just a few years earlier during the war. Indeed, construction of the cemetery on the Mount of Olives had begun immediately after Allenby's occupation of the city with the burial of 270 British soldiers who had been killed in the victory. Slowly, additional interments were undertaken through the transferral of human remains from neighbouring cemeteries where British and imperial troops had lain buried near to where they had been killed in action. By the time Churchill attended the memorial service on that afternoon in March the number of war dead interred at the cemetery had become larger still. In a moving address he spoke about the 'veteran soldiers' who lay amidst 'the dust of the Khalifs and Crusaders and the Macabees. Peace to their ashes, honour to their memory and may we not fail to complete the work which they have begun'.[8] Although the fundamental nature of that 'work' may have been in sharp dispute between Churchill and MacInnes, the sincere emotion of their shared moment amongst the British war dead would create a bond between them nonetheless.

In the meantime, the first part of Lawrence's return to Jerusalem had been spent mainly in the company of his old Arab Bureau chief, Sir Ronald Storrs. To Lawrence, 'Ronny' Storrs remained a kindred spirit: 'always first, and the great man among us', as he would describe him reverently in the pages of Seven Pillars of Wisdom, 'the most brilliant Englishman in the Near East'.[9] Storrs was only seven years older than Lawrence, but he seemed to embody a different generation's settled security and social confidence, which contrasted sharply with that of his maverick friend and colleague. The eldest son of a

Nova Scotia-born Church of England prelate, Storrs had been educated at The Charterhouse and later at Pembroke College, Cambridge, from which he graduated in 1903 with a first class degree in classics. Afterwards he had gone to Egypt to work in the Finance Ministry. Staying on there through the early war years, Storrs served in various capacities until in 1917 he was transferred out to become 'the first military governor of Jerusalem since Pontius Pilate', as he put it pithily.[10] A few years later in 1920 Storrs's role expanded when he was made governor of Jerusalem and Judea, the position in which he was serving when reunited with Lawrence in March of 1921. For the next few days in Jerusalem Lawrence apprised him of what had been decided at the Cairo Conference, as well as about the task that remained of aligning Abdullah's political future with the require- ments of the Sherifian Solution.

Storrs and Lawrence shared essentially the same view as to what should constitute the future of Palestine; that is, the need for it to be partitioned in order for Transjordan to come into existence as an independent Arab state under the kingship of Abdullah.[11] Each man knew the other extremely well, and they had a common under- standing of the crackling tension inherent in the metropole–periphery dynamic of what they had undertaken to achieve in the Middle East. The British imperial habit formed abroad over the preceding centu- ries was one that rested mainly upon the received policy of Indirect Rule.[12] In pursuing the Sherifian Solution, Churchill understood the obvious give and take inherent in this policy, as did Lawrence and Storrs.

On Saturday, 26 March, after a couple of quiet days spent in Jerusalem in anticipation of taking up his assignment, Lawrence departed the city to meet up with Abdullah on the east side of the Jordan River. He did so at Churchill's request and in accordance with what had been discussed earlier in both London and Cairo. The colonial secretary had charged Lawrence with informing Abdullah fully as to the scope and expectations of the British plan so that an agreement between the two parties might be achieved during his short stay in Jerusalem. As much as general agreement had been found at the Cairo Conference over the key features of the plan, the Sherifian Solution carried with it a sting in the tail, at least for Sir Herbert Samuel. As had been made clear to him during the final days of the conference, the creation of an Arab kingdom east of the Jordan River – 'Trans-Jordania' – would necessitate a territorial dismemberment of the original boundaries of Palestine.

At the meetings of the Palestine Political and Military Committee held on 17 and 18 March, Churchill had argued forcefully that the existing territorial footprint of Palestine would have to be altered substantially in order to accommodate the necessary creation of Transjordan.[13] Indeed, in a lively private discussion with Samuel at the British Residency on the evening of his arrival in Cairo on the 16th, Churchill had told him that Palestine needed to be severed in the manner described, with the historic Jordan River serving as a natural and useful boundary to divide Palestine from the proposed new state of Transjordan. This decision was in keeping with Churchill's stated position that, although most of the commentary about and reaction to the Balfour Declaration had focused on its promise of a national home for the Jews in Palestine, it contained nevertheless a second promise that guaranteed to Arabs their residential and territorial integrity. This promise was one that Churchill intended to keep. Both Samuel and Chaim Weizmann had strongly rejected any proposal that would change the traditional boundaries of Palestine. But to Churchill doing so offered the only solution to the festering problems between Arabs and Jews in Palestine. He saw in it the makings of a regional *via media* that could accommodate both resident groups while at the same time ensuring the maintenance of broader British imperial interests.[14]

In leaving Jerusalem on Saturday morning, Lawrence headed for the town of Salt. He travelled as a passenger in a government car via the Jericho road going east out of the city. The road pitches downhill quickly as it descends from an elevation of almost 2,500 feet at Jerusalem to well below sea level at the edge of the Jordan River. Once there Lawrence crossed the Allenby Bridge, built in 1918 by the EEF's engineers to span the Jordan and facilitate an attack on Ottoman positions farther east. The bridge is located just north of the Dead Sea and sits about 1,000 feet below sea level; nearby is the site reputed to be that of St John's baptism of Jesus Christ. The climb up the eastern side of the Jordan is equally steep. Upon reaching the plateau Lawrence and his driver then turned northwards for the last part of the 125-mile journey to Salt, where Abdullah was waiting for him to arrive. The town's few thousand residents were spread across a trio of hills. Though small, Salt was an historic town and later it would serve briefly as Transjordan's capital.

In meeting with Abdullah at Salt Lawrence's plan was to ensure that the Hashemite prince would be prepared fully for his first diplomatic encounter with Churchill, which was scheduled for the following day in Jerusalem.[15] Born in 1882 in Mecca as the second of Sharif Hussein's four sons, Abdullah was educated in Constantinople and in the years leading up to the war had sat in the Ottoman General Assembly as a deputy for the city of his birth. Committing himself increasingly to independence for the Hejaz however, Abdullah encouraged his father to sponsor the Arab Revolt and once it had commenced in 1916 came to occupy an important role in it, although in subordination always to that of Faisal. Lawrence's initial meeting with Abdullah in October of 1916 at Jeddah on the Red Sea coast had left him with a permanent dislike of the Hashemite prince. In blistering heat – 'the atmosphere was like a bath', Lawrence would write later – he had been unimpressed with Abdullah from the outset. He thought him overly theatrical, having arrived for their meeting, for example, galloping on a white horse, a mount reserved traditionally for use by sovereigns. Moreover, he was too merry, Lawrence believed, too fat, too insincere.[16] Lawrence could himself be prickly – as well as showy – but his negative view of Abdullah was one that had remained unchanged. Now however, five years later, Lawrence would be required to alter his view if the second plank of the Sherifian Solution was to be put in place, a task dependent upon Abdullah subscribing to its precepts.

Even more recently however, Abdullah had made it harder for Lawrence and the British in their attempt at regional state-building. A few months after Faisal's removal from the Syrian throne in the summer of 1920 Abdullah had decided to move north from the Hejaz into southern Transjordan to signal his intention to possibly re-take Syria. Earlier that year Abdullah had been proclaimed peremptorily as king of Iraq by the Iraqi National Council, only to refuse the honour that would go ultimately to Faisal. To the French, Abdullah's continuing presence in Transjordan remained a highly unwelcome provocation against their coming formal mandate in Syria. Unless, that is, he could be made to renounce any future designs on Syria by being given a state of his own over which to rule, one that could be carved out of the existing territory of Palestine. There was a method to what Churchill and the British were attempting to do therefore, and the major conduit to effect its success had become Lawrence and his presumed success in persuading Abdullah of the plan's attractiveness and viability. Abdullah had always held great respect for Lawrence, if also remaining wary equally of his manifest charisma and the mesmeric appeal he was able to exert 'among the tribes'.[17] He understood exactly why Lawrence had come over from Jerusalem to meet him at Salt, if not the precise details of the proposal that he was bringing along with him. In any event, Abdullah welcomed his old desert comrade with the usual large measure of Arab hospitality bestowed upon honoured visitors.

Arriving on Saturday afternoon, Lawrence spent the balance of the day in conversation with Abdullah before being entertained that evening at a splendid dinner put on by a local worthy.[18] The next morning, Easter Sunday, 27 March, Abdullah and Lawrence departed Salt for Jerusalem. On the way out of town they were 'mobbed' by a 'very enthusiastic and excited' crowd, Lawrence recounted later with satisfaction.[19] Passing through the countryside, more cheering came from groups of Palestinians who had gathered along the roadside. So engrossed were the two men in their conversation about the meeting with Churchill to come, however, that they ignored the loud shouts of acclamation as their car passed by the people. Arriving at the Holy City a few hours later they were met by a similarly warm reception in its streets before making their way to Government House. Here Abdullah was introduced formally to Sir Herbert Samuel, followed by afternoon tea. That evening an official dinner was put on by the high commissioner at which Abdullah and Churchill finally met. It marked the first time that either man had been in the presence of the other.[20]

This initial meeting between Churchill and Abdullah would act, in a way, as the fulcrum of the Cairo Conference's faith in the Sherifian Solution. To start, if the two-part plan were to work in the manner envisaged by the British then Abdullah would be required to dispense with all pretensions pertaining to the thrones of either Syria or Iraq. By this point in the run of events, such a decision, it was assumed by Churchill, had become all but assured. Certainly neither he, nor any member of the Middle East Department, nor anyone else in the British government had ever thought of Abdullah as being the right Hashemite legatee to preside over either country. The Iraqi National Council's appointment of him as their putative king during the previous year had suggested a different view, however. And the position of his father, Sharif Hussein, needed to be taken into consideration also. But ever since Faisal's ignominious expulsion from Syria the likelihood and desirability of the Iraqi throne being made for him alone had been accepted by almost everyone concerned, and certainly such was the view of the British.

Similarly, the good maintenance of Anglo-French relations militated against the British turning a blind eye to the sometime incursions made across the Syrian border by Abdullah's supporters. Moreover, the British were not about to back him in any attempt to reclaim Syria in the guise of some sort of recrudescent Arab liberator. Accordingly, in order that the Sherifian Solution should gain the necessary amount of traction locally, Churchill needed to make plain to Abdullah that his only real option was to accept what the British had in store for him in Transjordan, even if it meant dispensing with his broader Syrian dream. Indeed, less than a week earlier, on 22 March, the British Cabinet had ratified the decisions made at Cairo, recording that 'Feisal will be told privately that there is no longer any need for him to remain in England, and that he should return without delay to Mecca to consult his father'.[21] The communication of this instruction to Faisal had been Lawrence's to undertake, the second part of which would become Abdullah's opportunity to rule in Transjordan.

During the formal dinner at Jerusalem's Government House on that Easter Sunday evening, Churchill was seated next to Abdullah. Since the dinner had been designed mainly to be a social occasion it would have been bad form for the colonial secretary to proceed much beyond voicing mere pleasantries in their private conversation. But he would do so anyhow. Churchill pointed out to Abdullah that his taking up residence at Maan during the previous November – on what had been called euphemistically a 'tour of inspection', though Abdullah had been accompanied by 300 men and six machine guns – had greatly upset France's post-war equilibrium in Syria. Moreover, recent border clashes between armed Bedouin warriors and French troops were being blamed on Abdullah's presence at Amman – to which he had moved earlier that month – as well as on his sometime residence at Salt, which was even nearer the Syrian border.[22] Churchill noted that he had sent the French military commander in Syria, General Gouraud, assurances that neither the British nor Abdullah himself were supportive of such raids, a position that he would reiterate to Gouraud in person a few days later in Jerusalem.[23]

After listening to this litany of complaints from Churchill, Abdullah countered that Syria had been won honourably in the field by the Arabs in helping to defeat the Ottomans in 1918, only to see the country wrested away from them by the political machinations of the French. Therefore, he stressed, Churchill was in no position to blame the Syrians for having acted patriotically in response.[24] Despite Abdullah's reputation – at least as far as Lawrence was concerned – for being an 'indolent dilettante', and for enjoying too much social merriment and luxurious living, he was politically astute nonetheless. Earlier, before the war, as the historian Neil Faulkner points out, Abdullah had been effective as the 'go-between' with the British and his father.[25] Even Lawrence would come to admit as much in his favour.[26] And although Abdullah was not the charismatic political leader that Faisal had been during the Arab Revolt, 'his value', Lawrence believed, 'perhaps would come in the peace after success'.[27] Here then was the moment for that hoped-for value to show itself. Certainly for Churchill, despite some obvious points of friction between them, a good beginning had been made over dinner. Indeed, in his estimation Abdullah was 'a very agreeable, intelligent, and civilized Arab prince'.[28]

The three days in Jerusalem that followed proved to be an intense, even frenetic, experience for both men, especially Churchill. On the next morning, 28 March, they met again, and this time the British plan for the future of Transjordan and Palestine was reiterated to Abdullah. He was reminded by Churchill that the original borders of Palestine would need to be altered dramatically in order to accommodate the formal creation of Transjordan. But by so doing the British government would be acknowledging and fulfilling also the promise made in the Balfour Declaration to establish a national homeland for the Jews in Palestine. Abdullah objected immediately to this stance. He proposed instead that since a reconfigured Palestine would remain overwhelmingly Arab in population the only sensible course of action to take was to ensure that it be given an Arab governor. The animus between Arabs and Jews, he said, could best be 'overcome' under this sort of bi-national arrangement.[29] Churchill refused to accept Abdullah's proposal however, telling him that for the British to act in this way was impossible politically almost four years after the Balfour Declaration's promulgation. But regional balance could be achieved nevertheless, stated the colonial secretary, by ensuring that Arab rule prevailed in a newly demarcated Transjordan.

In the main their meeting that day would put in place a formal imprimatur on Abdullah's continuing presence in Transjordan, an acknowledgement by the British that his presence there was likely to be permanent. Indeed, a young British official named Alec Kirkbride had been waiting at Amman station a few weeks earlier to welcome Abdullah to Transjordan in the name of the so-called 'National Government of Moab', a glib reference to the local Mountains of Moab and the expected creation of a new Transjordanian state. Kirkbride had served under Allenby in the EEF and then had remained in Syria until Faisal's fall from the throne. Afterwards he had taken up residence in Transjordan to offer a tangible British diplomatic presence there in advance of the Cairo Conference. Upon his greeting of Abdullah the status of Kirkbride's place-holding 'National Government of Moab' had been discussed briefly between them. A mutual understanding was achieved quickly, with Kirkbride telling Abdullah that 'the question is largely of an academic nature now that Your Highness is here'. Abdullah is recorded to have replied knowingly, 'Ah, I was sure that we understood one another'.[30]

Subsequent discussions over the next two days in Jerusalem between Churchill and Abdullah solidified the parameters of what the British were prepared to offer him in Transjordan. During the six months predicted to be required for Faisal's enthronement and public acclamation in Iraq Abdullah's initial 'emirship' of Transjordan was to be provisional. Ultimately, the plan called for his status to be confirmed and then aggrandized to one of acknowledged kingship. The British – as they had done with Sharif Hussein and Ibn Saud and would do also with Faisal – offered Abdullah a substantial subsidy, in his case of £5,000 per month.[31] Key to their evaluation of his performance as emir would be a strict cessation of anti-French raids across the border with Syria, as well as an end to his speaking publicly about the possibility of reclaiming it for the Arabs. Churchill did not eliminate entirely the possibility of one day seeing Abdullah move to restore the Hashemite throne in Damascus – or indeed beyond it in a still-larger understanding of his Arab patrimony – but he offered absolutely no guarantee to him in this regard. Moreover, he emphasized to Abdullah that Zionist settlement activity west of the Jordan River must be allowed to proceed in future without inter-ference by Arabs coming across from Transjordan. If this provision were to be respected by Abdullah, said Churchill, then he could expect the British to prevent any future Zionist expansion eastwards. Altogether, the agreement achieved in their talks proved to be satis-factory to both parties, although Abdullah appears to have betrayed little enthusiasm for the plan at the time, only a certain resignation.[32]

At this juncture in the process, and in a demonstration of what it might mean to Abdullah to have British suzerainty over Transjordan remain in place, the two men drove the short distance from Jerusalem to Jaffa. Once there, they undertook a troop inspection prefatory to viewing an RAF fly-past. Having only recently ended his tenure as air minister, Churchill enjoyed this moment especially. For Abdullah meanwhile, a show of British military strength – especially the fly-past – acted as a salutary reminder of the nature of what he could expect to bolster his own regime's security in Transjordan. More pointedly, it was evidence also of what could be ranged against him if he chose to violate the terms of the agreement arrived at with Churchill.[33]

During these intense days of talks with Abdullah, of paramount importance for Churchill was regional state-building. Only this time the challenge lay not in Iraq, but rather in Palestine and Transjordan. The British had begun to put in place the political sinews of a new generation of Arab states whose aspirations for genuine independence would be recognized and endorsed, even if the specific date of this independence remained both unknown, and unknowable.[34] Accordingly, such new states would replace the Ottomans' old provincial *Vilayet* system and recast the Middle East as indelibly modern, at least in political form.

This manner of thinking would be top of mind for Churchill when he met with consecutive deputations of local Jerusalem officials representing first the Palestinian Arabs, and then the Palestinian Jews. At his meeting with the Arabs on 28 March, attended also by Lawrence, Churchill rejected outright their opening demand that the British overturn immediately the provisions of the Balfour Declaration and put a stop to Jewish immigration to Palestine. 'It is not in my power and it is not my wish to do this', he declared bluntly. Moreover, the promises contained in the McMahon–Hussein correspondence did not preclude a Jewish national home, Churchill maintained. Additionally, under the terms of the League of Nations and the San Remo Conference, the colonial secretary stated flatly that Britain as a mandatory power was required to fulfil its international obligations towards the Jews.[35] Not only that, but he was well aware that Faisal, as the recognized leader of the Arab Revolt, had had a meeting with Chaim Weizmann in June of 1918 in Arabia, during which he accepted the principle of a future and permanent homeland presence of the Jews in the long-held territories of the Arabs.[36] As Faisal had written earlier and even more broadly to the Jewish-American judge and delegate to the Paris Peace Conference, Felix Frankfurter, 'there is room in Syria for us both. Indeed, I think that neither can be a real success without the other'.[37]

Underlying Churchill's position in this regard, however, was his abiding belief that Palestinian Arabs were of inferior socio-cultural value to their desert-fighting Bedouin cousins, and what is more that during the First World War they had fought with the Ottomans against the British. Churchill's prejudiced undervaluing of Palestinian Arabs was hardly a position that he held alone. Lawrence had influenced him to think along these lines, as had Wilfrid Scawen Blunt. Even Faisal himself was known to rank-order Arabs in this way.[38] Indeed, the denigration of Palestinian Arabs and the concomitant romanticizing of the Bedouin, which had been undertaken over a long period of time, especially by various travellers and writers, had made such a view normative amongst leading British Arabists.[39] Given the various reasons that Churchill had itemized for enforcing the Balfour Declaration, he was never going to accede to the Jerusalem-based Arabs' persistent demands to end the longstanding Zionist dream of creating a Jewish homeland on the ancient soil of Palestine. But neither was it Churchill's intention to leave unfulfilled his wider ambition of creating a new state where both Semitic peoples could live and prosper side by side. Initially, life in such a state would come necessarily under Britain's League of Nations mandate, but to Churchill the ultimate end remained one of independence.

Accordingly, the exact same message was given by Churchill later that same day to the Palestinian Jewish National Council. He told its representatives that the success of a Jewish national homeland was dependent largely upon its ability to operate without prejudice towards both the Arabs and the Christians. They too, he emphasized, had every right to reside in Palestine and the guarantees for such, included in the Balfour Declaration, made that right clear for all to see.

If Churchill's view of what it might be possible to achieve in an ethnically shared Palestine was overly roseate to some in the British government, to others his position in 1921 had come to constitute a more fundamental betrayal of what had been promised to the Jews almost four years earlier. One of those in the latter camp was the wartime British intelligence officer turned Middle East Department staff member, Colonel Richard Meinertzhagen. His robust Zionism verged on the fanatical as he understood Churchill to be in the process of creating a situation in Palestine where Arab interests would be favoured clearly over Jewish ones: 'the atmosphere in the Colonial Office is definitely hebraphobe', Meinertzhagen opined at the time, in a reference to what he believed was its anti-Semitism. 'I exploded on hearing Churchill had severed the Transjordan from Palestine ...

Lawrence of course was with Churchill and influenced him ... This reduces the Jewish National Home to one-third of Biblical Palestine'. It may have fit Meinertzhagen's mercurial reputation to interpret the policy of the Colonial Office in this way. Indeed, it had left him 'foaming at the mouth with anger and indignation'.[40] But there were others of much greater equanimity than Meinertzhagen – namely Sir Herbert Samuel – who were just as dismayed by the planned partition of Palestine. They, however, were much more even-handed in response to it and would seek to implement the settled British policy regarding Palestine's future as best they could.

For Churchill, 28 March thus had been a day of intense meetings, which was capped by a not-very-sociable reception in the evening hosted by a deputation of Jerusalem's leading Zionists. The next day proved to be much the same for him, including a visit to the site of the newly established Hebrew University of Jerusalem located atop Mount Scopus. '[T]he hope of your race for so many centuries will be gradually realised here', Churchill stated in a speech given to mark its official opening. Following the ceremony Churchill attended yet another reception, this one hosted by Samuel back at Government House.[41] Lawrence accompanied him to all of these events. The following day, Wednesday, 30 March, was to be Churchill's last in Palestine. He spent it in much the same busy way as he had the previous six. It included a visit to the ancient city of Jericho, as well as to a group of new Jewish settlements – *kibbutzim* – both at and near the growing coastal town of Tel Aviv. That evening, his work in Palestine over, Churchill departed the country by train. He and Clementine were back in Alexandria the next day where they promptly boarded a ship bound for Italy, and thence by rail to spend a few weeks amidst the familiar and much-loved surroundings of the French Riviera.[42] On 12 April, Churchill returned finally to London. He had been out of the country for a total of some six weeks.

In less than seven days spent in the Holy Land, Churchill and his Middle East Department lieutenants had put the final touches on the work of the Cairo Conference. 'Mr. Winston Churchill', as Lawrence would praise him later, '... was entrusted by our harassed Cabinet with the settlement of the Middle East; and in a few weeks, at his conference in Cairo, he made straight all the tangle, finding solutions fulfilling (I think) our promises in letter and spirit (where humanly possible) without sacrificing any interest of our Empire or any interest of the peoples concerned'. In Lawrence's summative words, the constructive tension of the contemporary Middle East had been made plain: the juxtaposition of local crisis and metropolitan policy. The British government is 'well-disposed to the Arabs and cherishes their friendship', Churchill had reassured certain of his listeners in Jerusalem. But it was clear that a substantial caveat had to be attached to this statement in the form of Britain's unwavering commitment to the establishment of a new state in Palestine that would necessarily be at least partially Jewish in composition.

During his visit to Jerusalem Churchill had done his utmost to stress to both Arab and Jewish audiences alike that the future of Palestine under the British mandate would be one of engendering a surpassing mutuality in their relations with one another, so as to build a new land, one whose 'success will bring general prosperity and wealth to all Palestinians'. As rhetorical as Churchill's language could often be, he was staunchly of the view that the politics of inter-ethnic amity could me made to take root in the newly conceived Palestine. Especially, as he had emphasized during the same speech to the delegation of Palestinian Arabs he had met on 28 March, if 'instead of sharing in miseries through quarrelling Palestinians should share blessings through cooperation'. In Churchill's inimitable way he had sounded the trumpet of modern pluralistic nationalism, but also of a specific new nationality, that of the 'Palestinian', shorn of its historically exclusive Arab identity and infused with what he believed would be the undoubted 'benefits of Zionism'.[43] His sanguinity here was strong, perhaps too strong; certainly it would go largely unfulfilled. But his desire to see such a state take root in

Palestine was reflective of the progressive internationalism of the day, represented most obviously by the aspirations embodied in the League of Nations. Notably too, Churchill's position did not represent the apocalyptic millenarianism which had come to define the view of a large number of Zionists in Britain, the United States and elsewhere.[44] In other words, he did not believe that the creation of a modern state in ancient Israel was revelatory of the end times.

Upon Churchill's departure from Palestine on 30 March, Lawrence stayed behind in Jerusalem and got to work on fulfilling the agreements reached with Abdullah during the previous week. The Cairo Conference and its Jerusalem addendum meant, in Lawrence's estimation, that 'we were quit of the wartime Eastern adventure, with clean hands, but three years too late to earn the gratitude which peoples, if not states, can pay'.[45] If such indeed were true, over the next week or so Lawrence would go back and forth between Amman and Jerusalem in a concerted attempt to earn that very measure of elusive gratitude, especially from Arabs on either side of the Jordan River. From an individual perspective, however, as a figure of surpassing wartime heroism to most Arabs, Lawrence would never be less than showered with gratitude by the Bedouin. But acting now as the empowered agent of the British government had left him in a different and, from an Arab perspective, compromised position.

Still, as Churchill's bodyguard Detective Inspector Walter Thompson would attest, to the Arabs 'Lawrence was the man'. The Churchill party's arrival in Gaza the previous week had served as Thompson's introduction – as it had for everyone else on the special train from Cairo – to Lawrence's apparent spellbinding hold over the Bedouin. 'Aurens, Aurens, Aurens', was the cry that had rung out in the midst of a general ululation. 'No Pope of Rome ever had more command before his own worshippers', Thompson would write effusively about that moment at Gaza Station. 'Colonel Lawrence raised his hand slowly, the first and second fingers raised above the other two for silence and for blessing', continued Thompson. 'He could have owned the earth. He did own it. Every man froze in respect, in a kind of New Testament adoration of shepherds for a master'.[46] Notwithstanding a later generation's recognition of the Orientalist flavour of this description, Lawrence indeed needed every bit of his abundant charisma in order to confirm the agreement that had been struck between Abdullah and Churchill. Accordingly, in a cable to his colleague John Shuckburgh at the Colonial Office on 1 April, Lawrence informed him that as Samuel 'has asked me to begin things with Abdullah while he is arranging the appointment of a Chief Political Officer for Trans-Jordania, I move to Amman tomorrow for about a week'.

At the beginning of April therefore it was back across the Jordan River for Lawrence, passing by car through the familiar Salt and then on to the future Transjordanian capital of Amman. 'The country across Jordan is all in spring', he wrote happily to his mother in Oxford, 'and the grass & flowers are beautiful'. Upon his arrival in Amman he was lionized by the Bedouin in their customary way before settling down for some frank and far-reaching discussions with Abdullah over the geopolitical future of Transjordan. The week spent in Abdullah's camp at Amman was for Lawrence to be both a critical exercise in building what would become the Hashemite Kingdom of Jordan, as well as a welcome reminder of the hard but heady years of the Arab Revolt. Being there again 'was rather like the life in war time', he informed his mother, 'with hundreds of Bedouin coming & going, & a general atmosphere of newness in the air'. He added, however, that this time 'the difference was that now everybody is trying to be peaceful'.[47]

The week at Amman went exceedingly well. So well indeed that by 9 April, having returned to Jerusalem, Lawrence was able to report to Samuel that Abdullah's 'position is very strong. The people seem contented and comfortable and numbers of them are paying him visits and submitting to his judgement their tribal and family disputes'. But the most important piece of information that Lawrence had to convey to the high commissioner – indeed, what would clinch the work of the Cairo Conference – was to state that 'there is no possibility, so long as Abdullah believes we are sincere, of any large movement against the French or against our Zionist policy and little possibility even of small incidents. In public Abdullah has taken a strong line about this and his injunctions have been well received'.[48] Here was the final block of the policy edifice that comprised the Sherifian Solution, slid into place by Lawrence. All that remained was what most believed would be the trouble-free acclamation of Faisal to come at Baghdad. A short time later Lawrence informed Churchill that 'I know Abdullah: you won't have a shot fired'. And he was right, concord would prevail.[49] The next day, 10 April, a justly satisfied Lawrence flew back to Amman accompanied by four RAF Handley Page bombers to impress upon Abdullah once again the strong measure of British support that lay behind his new regime. Abdullah 'had been longing for aeroplanes' – to see some – Lawrence wrote home afterwards, glad to have obliged the new emir in this way, 'and gave us a great reception and a large lunch'.[50]

Clearly, these days were full and exciting ones for Lawrence. At that moment he had become almost a proper diplomat, an acting proconsul as it were, shuttling back and forth between Amman and Jerusalem. Then on 11 April he flew over to Egypt to meet up with Faisal, who had left England as planned not long before and was due to arrive that day in Port Said by ship. Lawrence and Faisal held an extended secret meeting that afternoon. During the meeting, Lawrence presented Faisal with the detailed plans for his future kingship of Iraq as considered and approved at Cairo.[51] 'Feisal expressed his appreciation of the general policy outlined and promised to do all he could to make his part of it work', Lawrence reported in a memorandum sent immediately to Churchill in London. He went on to say that Faisal was prepared to offer a 'guarantee' not to attack the French nor to intrigue against them, and that the establishment of 'friendly relations' with Ibn Saud remained a top priority also. Faisal requested of Lawrence that a British adviser be placed on his personal staff, but recoiled at what he understood to be the permanent conditions of the British League of Nations mandate in Iraq with 'its humiliating implications of dependency and colonial status'. Accordingly, wrote Lawrence, Faisal made clear to him that such inferior status would have to be renegotiated soon by the British and Iraqi governments if the Sherifian Solution were to prove a success.[52]

Following their meeting both men then travelled the short distance south to Cairo, with Faisal checking into Shepheard's Hotel while Lawrence, to allay any possible suspicion of their having been in direct contact, went to the nearby Continental-Savoy Hotel, a place that he knew well from his earliest wartime days in the city, when it had served as the headquarters of the Arab Bureau.[53] The next day, 12 April, Lawrence flew back to Jerusalem while Faisal stayed on in Cairo for a further week to receive various guests and colleagues at Shepheard's, including Lord Allenby. The impression left on Allenby by this meeting, as he observed in a letter home, was that he did not think Faisal 'has a very cheerful prospect before him'.[54] Meanwhile, arriving back in Jerusalem, Lawrence reported immediately to Samuel; the next morning they drove together across to Amman in order to interview Abdullah. The day after that they proceeded south with some of Samuel's Government House staff to Petra for a tour of the famous historic Nabatean ruin located not far from Aqaba. Lawrence knew the 'brilliant Petra' well, and was pleased to be back in its ancient precincts for what amounted to a brief holiday. Indeed, it might well have been an appropriate moment to 'finish my jobs out here', as he wrote home at the time. But his valedictory words were premature: a few days later Churchill would ask him to meet with Faisal yet one more time.[55]

On 21 April Lawrence thus flew to Egypt once again. The next day at Suez he had a second secret meeting with Faisal. By this point Faisal was about to depart for the Hejaz in anticipation of proceeding to Baghdad. There is no written record of their clandestine meeting, but at its conclusion on the afternoon of the 22nd Lawrence cabled Churchill to inform him that 'I leave tomorrow by air for Jerusalem, and I think that I might, unless you have other wishes, return thence to England'.[56] As a final precaution against the possibility of their plans going awry, at the eleventh hour Churchill instructed Lawrence to remain in Jerusalem for a further week before subsequently approving his departure for home at the end of the month. Finally, Lawrence would be released to return to London in early May.

Once home, Lawrence experienced a natural sense of relief at the evident success of what had transpired in the Middle East over the preceding nine weeks. Still, he was not entirely sure as to exactly what had been accomplished. Would the agreements hold up? Would Faisal succeed in Iraq? Would Abdullah rise to the occasion in Transjordan? Indeed, not long after returning to England Lawrence lamented to his friend and future first biographer, Robert Graves, that 'I wish I hadn't gone out there: the Arabs are like a page I have turned over: and sequels are rotten things'. Was it the anti-climactic nature of his return home, or an elegiac sense of what he had left behind in the desert in 1918, that had produced these regretful words? Or was it perhaps the fear of having failed the Arabs, yet again?

Not long afterwards, however, Lawrence would write in a completely different tone about what had just transpired at Cairo and Jerusalem, telling Graves that it 'was the big achievement of my life: of which the war was a preparation'. In time, Lawrence's return to London would seem to have steadied him, in part because he had completed his initial task and now was waiting upon others to do likewise. He would take credit properly for 'the knowledge and the plan' of the Sherifian Solution while praising Churchill for having had 'the imagination and the courage to adopt it and the knowledge of the political procedure to put it into operation'. He 'was my very friendly and kindly chief', Lawrence continued, 'and still has his career to make'. Indeed, Churchill remained Lawrence's chief until the following year, when the latter's appointment at the Colonial Office expired. It was then that he chose to leave British government service forever, a decision much regretted by Churchill. But for the time being, the decisions made at Cairo required to be operationalized and there was still much to do, beginning with Faisal's imminent arrival in Iraq.

Having departed Suez shortly after his final meeting with Lawrence, Faisal reached Jeddah on 25 April. Welcomed home heartily by his ageing but gratified father, Sharif Hussein, both men then journeyed to Mecca and from there began to make the final preparations for what was shortly to take place in Iraq. Letters were written, assurances given and plans made: 'If the people of Iraq wish for my presence, then I am prepared to come', Faisal cabled to Sayyid Talib, formerly a rival for the kingship and currently the country's interior minister.[57] In early June, Faisal was informed that the British would be sending a cruiser to carry the regal party to Basra. On the 12th of the month the *Northbrook* duly left Jeddah with Faisal on board, accompanied by many of his former advisers from Syria. In addition, he had made a number of new appointments, including that of a highly trusted colleague from the Arab Revolt, Colonel Kinahan Cornwallis. On 23 June 1921, Faisal's ship arrived at Basra where he was met by a handful of Iraqi government dignitaries, including Jafar al-Askari and St John Philby. On that day, for the first time in his life, Faisal set foot in Iraq.

CAIRO IN ACTION
IMPLEMENTING THE SHERIFIAN SOLUTION

As Faisal arrived in Iraq in June of 1921 to become king and set in motion the Sherifian Solution, earlier in London Churchill had moved to ensure that the plan made its way successfully through Cabinet and Parliament.[1] The Sherifian Solution's supporters understood themselves to be experts. Certainly they were bullish, a reflection, one might suggest, of Churchill himself. But the post-Ottoman Middle East's complicated geopolitics meant however that not everyone believed British policy as engineered by the colonial secretary was going to solve the region's problems. Indeed, while at Paris in 1919 Gertrude Bell had described the Middle East to her father exasperatingly as 'complex beyond all words'. And in the Peace Conference's depressing aftermath she had continued to wonder whether there remained any reason to think that 'an Arabian state is a possibility'.

The Cairo Conference had done much to change that understanding however, at least as far as Bell was concerned. In particular, she had developed great respect for the quality of Churchill's statesmanship, which she hoped would enable Britain to square the governance circle in the Middle East. But scepticism about the

British government's ability to achieve regional stability and political progress would remain nonetheless. 'We rushed into this business', Bell complained to some of her colleagues in Baghdad, 'with our usual disregard for a comprehensive political scheme ... How can you persuade people to take your side when you're not sure in the end whether you'll be there to take theirs?' In exactly the same vein, Wyndham Deedes, the civil secretary in Palestine, had remarked privately to Bell at Cairo: 'Does our Government know where it is going? If you ask Mr Churchill what he thought would be the position in these Arab countries in 20 years' time, could he give you the most shadowy answer? He does not know; he does not think; there is no coordination in what we are doing'.[2] Still, one might suggest that Deedes's dire prognostications – even if given quietly – were an extreme response to the prevailing situation in the Middle East. There were, after all, as far as the British were concerned, a number of drivers behind the Sherifian Solution, each one of them designed to coordinate with the others to achieve a comprehensive whole. Moreover, no one can ever predict the future with surety. As a determined Zionist, it might have been better had Deedes asked himself about the wisdom of imposing a Jewish homeland on an overwhelmingly Arab Palestine. If the Sherifian Solution had a defining weak spot it might very well have been the one which Deedes himself refused to accept. But given that by this point in time British government policy was firmly in favour of Zionist Jews settling in the ancient homeland of their ancestors, an ineluctable rebalancing of territory and re-vivification of rule in the Middle East had begun to occur already. The Colonial Office plan may well have been sound policy crafted within the prevailing internationalist spirit of the age, but many of those to whom it was supposed to apply would resist its logic nonetheless.

On the day that Faisal arrived in Basra and entrained for a whistle-stop tour of southern Iraq, Bell and Sir Percy Cox had chosen to remain in Baghdad. Faisal's reception at Basra would be 'lukewarm', with those in attendance implored by the local governor to, 'for Allah's sake, cheer!'[3] In greeting the arrival of their new king most Iraqis, both then and later, appeared to be apathetic.[4] Cox and Bell had stayed behind in the capital mainly to give the impression that the British had not orchestrated Faisal's arrival nor his accession to the Iraqi throne to come. Stage-managing of this sort may have been transparent but it also served a genuine purpose. Cox had sent his political officer, St John Philby, to Basra along with the Defence Minister, Jafar al-Askari, to meet Faisal. Sending Philby – an avowed booster of Ibn Saud – to demonstrate British even-handedness and in order that Faisal's strengths and charms might be recognized by him seems to have been Cox's motivation. Philby would never become convinced of Faisal's suitability to rule Iraq, however, and a short time later Cox decided to 'part company' with him to preserve a unified front alongside Faisal against anyone who remained opposed to his impending enthronement.[5] For her part, Bell saw Philby's departure from Iraq's governing inner circle as inevitable, having written to her father during the previous month to say 'I'm doubtful whether he [Philby] will stay if Feisal comes'. Bell and Philby were long-time friends, and she had told him that 'I wasn't going to let politics make a difference to our friendship'. But, she continued to Sir Hugh, 'it's no good for a Gov[ernment]t servant to be in opposition to official policy and he has done some harm in openly discussing a republic. Sir Percy has now stopped him but he can't be expected to put his back into the job and the Sharifians all look on him as an adversary. It's a great pity'.[6]

In both this and other regards Iraq's politics remained complex, although not necessarily more so than those of other contemporaneous colonial states as they moved towards independence by fulfilling the requirements for administrative unity and Western-style mass nationalism. To be sure, as a hallmark of their long period of rule the Ottomans had purposively inhibited the development of national feeling in Iraq, along with resisting the creation of internal political coherence. Their *Vilayet* system had kept the provinces of Baghdad, Basra and Mosul as separate from one another as possible, with a commensurately divided and intensely competitive political leadership all vying now to take power in the post-war vacuum created by the Ottomans' defeat. While this situation would have had the necessary and desirable effect during the Ottoman period of blunting the impact of indigenous opposition to the regime, it had left a significant political gap to fill once their control had been removed by the victorious British in the spring of 1917. Arab Muslims – both Sunni and Shia – as well as Kurds, Persians, Christians, refugee Assyrians and Armenians, city-dwellers or rural tribesmen all, meant that Iraq was greatly diverse socio-politically.

For the time being such cleavages had been forcibly overlain by the presence of some 100,000 British troops whose government wished to see such high and costly numbers decline drastically as Iraq moved into a more united and progressive phase of its post-war political development. Full independence for Iraq was the ultimate British goal even if they believed that it would have to arise gradually and with due regard to the country's status as a League of Nations mandate. Britain's prevailing imperial interests remained of constant import too. None of these interrelated political realities made accomplishing the task of governing Iraq anything less than extremely difficult. Bell understood this highly complicated situation better than most, which as we have seen was reflected in her comprehensive memorandum, *Review of the Civil Administration of Mesopotamia*, published not long before the Cairo Conference. 'The rank and file of the tribesmen, the shepherds, marsh dwellers, rice, barley and date cultivators of the Euphrates and Tigris', she wrote, 'whose experience of statecraft was confined to speculations about their next door neighbours, could hardly be asked who should next be the ruler of the country, and by what constitution'.[7] The paternalistic authoritarianism of this passage is obvious to modern ears. But in the post-war world in which the leading democracies had only just begun to approach – much less implement – universal electoral enfranchisement, one might argue that even to consider undertaking the establishment of a form of representative government in Iraq in 1921 was to aspire after something determinedly progressive, if perhaps naively so.

Bell was under no illusions therefore about the political challenge that lay ahead in Iraq. But neither did she think that the British and the Iraqis together were attempting the impossible. She agreed that the Iraqi Revolt in 1920 had represented an 'immense failure' on the part of the British after having defeated and expelled the Ottomans three years earlier. The uprising had come about, as she put it, because even though 'the Turks didn't govern . . . we have tried to govern too much'. The desire to implement 'British efficiency' – as Sir Gilbert Clayton, the former head of the Arab Bureau whose experience in the region had been tapped by the Middle East Department, had earlier written to Bell – militated against what should have been a 'light hand' in governing the country.[8] Accordingly, if the initial challenge had been to enthrone Faisal, the longer-term aspirations were to see good government prevail in Iraq. As Bell had written at the beginning of 1920 to Edwin Montagu, secretary of state for India and therefore at that time still responsible for Iraqi governance, 'I don't want to make money out of this country; nor do you. I want the natives to make it. It's their country. We are here, not for financial advantage, but because if we leave Mesopotamia to chaos it will be a fertile breeding place for international jealousies, and that ultimately means European war'.[9]

Much has been written suggesting that the British had become so enamoured of the potential for Iraqi oil to power the Royal Navy that *all* other considerations regarding the country fell under this commercially driven motivation.[10] For some British officials, such as Arnold Wilson, late of Cox's staff in Baghdad and now the managing director of the Anglo-Persian Oil Company, this interpretation is likely true. Bell herself thought so, saying to her father of Wilson's APOC appointment that there had been 'a good deal of hanky panky about the business. He had the offer up his sleeve, I think, for a long time. I hear now that he kept all the APOC business in his own hands always – the files were absolutely secret'. But what may very well have been true of Wilson was certainly not true of Bell. 'Oil is the trouble, of course – detestable stuff', as she had put it bluntly. For her, Britain's political responsibilities in Iraq were supremely serious and morally defensible and the plan to establish for it a modern, civil and ultimately independent government she believed to be an honourable one, transcendent of oil's reach. About this aspiration Bell was unequivocal, stating forcefully: 'I am so sure I'm right I would go to the stake for it'.[11] Moreover, as decisive a place as oil would come to occupy eventually in most Middle East power calculations – especially those made later by the United States through Standard Oil – extensive oil reserves were not discovered in Iraq until 1927 and commercially significant oil production did not occur until 1934, both dates which came well after the governmentally formative period of 1917 to 1921.[12]

After completing his tour of southern Iraq, Faisal entered Baghdad on 29 June riding on a train specially fitted out for the occasion. Bell herself had taken charge of the arrangements for his arrival in the capital.[13] A delay on the track meant a late entry into the city, but around 6 o'clock in the evening Faisal's train steamed into Baghdad Central and this time, unlike at Basra, he was received by a loud and enthusiastic crowd. Both Cox and Bell were there of course, as were a number of Iraqi National Council officials and dignitaries. Indeed, on 11 July, within two weeks of his arrival in Baghdad, the council would formally declare Faisal king of Iraq. Only then, however, would the hard work commence of trying to convince all Iraqi stakeholders that Faisal should be confirmed as king by a general plebiscite as the choice of Iraq's people and not simply as that of the mandatory British and the National Council. Owing to the country's political complexities, such a task was immensely difficult, though not impossible. Faisal himself, probably more acutely than anyone else, was highly cognizant of the challenges that lay ahead. Indeed, his first week in Iraq had not been reassuring as to the wisdom of seeking to sit on the throne of a country in which he had neither been born nor had ever visited before in his life. Faisal's tepid reception at Basra had been deflating, to be sure, and thereafter as he travelled throughout the south not much had changed to suggest that his presence in the country was desired by the people. At one stop during his tour, for example, made at the town of Hilla, Faisal's welcoming party had consisted of just two people. During his brief visit one of the two, the local deputy administrative officer, Bertram Thomas, had had the temerity to tell him flatly that 'the people don't want you'.[14] Accompanying Faisal at the time was Jafar Pasha, who was outraged by this kind of calculated humiliation of Iraq's soon-to-be king, especially coming as it did from a government official. The insulting behaviour had in fact been Philby's doing, as would be made clear later, which provided yet further evidence for Cox to sack him.[15]

The grand welcome that Faisal received at the much friendlier Baghdad, however, reassured him that the National Council, as well as most of Iraq's British administrators together with a large swathe of the city's people, indeed did see him as their expected and rightful king. He would be the one to fill the political lacuna that had resulted from the defeat of the Ottomans. A short while earlier, after the ignominy of losing the Syrian throne, Chaim Weizmann had described Faisal as a 'broken reed'.[16] But not on this day in Baghdad. The city was decorated with 'triumphal arches, Arab flags, and packed with people, in the street, on the housetops, everywhere', as Bell exulted. Almost 700 years had passed since Baghdad's medieval glory days, when it had served as the capital of the Abbasid Caliphate, so the first few days of July were celebratory in a way that no one living there had ever witnessed before. The *naqib* of Baghdad and sometime rival for the Iraqi kingship, the elderly Sayyid Abd al-Rahman, was especially welcoming of Faisal. So too were Cox and General Haldane, both of whom, like Bell, had been working diligently since the end of the Cairo Conference to ready Iraq for Faisal's arrival. In Cox's case such work had meant taking the drastic step in April of arresting Faisal's main political rival, Sayyid Talib – whose disruptive presence in the country had been discussed in earnest by the delegates at Cairo – and sending him into exile in Ceylon after seeing evidence of his complicity in public violence and conspiracy. Talib, Bell wrote to her father, had led 'an incitement to rebellion as bad as anything which was said by the men who roused the country last year, and not far from a declaration of Jihad'. At Cox's request, Churchill had approved Talib's expulsion, notwithstanding the bad optics that it might produce publicly. However, Talib's dangerous reputation, combined with what was understood to be in the best interests of Iraq's immediate political development, meant that removing him from the scene at that particular moment had probably been the height of wisdom. Later, he would be given a pacifying pension by the British.

The National Council's subsequent declaration of Faisal as king of Iraq on 11 July proved to be a superbly culminating moment for Bell. To her, Iraq was 'my country', as she called it, and its future success in becoming a politically modern Middle Eastern state mattered to her more than anything else in life. Unmarried and without children, Bell's world revolved around her position on Cox's staff and in what became quickly a close advisory capacity to Faisal. 'The extremely interesting events we shall be passing through', she had forecast, had begun to occur from the moment of Faisal's arrival in Baghdad at the end of June until the declaration by the National Council of his kingship a fortnight later. Indeed, Bell had been living within a greatly heightened atmosphere locally ever since she herself had come home from the Cairo Conference on 9 April. Even by that early date, word of the strong likelihood of Faisal becoming Iraq's king had become public and because of it, she said, in Baghdad 'passions' were running 'very high'. As much as the Sherifians were looking forward to enthroning Faisal, there were others, however, who did not share their excitement. Talib, whose following was significant, was one. For Bell therefore, any delay in Faisal's arrival in Iraq was time wasted. 'I'm egging Sir Percy on to bring Faisal over by air', she had written to her father even earlier, on 3 April: 'the sooner we put an end to the suspense the better'. In the meantime, Talib's rebellious behaviour was a constant worry until Cox had had him expelled later that month. To Bell, Talib's expulsion was to be 'Sir Percy's great coup', an act that lowered the political temperature in Iraq. 'Not a voice has been raised against it', she related to her father, 'on the contrary the whole country is immensely relieved ... everyone was afraid of him'.

In fact, throughout this period of tension leading up to Faisal's arrival in Iraq Bell had been careful to refrain from making public her strong opinion as to the desirability of his impending accession. This guarded stance was no mere political artifice, however. In the febrile atmosphere of that spring in Baghdad Bell may well have been, as she stated, quite happy to be 'identified as a Sharifian', but that did not mean she went around announcing the fact. Iraqi politics were divided sharply between demands made by the British for supervisory control on one hand, and nationalist expectations for independence on the other. Consequently, Bell was both careful and sincere in saying about Faisal's enthronement 'that the choice must rest with the people'. Still, in her mind there simply was no possible alternative to Faisal: 'the people will not accept a local Arab because there's none they trust to refrain from grinding his own axe. And after all, Muhammed is Faisal's direct ancestor'.[17] In the view of some later commentators, these moves made by Bell and the other British actors involved in Faisal's monarchical appointment are evidence of little more than self-serving political machinations to place the most pliable candidate on the Iraqi throne.[18] Faisal, however, would prove to be nobody's political plaything. If having a local automaton as Iraq's king was what the British had truly wanted, then the readily pliant *naqib* would have been a much better choice for them to have made than Faisal. They may not have selected the most cooperative candidate, but there can be little doubt that at this moment in Iraq's modern political development Faisal appeared to be the best one available. Certainly Bell herself never wavered in supporting Faisal's cause as leading to 'what', as she put it, 'I [b]elieve to be the best thing for this country and the wish of the best of its people'.

Into the month of May therefore, with the intense heat of summer coming on and with 'Our politics hanging fire', Bell had continued to anticipate Faisal's imminent arrival. Her work rate throughout this highly expectant period was phenomenal. She conversed steadily with Cox; she debated policy and wrote memoranda; she considered where the lines on the new map of Iraq should be drawn; she hosted dinner parties for nationalists such as the ever-present Jafar al-Askari, his brother-in-law Nuri al-Said, and the fiery young Naji al-Suwaidi. All of them 'were very good and reasonable but they rightly said that it would be best for the country if things were settled', she observed to her step-mother, Lady Florence. 'At present', she continued, 'I [b]elieve most people if they were asked would go for British adminis-tration, which of course they can't have'.[19] Bell even gave considera-tion to a national anthem for Iraq, the design for a national flag, and served as president of the Baghdad Public Library, to which she was elected later that summer. Also on the library committee was her good friend and ally, Sassoon Eskell.[20]

During the month of June, Bell had continued to work in much the same way. As the heat rose to reach upwards of 40 degrees Celsius daily, the political temperature appeared to mimic the thermometer. Anticipation grew, especially in Baghdad, about the imminence of the political sea change to come. Later, Bell would describe herself during this period as having become absorbed completely by political events. These events ranged from witnessing street demonstrations, to conducting interviews and writing policy prescriptions, to participating in a good deal of politically based socializing. The first two activities she relished; the latter, on the other hand, she did not much like doing, especially if it meant attending the seemingly endless number of dances and balls put on by the British Club in Baghdad. The dances were 'a perfect mania', she called them disparagingly. Participated in by a host of government officials, but even more keenly by their wives, they obscured the importance of the real political business of the day, Bell believed. '[C]onfound them', she wrote in frustration to her father Sir Hugh of such women: they 'take no sort of interest in what's going on, know no Arabic and see no Arabs. They create an exclusive (although it's also a very second rate) English society quite cut off from the life of the town. I now begin to understand why [the] British Gov[ernmen]t has come to grief in India where our women do just the same thing'.[21] Later on she would state bluntly: 'I dance no longer'.

In early July, almost exactly at the same time that Bell was helping to welcome Faisal to Iraq, in London Lawrence readied himself for his next significant Sherifian Solution assignment at the Colonial Office. In fulfilling it he would be required to report also to the foreign secretary, Lord Curzon. On the 8th of that month Lawrence departed London, bound for the Hejaz. He had been instructed by Churchill and Curzon to confer directly with Sharif Hussein in order to put in place a treaty that would bind the Arab king to Britain in the manner prescribed at the Cairo Conference. Lawrence went to the Hejaz with full British plenipotentiary powers, making him a diplomat in way that he had not been earlier. In addition to affecting what had been decided at Cairo, Lawrence was charged also with convincing Hussein to sign the Treaty of Versailles. The British wanted the king to formally recognize France's preponderant position in Syria and its due mandatory power. By this point in time Lawrence had begun to alter his thinking as it concerned Syria and was ready to advocate for London's position in the way that he had been instructed to do. As he explained to a friend on the day before departing anew for the Middle East: 'I'm not anti-French anymore. Feisal has swept Mesopotamia, & that is amends for his scurvy treatment in Paris'.

Once his work in the Hejaz was complete, Lawrence had been further instructed to head north to Palestine and Transjordan where, if possible, he was to put the finishing touches to the Sherifian Solution in the company of both Sir Herbert Samuel and Prince Abdullah.

Feeling like a 'shuttlecock, tossed between the Colonial & Foreign Offices', as he wrote to Wilfrid Scawen Blunt on the eve of his departure, Lawrence stopped off in Cairo for over a week before arriving at Jeddah on 29 July. As it transpired, he would be out of England for the next five months, having expected to be gone for only eight weeks. He would not return home until just before Christmas.

Negotiating with King Hussein proved to be a trial of unexpected proportions for Lawrence, the 'mental strain' of which, he told a military colleague later, 'had been worse than anything he had known' during the Arab Revolt.[22] Beginning on 30 July in Jeddah he initiated a series of meetings with Hussein. Unexpectedly for Lawrence, their time together would be shorter than anticipated: the king was due to depart imminently for Mecca to observe Eid al-Adha, the Islamic feast of sacrifice. Consequently, Lawrence attempted to move more quickly than planned in the negotiations with Hussein. He suggested also a contingency to the Foreign Office which would see him use the month or so that the king was to be away to travel to Aden for discussions over Yemen's future. Despite their abbreviated beginnings Lawrence's discussions with Hussein would become frustratingly protracted, as well as almost operatic at times. Initially, a draft treaty that had been prepared in London and brought along by Lawrence was presented to Hussein. However, upon reading it he refused to acknowledge its suggested provisions. Instead, he made an outrageous claim that the kingship of Iraq should be his, even though at that moment it was about to be awarded to his son Faisal. Indeed, as Lawrence informed Curzon immediately, Hussein's 'ambitions are large as his conceit, and he showed unpleasant jealousy of his sons'.[23]

As the talks continued, Lawrence's reports to London became eye-watering. The king 'raises absurd new ideas daily'; he is 'greedy and stupid'; 'he was only playing with me so I changed tactics and forced him to make exact statements'; 'the King burst into tears'; 'reason is entirely wasted on him since he believes himself all-wise and all-competent, and is flattered by his entourage in every idiotic thing he does'; on it went. On a couple of occasions Lawrence related that he simply could not stand to be in Hussein's presence any longer and therefore had stood up and 'walked out' of the room. Still, despite these frustrations, Lawrence was determined to reach a treaty with Hussein that would guarantee the implementation of the Cairo Conference's plans as British policy. 'The need is not so much to secure his signature', Lawrence wrote in a memorandum to Curzon, 'as to break down his convictions that we are dependent on him for our prestige in the East, and will pay any price and swallow any vexation to keep his friendship'. Finally, a tentative agreement was struck just before Hussein was required to leave for Mecca. Lawrence himself then departed Jeddah for Aden, where he undertook to conduct a cursory examination of its position in relation to that of neighbouring post-Ottoman Yemen. Otherwise, he found himself with plenty of time to continue working on a draft of *Seven Pillars of Wisdom*.

Once he had finished his diplomatic work at Aden, Lawrence then returned north to Jeddah in what was becoming for him 'the beastliest trip I ever had', as he lamented in a letter home to Oxford. He arrived on 30 August and conferred once again with King Hussein. Since departing for Mecca the king had had sufficient time to mull over his agreed position, which he proceeded now, however, to reverse. All the states in Arabia, he insisted, would be required to return to their pre-war boundaries. Moreover, Hussein now demanded that his supremacy over all other Arab rulers everywhere be recognized. Lawrence's chilly response to these outrageous demands was immediate, although it is not clear exactly what he said in this regard to the king. But whatever it was, it had the immediate effect of prompting Hussein to 'send for a dagger and swear to abdicate and kill himself'. Apparently, the manifest melodrama of such an outburst was too much to bear even for some of Hussein's own inner circle of advisers. Consequently, his eldest son and heir Prince Ali chose this moment to intervene and have his father removed from the deteriorating situation. To continue the talks afterwards a small committee of just three members was formed: Ali, his youngest brother Prince Zeid, and Lawrence. The change in tone of the discussions made by Ali's timely intervention was felt instantly. 'Things are now going in a most friendly and rational way', a relieved Lawrence reported to London. 'The King is not formally superseded but has certainly lost much of his power'.

Directly, this new arrangement yielded a basic agreement between the two parties. Still, three weeks would elapse before a draft treaty could be finalized, sent to London for approval, and then returned to Jeddah. In the meantime, while the diplomatic wheel turned, Lawrence would journey further north to Palestine and Transjordan. But before so doing he awaited the king's promised signature on the treaty. 'Ali and Zeid have behaved splendidly', he wrote to Curzon, but their level-headedness was to no avail as the king, who an exasperated Ali had himself even called 'mad', refused to sign. After almost two months of diplomatic toil a dejected Lawrence was left with no choice but to depart Jeddah for Jerusalem and Amman keenly disappointed that the Anglo-Hashemite Treaty had yet to be signed and ratified.

Before moving on however, Lawrence stopped first at Cairo. Exhausted and depressed by the apparent diplomatic debacle in the Hejaz – and the accompanying blow that it might land against the Sherifian Solution – he could muster little enthusiasm for the second major task of his mission. Still, he wrote positively to Eric Kennington, he had made progress in writing *Seven Pillars of Wisdom*. But as to what lay in store for him in Jerusalem and Amman, he said only that he was 'bored stiff: and very tired, and a little ill'. Indeed, Lawrence assumed that what he would find in Transjordan, as he wrote to Kennington, was probably going to be no better than what he had left behind recently in the Hejaz. He was going there, Lawrence stated dejectedly, 'to end that farce. It makes me feel like a baby-killer'.

But, much to Lawrence's surprise and relief, his return to Transjordan would prove to be the opposite of what he had experienced at Jeddah. After spending a little over a week in Jerusalem conferring with the high commissioner, on 12 October Lawrence drove with him along the familiar six-hour route to Amman. Expecting still to find Abdullah discontented with his lot and coming near to the end of his trial period as emir, he discovered instead that such was not the case. Remarkably, in Lawrence's estimation, Abdullah had grown secure in his new position. Moreover, he seemed to have developed a much more mature recognition that he had few if any other viable options and none better than the one that he had been given by the British. Accordingly, Abdullah's emirship was beginning to have about it the appearance of permanency. Ironically, Lawrence had found now that Abdullah, whom he had long underestimated, presented the best option to proceed with and guarantee the Anglo-Hashemite Treaty. On 28 November therefore, after having spent well over a month shadowing Abdullah daily as his principal British adviser, Lawrence informed Churchill that he was willing to sign the outstanding treaty. As Abdullah was his father's representative only, the treaty would require due ratification by King Hussein himself. But Lawrence had made a breakthrough nonetheless. A highly relieved Churchill approved immediate action, and in Amman on 8 December the document was signed jointly by Lawrence and Abdullah. A few days later an elated Lawrence departed Transjordan, and travelling via Egypt once again made for home. Just as at the time of his return to London to advocate for the Arabs after the ecstasy of victory in October of 1918, there was still much work to be done. But for Lawrence himself, his diplomatic mission in the service of the Sherifian Solution had come to an end. In fact, he would never again return to the Middle East.

As disappointing as Lawrence's experience in Jeddah had been, the move to Jerusalem and then on to Amman had revived in him a sense of confidence in the potential for the Sherifian Solution to succeed. Establishing Abdullah as ruler in Transjordan had been made almost a certainty, which coincided well with the fact that in Iraq Faisal was officially now the country's king. Still, Hussein's ultimate refusal to ratify the Anglo-Hashemite Treaty would prove three years later, in 1924, to be one of the reasons for his own downfall, at the hands of his chief rival, Ibn Saud. Subsequently, the Hejaz would be absorbed by Ibn Saud's opportunistic strategy of sponsoring his own pan-Arabian state. But that event belonged to the future. For Lawrence, as the New Year of 1922 dawned he could be well pleased. In Transjordan he had seen clear evidence that Abdullah was moving in the right direction. Altogether, it was a promising development when put alongside the positive trajectory taken already by Faisal in Iraq.

'We've thrown our die – the next few days will show whether it's a winning number'. So had written Gertrude Bell back in June of 1921. The rest of that summer in Baghdad had proven to be 'frightfully interesting' for Bell, especially the lead-up to the promised national plebiscite that would attempt to gauge the level of Iraq's public support for Faisal's accession as king.[24] Altogether, the plebiscite would represent a halting exercise in a jejune form of democracy. But it was not illegitimate nor, as some critics would charge later, a mere farce.

Following the declaration of Faisal's kingship, over the course of almost four weeks from 16 July until 11 August a series of meetings were conducted around the country. During these meetings selected representatives made known their views about the new king in the form of *madhbatas*, or declarations. While it is beyond dispute, as Faisal's biographer notes, that 'Every effort was exerted by Cox and his administration to ensure the desired outcome would be achieved', dissent directed towards the process itself, as well as towards individual candidates, was duly registered. During the weeks leading up to the plebiscite Faisal had spent a good deal of time speaking to those groups in Iraqi society where cleavages ran most deeply. As a

Sunni, Faisal's addressing of the small but important Iraqi Shia minority was of obvious importance; but so too were the Kurds, as well as the Turcomans – as the resident Turks were called – along with the Chaldean Christians. Significantly, one of the highly influential ayatollahs, Sheikh Mahdi al-Khalisi, qualified his *bayah*, his statement of allegiance to Faisal, by demanding that a constituent assembly be established that would be empowered to act independently of the king.[25] As a potential monarch, Faisal's pedigree and stature as an Arab leader were enormously attractive, and not just to the British. As Bell wrote: 'What helps everything is that Faisal's personality goes three-quarters of the way'.[26] Increasingly, many Iraqis themselves were attracted by his charisma, his lineage as a direct descendant of the Prophet Muhammad, and by their understanding of his heroic leadership of the Arab Revolt. Moreover, the fact that he had been well received by the Syrians as their king, if only briefly, was impressive also. Most Iraqis understood too, especially those who were informed politically, that there was no real alternative to Faisal.

In determining the results of the semi-democratic plebiscite, the official published figure would show that an astonishing 96 per cent of those casting ballots had voted in favour of Faisal. As important as this overwhelming measure of support was, it mattered less to Faisal himself, however, than it did to his Sherifian supporters. To the new king a much more pressing issue than the precise result of the plebiscite was Iraq's continuing relationship with mandatory Britain. Faisal was determined to move as quickly as possible to substitute the existing mandate with a bilateral treaty so as to reinforce the idea that substantive Iraqi independence was in the process of becoming political reality. Faisal believed that he had good grounds for holding this forward position, but in the run of events that summer Churchill would prove unwilling to grant him the point. On 9 August, for example, the colonial secretary insisted to Cox that 'the Mandate has been accepted by him and until it is replaced by some other relation he must work with it'.[27] In what Bell called a 'red tapy' moment of crisis, both she and Cox supported Faisal's view against that held by Churchill. 'We are going, as you know', she reminded her father, 'to drop the mandate and enter into treaty relations with Mesopotamia. Faisal says that from the first we must recognize that he is an independent sovereign in treaty with us, otherwise he can't hold his extremists. Sir Percy, bless him, wobbled a little, but my view was that as it came to the same either way, in the end, there was no point in claiming an authority we could not enforce. We are not going to reconquer Mesopotamia'. Thanks to both the man and woman on the spot, cooler heads indeed did prevail, and a reciprocal climb-down was made. Faisal agreed to leave aside an explicit definition of the country's status until sometime later, and Churchill moderated his authoritarian tone concerning the primacy of the requirements of the existing British mandate.

Accordingly, Faisal's coronation went ahead on 23 August. The ceremony – 'admirably arranged', according to Bell – reached its climax at the moment when Cox intoned, 'Long live the king!', followed by the loud and symbolic crack of a twenty-one-gun salute. 'It was an amazing thing to see all Iraq', Bell continued exuberantly to her father, 'from north to south gathered together. It is the first time it has happened, in history'. Bell could hardly contain her sense of pride in the moment, although it was mixed with a degree of trepidation for the future of the country as well as for Faisal's own future as king. Nonetheless, she was certain that both she and the other Sherifians had done the right thing at Cairo in backing Faisal's candidacy for the Iraqi throne. In so doing they had helped give birth to the modern state of Iraq, a country of some 3 million people at the time, spread over almost 200,000 square miles of territory. Speaking of the task at hand Bell expressed passionately to her father 'that we are not building here with lifeless stones; we're encouraging the living thing to grow and we feel it pulsing in our hands. We can direct it, to a great extent, but we can't prevent its growing upwards, that is, indeed, what we have invited it to do'. As a statement summarizing what the Cairo Conference had set out to accomplish in planning for Iraq's future, Bell's words had captured the situation well. The post-coronation road ahead in Iraq would not be easy, as she well knew, but the superstructure for its potential success had been put in place. Upon it could be built an enduring Iraqi state, Bell believed, a model to help much of the Middle East move more firmly in the direction of political modernity.

Nineteen twenty-two would prove to be a watershed year in the history of the impact of the Cairo Conference on the creation of the modern Middle East: in Iraq, to be sure, but also in both Palestine and Transjordan. Moreover, it would see Lawrence conclude his service at the Colonial Office, as Churchill did also. For Iraq, the year would culminate in the Anglo-Iraqi Treaty, which Faisal and Cox had begun to negotiate in earnest during the autumn of 1921. Of course, Faisal's first task upon becoming king in August had been to form a government comprised of the 'new Sharifian party', as Bell described its membership, 'of all the solid moderate people'. As ministers, they needed to be both loyal to him and acceptable to Cox. Carrying out this task would preoccupy both men in the latter days of August and into the early part of September.

Later that autumn, the creation of Mandatory Iraq's first government ministry under the leadership of the *naqib* as prime minister was the result. Bell was well pleased with the *naqib*'s appointment (it was in her estimation 'a very, very wise move'), although not nearly as pleased as the man himself. He was 'embarking on a promising political career at the age of 77. Good, isn't it,' Bell wrote happily in a letter to Sir Hugh. Cox agreed with Faisal's choice of the *naqib* to lead the government, although he objected to his choice of Naji al-Suwaidi for the key post of interior minister. As a leading figure in the nationalist rebellion of the previous year, Cox distrusted al-Suwaidi and had counter-proposed to Faisal the name of Tawfiq al-Khalidi as a more moderate alternative candidate. This time, however, it was the new king's turn to object. The resulting disagreement between the two leading figures in the Iraqi government turned into a three-week struggle for primacy. Bell, assisted by one of Faisal's closest advisers, Kinahan Cornwallis, was able to ameliorate the dispute by moving the various pieces of the cabinet chess game about the board until a consensus could be reached by all. But this period of intense negotiation was an early example of the ways in which Cox was required to adjust his thinking; that is to say, the need to alter the long-time habit of exerting supreme politico-administrative authority in the Middle East became clear to him. At the same time, it underscored in Faisal's mind the need for Iraq to achieve full independence as soon as possible.

But regardless of such differences of opinion in making hard political choices, these first days in the reign of King Faisal I were heady and acclamatory ones. On the morning after his coronation Faisal had held a levy, attended en masse by all kinds of government officials and dignitaries. Included amongst them was an overjoyed Jafar Pasha, who had been reappointed as Minister of Defence. The composition of the new government was on the lips of everyone. 'Nothing else is being talked of, naturally ... There's no doubt that this is the most absorbing job that I've ever taken a hand in', a breathless Bell wrote home. Even though Bell had just passed her fifty-third birthday in July, some of her reportage at the time reads as if she were in an almost youthful state of mind. 'Oh Father, isn't it wonderful. I sometimes think that I must be in a dream', she gushed, after having been told by Faisal that she was going to have a regiment named for her – the 'Khatun's Own' – in the new Arab Army.[28] Such a regiment was never to be formed, but for Bell the prospect of it was suggestive of the joyous expectations that were very much alive in Baghdad during the early days of Faisal's rule. In the summer and autumn of 1921 all seemed possible – at least to Bell – in the new state of Iraq.

Once cabinet-making and the king's coronation were complete, Faisal and Cox, together with Iraq's newly appointed ministers and government advisers, proceeded to engage directly in the demanding business of state. In the few months that the king had been resident in the country he had endeavoured to build support for his regime by constructing firm alliances and engendering personal loyalty. To some extent the adhesives required of political life in early developmental Iraq were no different than those required elsewhere. Regimes of all types and in all places must create connections that provide them with a carapace resistant to easy breaking. Indeed, this task is exactly what Faisal had begun to undertake from the moment that he had arrived in Iraq. But now that he had assumed monarchical control of the country, both asserting his authority and having it respected became even more necessary. For Faisal, of great importance too was achieving a treaty with the British that would signal Iraq's growing independence, even if it were to be attenuated for the time being under the constraints of the mandate. Not only would achieving such a treaty bolster his own bona fides as the country's leader and the one who could deliver political results for his people, but it would lessen the influence of the British on Iraq's (internal) affairs of state. Faisal was absolutely determined to succeed in this way. And while Cox did not actively resist Faisal's aspirations, he advised him nonetheless to adhere to a slow and steady constitutional maturation. Just then this same pattern was being followed in Egypt, he pointed out for example, under the high commissionership of Lord Allenby.

Regardless of these various caveats, firm negotiations over the proposed treaty commenced between Faisal and Cox in October of 1921.[29] From London, Churchill sent over a veteran from the Cairo Conference, Hubert Young of the Middle East Department, to engage in the talks and to act as his eyes and ears for their duration. At the time that these negotiations took place, Churchill as colonial secretary was being pulled in a number of different directions. The Irish War of Independence was nearing its climax, meaning that soon he would be required to preside over the extremely tense negotiations leading up to the Anglo-Irish Treaty in December. Meanwhile,

Palestine continued to be a place of turmoil between Arabs and Jews, which demanded his close attention also. Additionally, under their determined new post-war leader, the former army commander Mustafa Kemal, the Turks had refused to sign the Paris Peace Conference's Treaty of Sèvres. Meanwhile, they were battling and beating the Greeks in the eastern Mediterranean, much to the satisfaction of Islamic populations everywhere. Soon Churchill would be drawn into that conflict's Chanak Crisis with its unwelcome patina – for him especially – of 1915's Dardanelles disaster. As well, Chanak held the potential for sundering the close imperial ties that had been built up during the war between Britain and her dominions, especially with Canada.[30] All told therefore, the Anglo-Iraqi Treaty was but one of a number of contentious issues facing Churchill in 1921–22.

For Faisal and Cox of course, the as-yet unanswered Turkish question made their own job in Iraq that much more difficult. The Turks, it was feared, might well act with hostile intent towards Iraq – possibly at oil-rich Mosul – and there existed within the country plenty of pan-Islamic sympathy too, including to an extent that held by Faisal himself.[31] In an attempt therefore, to counter pro-Turkish sentiment where it remained most rife in northern Iraq, Faisal began to tour the region in mid-October. His subsequent presence at Mosul and elsewhere would have the welcome effect of letting some of the steam out of the nationalist kettle. Simultaneously, he also turned his attention to the ever-vexatious question of the Kurds. But the requirements of nation-building and regime loyalty needed more of a masterstroke than mere soothing words, and this is exactly the place where the aspiration for a treaty with the British resided. If Faisal was to counter the cry of *Al Istiqlal al Tamm* ('complete independence') – 'the catch word of the extremists', warned Bell – then a treaty that offered a staged independence to Iraqis in the form of a soon to be reached constitutional agreement with the British must be achieved. The strongly independence-minded people of Kirkuk, for example, had voted against Faisal in the recent plebiscite and had positioned themselves in the nationalist vanguard. To many such nationalists, Faisal represented a roadblock on the way to independence rather than an effective conduit to achieve it. Even though those at Kirkuk might be described bluntly as 'asses' by a frustrated Bell, the strong but unfocused nationalist sentiments of both them and many others in Iraq had to be met with an irresistible answer if criticisms of the regime were to be assuaged.[32] The answer, both Faisal and Bell believed strongly, was a mandate-superseding treaty with the British.

In the weeks after commencing treaty negotiations with Cox, therefore, Faisal sought to consolidate his pan-Iraqi appeal as monarch. The most important part of doing so, he believed, was to deliver on the promise of a treaty to the people of the country, which would demonstrate to them that he was not merely a British puppet. The charge of 'puppetry' has been made always in imperial situations such as was Iraq's in 1921, but in Faisal's case it is not necessarily convincing.[33] None of Cox, Bell, Cornwallis, Young or Churchill understood Faisal to be suspended on a string at the centre of a mere papier-mâché Iraqi regime of their own construction. As much as the Sherifian Solution was a plan of the Colonial Office's devising and served partially as the means by which to uphold Britain's regional interests, it was one also whose teleological end remained genuine independence for Iraq. The real question for all concerned was not if but when independence would happen. Of course, disagreement over the pace of events was endemic. But in Iraq there was little doubt that ultimate independence was the shared goal of Faisal and his circle of British advisers.

Accordingly, the latter months of 1921 passed in the same charged way as the year had begun. As Lawrence sought a treaty with King Hussein in the Hejaz and then worked successfully to consolidate Abdullah's ruling position in Transjordan, in Iraq, Faisal and the British moved towards achieving their own form of bilateral agreement. A little later, in March of 1922, the process in Iraq was given a sharp, destabilizing jolt, however, when a raiding party of hundreds of

Ikhwan tribal fighters from the east attacked a large number of essentially defenceless Iraqi pastoralists in the southern part of the country. Having come across to Iraq from lands controlled by Ibn Saud, the Ikhwan were members of the ultra-conservative Wahhabist sect. Since its founding in the eighteenth century, the Wahhabists had been the most uncompromisingly fundamentalist of Muslim sectarian divisions, devoted to an exclusivist reading of the Quran, which would yield offensive action. In the attack of that March some 700 predominantly Shia Iraqis – men, women and children – were killed.

For Faisal and Cox, the attack – for which Ibn Saud himself, it became clear, was not responsible – was a direct challenge to the king's authority, as well as to the British commitment to provide Iraq with military defence. Since the end of the Cairo Conference Britain's military responsibilities had begun to be altered – as planned – by moving away from heavy dependence upon ground troops and towards greater deployment of the Royal Air Force. But after an RAF plane had been shot down during a reconnaissance mission over the area where the raid had taken place, Cox proved reluctant to court further losses by authorizing additional flights. His conservative position in this regard played badly, however, with both Faisal and the Iraqi population, as it was understood to have signalled an overly permissive approach to the hated Wahhabists and therefore to their overlord, Ibn Saud.

The outcome of the Ikhwan crisis put even greater strain on the relationship between Faisal and Cox, the result of which was the calling of a special conference at Karbala in April by an angry group of leading ayatollahs. The conference took as its focal point the Wahhabist attack. But it quickly offered a platform too for anyone wishing to denounce the ongoing British mandate, and the refusal by Cox to intervene against the Ikhwan raiders in the way that they believed had been necessary to protect the lives and property of a group of especially vulnerable Iraqis. Faisal, who did not attend the conference at Karbala, was greatly commendatory of it nevertheless, praising the delegates for their 'noble sentiment, true patriotism and wisdom'. Meanwhile, Cox viewed the Karbala gathering as being 'ill-advised and dangerous', which for him would put the question of the sustainability of the British mandate into even sharper relief.

The acute tension in contemporary Iraqi affairs would continue throughout the spring of 1922. But at length, on 22 June, Faisal and his cabinet received from Cox a draft of the proposed Anglo-Iraqi Treaty. After spending a month contemplating its provisions, Faisal moved to accept it, but with the proviso – insisted upon robustly by the lately emboldened *naqib* as prime minister – that ratification of the treaty could be undertaken properly only by a future Iraqi constituent assembly. Cox, however, resisted this demand. In the event, the Iraqi government was no less determined to ensure that this demonstration of its putative sovereignty should command British respect and cooperation. Later, in August, the process was hindered further still when Faisal fell ill with appendicitis. As the king recovered, the gravity of the deteriorating local political situation between palace and Residency continued to be debated long-range by Cox in Baghdad and Churchill in London. The colonial secretary's position, though a resistant one, was not recidivist, and he understood well the countervailing pressures that had been placed upon Faisal by the mandate-decrying nationalist opposition. Still, in the midst of the debate Faisal's own growing tendency towards autocracy had become evident, both to the British as well as to his own cabinet and some of his subjects.[34]

On 29 August, as the crisis neared its climax and with Faisal convalescing after surgery, Churchill informed Cox sharply that 'It should be made clear to him [Faisal] that we will not allow his obstinacy to wreck our whole policy ... He was brought to Iraq not to play the autocrat but to settle down into a sober and constitutional monarch'.[35] Preventing the treaty from being scuppered was what mattered most to Churchill and Cox, as it would ultimately also to Faisal. Although he understood the purpose of the treaty differently than did his British counterparts, Faisal knew that he could not push them too far on the issue. After all, it was they who had made him king. Consequently, on 10 October, Faisal agreed to sign it. The Anglo-Iraqi Treaty had been achieved at last, confirming in the process Iraq's approaching independence as a significant feature of the Cairo Conference's plan for Britain's 'whole policy' in the Middle East, as it had been termed by Churchill. Notwithstanding Faisal's considerable reservations, he praised the treaty in both voice and print as having constituted a significant achievement. It was evidence, he said, of 'the continuance of the friendship of our illustrious ally, Great Britain, and to carrying out the elections for the convening of a Constituent Assembly'.

Throughout this period of almost unrelieved tension, Gertrude Bell had begun to ponder whether the political achievement that had been the creation of modern Iraq, and of Faisal's enthronement, might well be coming to naught. 'You may rely on this', she remarked wearily. 'I'll never engage in making kings again. It's too great a strain'. Bell had even gone so far as to consider leaving the country permanently, recognizing the potential for it to sunder over the issue of the treaty. 'Before every noble outline had been obliterated', she had written to her father in near-despair in June, describing an interview she had had recently with Faisal, 'I preferred to go; in spite of my love for the Arab nation and my sense of responsibility for the future, I did not think I could see the evaporation of the dream'.

For Bell, the saddest part of the dispute over the proposed Anglo-Iraqi Treaty was her belief that Faisal had been less than honourable in his dealings with Cox: that he had been too ready to appease opposition extremists and had shown himself, in her condemnatory words, 'amazingly lacking in strength of character'.[36] Bell's stance here is a hard one, and betrays to some extent a metropolitan bias and an inability to appreciate fully the narrow scope of action available to Faisal. Her charge was little short of a full indictment of the king, however, as it came from someone who had respected him always and who had held onto the aspiration for Arab independence longer than any other British person – man or woman – in the Middle East.[37] Hence the supremely welcome final settlement that had yielded the treaty. It would act for Bell as a vindication of Faisal, as well as a summing up of her labours in Iraq over many years.[38] As one of the king's ministers had told her just prior to the coronation, 'People like to see you at the meetings for Faisal. Wherever you are they know it will be all right ... People know that you always advocated an Arab state and it gives them confidence to see you'. It should come as no surprise, therefore, that for Bell the less than four years of life left to her would be valedictory in their personal satisfaction over what had been achieved in Iraq: 'I've got the love and confidence of this country ... I couldn't have expected a better destiny'.[39] But these years for Bell would be poignant also. Her own position and influence would decline in the face of greater and greater Iraqi independence under Faisal, about whose rule she began to grow disillusioned.[40]

In London, from Churchill's perspective, the signing of the Anglo-Iraqi Treaty could not have been timed better. It had come just over a week before he was forced out of office by the termination of Lloyd George's six-year coalition government at the hands of the resurgent Conservatives. Despite his precipitous fall, the so-called Welsh Wizard would remain a fixture in Parliament for years to come, but, unlike his sometime colonial secretary, Lloyd George's career in high office had reached its end. For Churchill, the Iraq treaty had put something of a seal on his productive twenty months at the Colonial Office, the last number of which had seen him attempt to fulfil the other constituent parts of the British plan laid down for the Middle East at the Cairo Conference.

Lawrence's return to London in late December of 1921, following his protracted diplomatic mission to the Hejaz, Jerusalem and Transjordan, had signalled his own coming end point at the Colonial Office. Turning, as he did now, his full attention to completing the

Seven Pillars of Wisdom, had much to do with a prevailing sense of finitude. Lawrence's belief that everything he could have done to help enact the Cairo Conference's Sherifian Solution had been done would clinch it. Additionally, these months for Lawrence were marked too by a persistent sense of existential angst. His one-year contractual commitment to the Colonial Office had almost expired, and he had decided both to leave its service and to take a pronounced turn inwards by changing his surname (to 'Shaw'; he would later alter it again to 'Ross'), and by anonymizing himself within the RAF. 'You know', he wrote early in 1922 to Air Marshal Sir Hugh Trenchard, whom he had got to know at Cairo, 'I am trying to leave Winston on March the first. Then I want about two months to myself, and then I'd like to join the RAF – with the ranks, of course'.

For Lawrence, a life of fame and unrelenting celebrity, of government service, and of exhausting diplomatic negotiation, had lost its previous allure. Indeed, nothing of this life seemed endurable any longer, and so he had begun to anticipate taking up something wholly different, although an explanation of his actions was never to become obvious to anyone, perhaps even to himself. As Lawrence often did during this period of vexation, he confided in his friend, Robert Graves. Later that year, for example, in an attempt to explain his actions regarding the RAF, he would tell Graves that 'Honestly I couldn't tell you why I joined up ... I sat up and wrote out all the reasons I could see or feel in myself for it, but they came to little more than that it was a necessary step, forced on me by an inclination towards ground-level, by a little wish to make myself a little more human ... It's going to be a brain-sleep, and I'll come out of it less odd than I went in'.[41]

Churchill, unaware of Lawrence's strained state of mind, pressed him to stay on in his service. Indeed, all the way through to Lawrence's early death in 1935, Churchill would remain, as he wrote to him later in 1927, 'always hoping some day to get a letter from you saying that your long holiday is finished, and that your appetite for action has returned'. Alas for Churchill, that day for Lawrence would never come, although he did agree to extend his stay at the Colonial Office by a few months beyond his original one-year commitment, telling his chief that 'I needn't say that I'm at your disposal when you need me'.[42] By July, however, Lawrence had resigned and was poised to begin a new life far from Whitehall and diplomacy, indeed far from conventionality itself.[43] 'I very much regret your decision to quit our small group in the Middle East department of the Colonial Office', Churchill wrote to him in an elegiac tone, '. . . I hope you are not unduly sanguine in your belief that our difficulties are largely surmounted'.[44]

In mentioning 'our difficulties', Churchill's reference was to the prevailing situation in Iraq, although the issue of the Anglo-Iraqi Treaty itself would be resolved by that autumn. Even more pointedly, however, Churchill meant the state of terminal political unrest in Palestine, as well as that which remained in Transjordan. Within the newly delimited Palestine the political situation had deteriorated markedly during the year that had followed the conclusion of the Cairo Conference. The persistent enmity between the Arab and Jewish populations had yielded mass protests. The Arabs were especially upset as they understood themselves to be under siege from a government intent on allowing more and more Jews to settle in Palestine, a process that they believed in time would squeeze them out of the territory altogether. The British high commissioner, Sir Herbert Samuel, listened patiently to Palestine's Arab leaders on this point. In response, he mandated the creation of a Supreme Muslim Council, and had appointed a grand mufti of Jerusalem, to show that he was committed to the creation of a predominantly Arab polity. But Samuel remained unmoveable on the question of whether Palestine would continue to contain a Jewish homeland. For him, the issue was fundamentally non-negotiable. As he reiterated in a speech made a few years later, 'the strength of the Jewish spirit is dependent upon the creation of a national home in Palestine. It cannot live without a centre. The centre can only be there'.[45]

The existence of a permanent Jewish homeland, however, as promised by the Balfour Declaration and confirmed by Churchill's post-Cairo visit to Jerusalem in late March 1921, was at the time never less than anathema to Arabs. A short time thereafter, in early May, widespread anti-Jewish rioting broke out, during which thirty Jews and ten Arabs were killed in Jaffa. For Churchill, the current anti-Turkish, pro-Greek policy of the Lloyd George government was more to blame for continuing Arab disaffection in Palestine than were local Zionist politics. His frustration with the prime minister's position on the issue had grown apace, so much so that he even suggested Britain ought to pull out of Palestine altogether to reduce Muslim opprobrium elsewhere. Unsurprisingly, Lloyd George had refused to countenance this radical line of reasoning, but Churchill continued to insist that his role in the Middle East as the chief broker of British policy would be made much easier if the prime minister would only make peace with the Turks. Indeed, Churchill proved relentless in pushing Lloyd George on the Turkish question. As late as September of 1922, just ahead of Lloyd George's ousting as prime minister the following month, Churchill would tell him that the 'victories of the Turks will increase our difficulties throughout the Mohammedan world'.

Exacerbating the Turkish issue was the fact that none of Samuel's concessions to Arab opinion in Palestine – not the creation of the Supreme Muslim Council; not the elevation of the prominent Arab leader Musa al-Husayni to the position of grand mufti of Jerusalem; not even the move by the government following the Jaffa riots to suspend temporarily Jewish immigration 'until immigrants now in the country are absorbed' – had served to mollify Arab opinion.[46] Even in its barest form, the presence of Zionist Jews in Palestine under the remit of the Balfour Declaration was totally unacceptable to Palestinian Arabs, and they would resist permanently the British policy that sought to make it normative.

Throughout the rest of 1921 and into the following year the essential Arab–Jewish divide would continue to cleave Mandatory

Palestine in a manner suggesting that it might be impervious to resolution. Indeed, Churchill's frustration with Britain's inability to bring
to pass a settlement in Palestine allowing for a civil residential relationship to develop between Jews and Arabs became intense. He
clung resolutely to the fundamental belief that two such peoples
should be able to work out the means by which to accommodate one
another in ways that were seen elsewhere in the world, both within
and without the British Empire. In taking this position was Churchill
naïve, or merely in thrall to a 'chimera' of his own making, as some
have written?[47] Churchill's assumption that Jews and Arabs might be
able to work out an acceptable political arrangement in order to share
the same territory and live alongside one another in essential harmony
was not an unreasonable expectation. In a world where the founding
principles of the League of Nations had come to provide an organi-
zational model for modern statehood, Churchill's own expectations
for Palestine were similar. Churchill agreed with Samuel, for example,
that the creation of participatory political institutions for the Arabs
should be part of the way forward in Palestine, just as they had begun
to develop in neighbouring Transjordan. 'I am strongly in favour of
introduction of representative institutions in Palestine', Churchill
wrote to John Shuckburgh of the Middle East Department in June
of 1921, 'and I consider it impossible to deny them to a country while
little backwards places like Trans-Jordan are given them'.[48]

Then and later, however, it is true that Churchill can be seen to have
held apparently contradictory positions on the linked questions of
representative institutions, local autonomy and national independence as features of colonial constitutional development within the
British Empire.[49] One need only instance Ireland and Egypt in the
1920s, or India in the 1930s, to find ample evidence for such apparent
contradiction, or at least inconsistency. But whatever may be said of
these other situations, over Palestine in 1921–22 Churchill remained
essentially consistent in his thinking, which is why he became discon-

solate about the problem as it continued to persist. To him, the Gordian knot of Palestine's interminable politics seemed to grow tighter with every passing day.

As much as Arab intransigence over the Zionist question seemed immoveable, so equally was the provocative and dogged nature of the Zionist lobby, led by Chaim Weizmann. Gradually but firmly, Weizmann and the Zionist Organisation had taken the position that the language of a 'national home for the Jewish people', as contained in the Balfour Declaration, had signalled but a starting point for the development of an eventual Jewish state. Accordingly, any political concessions made to the Palestinian Arabs by the British carried with them the implication, for Zionists, that Palestine was on the road to becoming a shared state. Throughout this period Weizmann believed, as he wrote to the other executive members of the Zionist Organisation from Jerusalem in March of 1920, that 'Allenby, and with him all the rest' were Arab apologists who 'have sold us over to Feyzal [*sic*] without the slightest compunction'. As a result they 'have entirely forgotten about Zionism'.[50] The founder of the Jewish Legion which had fought in the Palestine campaign, Ze'ev Jabotinsky, was of the same opinion. He had complained to Allenby in 1919 about what he believed to be Britain's weakening commitment to Zionism.[51] However, nothing could have been further from the truth. The British – specifically Churchill – believed that Arab–Jewish accommodation could be achieved in Palestine. But it was this kind of shared outcome in Palestine that the Zionists rejected. Moreover, Churchill's position was weakened by the fact that within British high political office he seems to have been the only person who had chosen to understand the implications of the Balfour Declaration in this broad and inclusive manner. Lloyd George, for one, certainly did not, and had told Churchill so plainly.[52]

By the end of 1921, and with the pressing political situations of both Ireland and Egypt to contend with, Churchill therefore had begun to retreat from close involvement in the Palestine question. Eventually, in June of 1922, he consigned the totality of the issue to a government White Paper, the direction of which he had discussed closely with Samuel in London during the previous month.[53] Written mainly by Hubert Young, the White Paper enunciated a tripartite policy to be adopted henceforth by Britain. After much contemplation by Samuel, as well as discussions with the Arab Executive Committee that had been formed in Jerusalem in late 1920, the White Paper confirmed that under the British mandate Palestine would remain a shared state. To be sure, it would continue to contain a Jewish national home. But Palestine itself was not be subordinated constitutionally to its Jewish population. Second, a legislative council was to be formed in Palestine, following in the British colonial tradition of creating a means by which to share power between the executive and the representatives of the people. Third, Jewish immigration to Palestine would be regulated and based on the concept of 'economic absorptive capacity'.

In theory, the White Paper's closely considered three-pronged policy might well have worked as the means by which to establish a modern, pluralist political culture in Palestine. Certainly, Samuel both believed in and was committed to its implementation. But the White Paper's recommendations would never come to pass. Two-stage elections for the legislative council were mooted later in 1922, but amidst boycotts by Arabs and low turnouts by all electors for the first stage, Samuel suspended – it was thought temporarily at first – this initial attempt to create representative political institutions in Palestine. The ultimate result of this action was that for the duration of the existence of British Mandatory Palestine, all the way until 1948, an elected legislature would never be established.[54] When assessing the content of Churchill's thinking in 1922, the failure of these proposed measures helps to explain why he grew weary of navigating fruitlessly through Palestine's dead-end politics in search of a solution to the interminable Arab–Zionist question.

The White Paper of that June was to be Churchill's final attempt to balance the interests of the Jews and Arabs of British Mandatory Palestine while serving as colonial secretary. Until the end of his term of office, and well beyond, he would however remain baffled, angry even, that such internecine enmity in Palestine could not be assuaged and an agreement to live together in peace be found. A political settlement in Palestine allowing for civil society to flourish, economic prosperity to spread, and representative governmental institutions to take root, was in Churchill's view there to be achieved. But as long as the Arabs remained implacable in their desire to have the Balfour Declaration reversed, and the Jews were committed equally to the development of an exclusively Jewish state, a resolution appeared impossible to reach.[55] Certainly, Churchill himself had remained determined to work out an enduring compromise that neither of the two antagonists really wished to see achieved. In the House of Commons on 14 June, therefore, he gave a speech that was to become his capstone utterance on the situation as it prevailed in Palestine. We cannot 'leave the Jews in Palestine to be maltreated by the Arabs', he stated. Equally it was 'illusory' that the Arabs were destined to lose their land. However, by the time he uttered these words, the vision that Churchill had shared with the Middle East Department at Cairo for a truly bi-national Palestine was looking likely to go unrealized.

If Palestine in the early 1920s had proved itself resistant to adopting Western representative political forms that might have achieved success in binding together a cleaved population, a short distance to the east, in Transjordan, the Sherifian Solution was destined for a very different and more unifying outcome. In Transjordan, what had been hoped for by the chief delegates at the Cairo Conference was beginning to manifest itself in the person of Abdullah as emir, and in the regime that was consolidating itself under his control. Abdullah would spend a considerable amount of time in Britain during the autumn of 1922, trying to work out the parameters of his increasingly successful rule.[56] To be sure, tensions persisted between his desire to be fully independent, and the insistence of the British on ensuring that diplomatic equipoise continued to mark Transjordan's relations with both of its neighbours, Syria and Palestine. But such tensions would never become destructive, and in May of the next year Britain chose to recognize the formal independence of Transjordan.

In the span of just fourteen months, following the conclusion of the Cairo Conference the British had created two new states in the Middle East, both of which were constitutional monarchies and based on the principle of representative government. As an exercise in state-building, first in Iraq and then in Transjordan, the early results were promising. In the midst of both the widespread upheavals brought on by the First World War and the statist expectations championed at Paris and San Remo, the Cairo Conference appeared to have been a success.[57] Under Faisal, Iraq had begun – albeit with significant difficulty – to find a serviceable political balance amidst an array of countervailing domestic forces. Such is the essential nature of all modern pluralist polities. Churchill was under no illusion about how hard the job of achieving political stability in Iraq would be. 'The task you have given me', he wrote to Lloyd George in September of 1922, 'is becoming really impossible'. Indeed, in a moment of acute frustration, Churchill had called Iraq an 'ungrateful volcano' and wondered whether the effort put in by the British would yield anything there 'worth having'.[58]

Meanwhile in Transjordan, Abdullah sought to achieve a similar stability, albeit on a much smaller and less complicated scale. The Cairo Conference had formulated a plan which had been put together by the best and most experienced minds working on Middle East affairs that the British could muster. The outcome they hoped for in the two new countries was both well reasoned and potentially durable, if highly optimistic. That the plan was committed to engendering a contemporary form of Western constitutional politics is clear. Indeed, in the form of the new states of Iraq and Transjordan, the Cairo Conference had attempted to create the first iteration of the modern Middle East. Ultimately, however, the results of the Sherifian Solution would redound mainly to failure. It remains only to answer why this was.

CONCLUSION
THE CAIRO CONFERENCE IN
HISTORICAL RETROSPECT

What then went wrong in the aftermath of the Cairo Conference? If, as the British believed, the Sherifian Solution had established a workable blueprint for modern government and politics in large parts of the Middle East, why was it unable to point the way towards an enduring form of regional state-building? If Cairo's universalist aspirations were so closely in line with the prevailing desire for self-determination and statist solutions in the post-First World War period, then why did its prescriptions fail to take hold? In the concluding chapter of this book some suggestions will be made as to why state-building proved elusive, where some success did emerge, and what might be said to offer a fuller way in which to understand the history and impact of the Cairo Conference.

To begin, in Iraq during the mid to late 1920s, Faisal continued along the path of attempting to forge a unifying national government. In so doing, the intention remained of trying to create pan-Iraqi Western-style nationalism designed to smooth over the various long-standing and variegated cleavages in the country. In the manner of the growth and development of traditional European-style nineteenth-century mass nationalism that had been inherited by Iraq's controlling political elite, Faisal's task was much the same as that found in any number of developing states around the world, both beforehand, at the time, and later.[1] Indeed, from the American War of Independence in the eighteenth century, to the classic versions of nineteenth-century European revolutionary nationalism, to the early twentieth-century colonial nationalism of the British dominions, to the post-Paris Peace Conference era of small-state internationalism, Iraq's history and its constitutional trajectory were not unique. Of course, every nascent state, no matter its size, can and should claim a degree of exceptionality, and due regard must be paid to local political conditions. But in moving towards the establishment of a modern and sustainable political model in Iraq, the challenges were not necessarily insurmountable, and certainly they were no more vexatious than those found elsewhere in the transitioning colonial world. In fact, after four centuries of Ottoman rule it might be said that Britain, first as military victor and imperial overlord, and then as mandatory administrator, had given Iraq a necessary and useful gestational period during which to indigenize the requirements and expectations of new and modern political and social forms.[2]

From the moment of Faisal's accession as king of Iraq in 1921, until his death twelve years later in 1933, he would attempt to use the scope of rule confirmed for him at the Cairo Conference to create a modern political state in the country, one designed to erase forever what most considered to be the baleful shadow left by the Ottomans. The Anglo-Iraqi Treaty of 1922 was a highly significant step in this process, allowing as it did for a large measure of national independence to occur in tandem with the maintenance of the traditional British imperial doctrine of gradual constitutional development. Semi-independence as the right way forward in Iraq is hard to argue against when put beside the rush to decolonization that would come elsewhere later in the twentieth century and which appears, for

example, to have played a significant role in condemning large parts
of Africa to a permanent state of political instability and violence, in
addition to economic precarity and poverty.[3] The sustaining presence
of the British administrative apparatus during the early days of Iraqi
independence can be viewed as having provided a form of governmental ballast, a pronounced stabilizing influence, while Faisal
sought to make normative the modernizing political practices of his
new regime. 'I don't see how I'm ever going to tear myself away from
this country', wrote Gertrude Bell without regret during this early
period, and she never did.[4] Indeed, she would die in Baghdad in
1926 at the age of fifty-seven – likely by her own hand – and lies
buried in the city's Anglican Cemetery in a grave that has continued
to be honoured and tended by Iraqis long after her death.[5] 'The Iraq
state is a fine monument' to Gertrude, Lawrence wrote in commen-
dation to her father after Bell's death.

During Faisal's period of rule his first task had been to understand,
and then to ameliorate, the natural fissures in the Iraqi body politic,
about which probably no one had greater knowledge at the outset
than did his chief British adviser, Bell. Doing so was a daunting
and continuous task, to be sure, but neither was it an unreasonable
nor an unexpected one. Certainly, it was much preferred by most
Iraqis to that of having to live for any longer under either form of
prevailing imperial suzerainty – Ottoman, or latterly British – that
had defined the history of the country over the preceding 400 years.
None of Churchill, Lawrence, Cox or Bell saw the Cairo Conference's
Sherifian Solution as merely the means by which to perpetuate a
species of permanent British imperial control over Iraq that would
extend indefinitely. That Britain sought to maintain good governmental relations with a constitutionally evolving Iraq, and would, at
least for a time, make safeguarding its vital regional interests a feature
of that relationship, is a commonplace in the history of states. Bell in
particular – though she was far from alone in holding this view – was

well pleased to see Iraq step out on its own constitutionally, and had she lived doubtless would have been overjoyed to see Iraq achieve full independence in 1932, just a year before Faisal's own death.

In the immediate aftermath of the Cairo Conference and of his accession, Faisal had worked to create and maintain a balanced and representative cabinet reflective of the Iraqi polity. Later, prominent critics such as the historian Elie Kedourie would argue to the contrary, however, charging that Faisal's regime had been little more than a façade; that loyalty to him did not exist outside of his inner circle, which included of course a cadre of British administrators like Bell; and that minorities – such as the Kurds, the Jews and the Assyrians – had always been treated badly in Iraqi society and were severely under-represented in the new government. Moreover, Kedourie suggests that democracy, pluralism, civility, equality and other such watchwords of modern political society were little more than urban, mainly Baghdad-based, Western conceits, having no purchase amongst the people living in the vast swathes of rural Iraq.[6] Certainly, Bell herself had been concerned greatly about this problem. As she had explained it in 1920 to Edwin Montagu, the Indian secretary, a new Iraqi administration must 'prevent the rural population from being run by a handful of Baghdad effendies, and that is probably the most difficult task of all'.[7]

To be sure, that the facts upon which Kedourie's argument are based are true cannot be doubted. But that Faisal made at least some attempt to alter these political realities, though he failed to do so successfully, is equally clear also.[8] That the nationalist elite of Iraq, as well as the large majority of the country's population, could not or would not be made to understand and embrace modern mass politics is abundantly evident. 'There is still', lamented Faisal not long before his death in 1933, '... no Iraqi people but unimaginable masses of human beings devoid of any patriotic idea'.[9] Breaking down Iraq's traditionally hierarchical and tribal society in the service of modern mass nationalism was extremely difficult and, probably, the new regime did not try hard enough to do so. But ultimately, the salient question to be asked as it concerns the period after 1921, is what might have made for a better alternative to the attempt at building a modern state in Iraq than that which had been undertaken by the delegates at the Cairo Conference? What was the range of options available to any and all of those engaged in trying to chart the direction of Iraq's future course? If anything, animated by aspirations for Western-style democracy, equality and social civility, exponents of the Sherifian Solution were carried along too readily by their own lofty ideas about the capacity for indigenous modern government to take root in the country. Bell believed that under the Ottomans any inkling of progressive politics in Iraq had been a 'farce'. But she had been careful to point out also that unless the British plan for Iraqi governance reflected a realistic understanding of the capacity for political reform to take hold Iraqi progressive politics 'must still be a farce under anybody else'.[10] The Cairo Conference delegates had displayed, she believed, a reasonable expectation that, if properly nurtured, civil society in Iraq could flourish under the sort of leadership projected to be offered by Faisal. After a decade or so of such leadership, however, the sanguinity of the Sherifians in this regard would begin to be doubted. As Stephen Longrigg, a contemporary of Bell's in the Iraqi government, later scathingly observed: 'In 1932 the Government of Iraq consisted of a facade of democratic forms'.[11] Had Bell still been alive at that moment she might well have been tempted to point an accusatory finger in the direction of Faisal, at his advisers, and likely at herself too. As she had commented in 1920, 'British officials, if they have a free run, will create institutions which suit themselves but may very well not suit Arabs, with the result that when the Arabs take over, as some day they must, the work will have to be done all over again'.[12]

That the delegates at the Cairo Conference had overshot in their projections; that they had overestimated the capacity of Faisal to lead the way, and for Iraqi political culture to rise to the level envisioned by its own nationalist partisans; that they had failed to engender the creation of a Kurdish state is clear. Moreover, international expectations – even demands – of a world suffused with the language and aspirations of modern mass nationalism were almost impossible for the infant polity of Iraq to meet. And British administrators, as well as Faisal, could have been more effective in transcending internal political divisions, as challenging a task as that proved to be. Selecting Faisal to be king of Iraq at the Cairo Conference in 1921 may well have been a far-sighted piece of British statecraft. But its ramifications ultimately could not be brought to fruition through a combination of British over-confidence and the narrow nature of Iraq's own leadership and nationalist political class. Still, to describe – as some have done – the outcome of the Cairo Conference merely as 'Churchill's Folly', or as 'hot air, Arabs and aeroplanes', does not seem to reflect the seriousness of purpose of what was attempted there in 1921.[13]

Shifting the focus to Jordan, what can be observed as constituting the historical impact of the Cairo Conference? The voluminous Churchill record contains a line from a speech that he gave to the House of Commons in March of 1936, during which he stated that 'The Emir Abdullah is in TransJordania where I put him one Sunday afternoon at Jerusalem'.[14] Indeed, by that time, exactly fifteen years after having had his position in Transjordan confirmed, Abdullah was in Amman to stay. The remark may be vintage Churchill, but it points also to the relative success and durability of the Sherifian regime in Transjordan in the generation that followed its inauguration. To extend the point further, Jordan today is the only one of the monarchical states created in the Middle East after the First World War to have survived into the twenty-first century. Equally remarkable is the fact that it has done so under the same Hashemite dynastic line, currently in its fourth generation as represented by King Abdullah II, the great-grandson of Emir Abdullah, put in place by the actions of Churchill and the Cairo Conference in 1921.[15] Given Lawrence's perennially low estimation of Abdullah's abilities – 'a tool too complex for a simple purpose', he had remarked acerbically about him in the lead-up to the Arab Revolt – it must come as one of history's ironies that his descendants have succeeded in fulfilling the Sherifian destiny given to him at Cairo, and through his agency maintained one of the most stable states in the modern Middle East.[16]

This outcome was not much planned for by the British until just before the trajectory for it got underway formally on 11 April 1921 when the 'Emirate of Transjordan' was established by the Lloyd George government. Historically, modern Jordan had been a sparsely populated Ottoman-ruled territory with a population in the early 1920s of only some 225,000. Moreover, it lacked clear cartographic boundaries and was without what might be called 'national feeling', much less a more developed sense of modern political nationalism. Additionally, the country was bounded on all sides by bigger and more robust states.[17] Still, Transjordan would survive the decade of the 1920s intact, and despite Abdullah's assassination many years later in 1951 during a visit to Jerusalem (his killer an enraged Palestinian Arab who viewed him and his regime as fundamentally traitorous), the country would persevere. In large part, Jordan's durability, as well as its stability, resulted from the essentially *tabula rasa* nature of its founding in 1921 and the way in which Abdullah would work gradually to imprint his personal rule upon the country with the resolute assistance of the British. The demographic make-up of the country was overwhelmingly Sunni Muslim, to which were added a small number of Shia, as well as other lightly represented minorities, such as Circassians and Armenian Christians. Jordan's national history was linked always too with that of Palestine, and then with that of the State of Israel after 1948. The two states, Transjordan and Palestine, had been created side by side at essentially the same time and in this way they had developed a mutual, if at times highly strained, tolerance. A major dispute between them over the West Bank, for example, would persist far into the future, until in 1988 Jordan formally renounced its claim to the territory.

For the first quarter-century of its existence, from 1921 until 1946, Transjordan would remain under the authority of the British mandate.[18] Nevertheless, throughout these years the country exercised considerable autonomy, leading ultimately in 1946 to the signing of the Treaty of London, and with it the recognition of Transjordan's full independence. Three years later, in 1949, the country's name would be changed officially to the Hashemite Kingdom of Jordan. During the twenty-five years of British mandatory supervision Jordan had moved from being a small and underdeveloped desert quasi-state to become a much more sophisticated, sure-footed and modern polity. Along the way, Abdullah would push hard for greater autonomy, even for independence, from the British, but in the interests of maintaining both internal and regional stability the latter was withheld until 1946.

Throughout this period the British continued to fulfil what was required of them internationally as a mandatory power. Abdullah's own stability as king was maintained by the British, both through administrative means and by the key presence of military force in the form of the Arab Legion. The historian David Fieldhouse does not overstate the case when he writes that 'The Legion was in a sense the core of the state; without it there would have been no state'. Indeed, he suggests rightly that Jordan's stability and survival owes much to consistency of leadership in the form of King Abdullah, and later in that of King Hussein. As well, the essential cooperation in the early period between Jordan and Palestine/Israel was important, including employing expelled Palestinians in government after 1948. But it was the Arab Legion's provision of a high standard of military service and of unimpeachable loyalty to the constitutional monarchical state that Fieldhouse contends were decisive. 'That tradition of military loyalty', he concludes, 'may well have been the greatest gift of the British to Jordan'. Still, despite its stabilizing features, military force could be and was employed repressively from time to time in Jordan, an unwelcome fact of political life in the country.

Fieldhouse is persuasive on this point, but the immediate foundational period of Jordan's modern history in 1921–22 was of equal indispensability, it may be argued, to its later success as a bastion of relative political civility in the Middle East. The four weeks that Lawrence spent with Abdullah in the autumn of 1921 had worked to assure him of the essential viability of the Sherifian experiment in Transjordan as proposed at Cairo. Lawrence's summative report of January 1922, which he wrote for the British government, had made clear his confidence in Abdullah. Nevertheless, he recommended that certain caveats be put in place, such as that the British governmental subsidy should be paid through its own representative in Transjordan rather than directly to Abdullah himself. Still, as qualified as was Lawrence's formal endorsement of Abdullah, the new emir remained a stellar choice to continue and ultimately to complete Cairo's Sherifian Solution of achieving long-term governmental stability and independence in Transjordan. By the time that Lawrence submitted his report early in 1922, however, he was moving quickly to escape from his life as a warrior-diplomat. Churchill persuaded him to stay on longer than he had planned, but in the end he chose to go. Thus it was that on 1 March Lawrence departed Whitehall; in his mind, the work of the Cairo Conference had been made complete. What would become the long-lasting state of Jordan was mainly the result of the undoubtedly swift but prescient work of both Churchill and Lawrence, its two chief executors.

What of the final part of the Cairo Conference's geopolitical triptych, Palestine? Truncated necessarily by the creation of Transjordan and not part of the Sherifian Solution directly, Palestine was integral nevertheless to the totality of Britain's post-First World War policy in the Middle East. In the immediate aftermath of the Cairo Conference the British plan for Palestine's political future remained essentially unchanged. Both Churchill and Lloyd George were immoveable in their support of the government's fulfilling of Britain's

209

1917 commitment to create a national homeland for the Jewish people in Palestine. Despite strong and persistent diplomatic representations and public protests within Palestine against the move, the two men continued to affirm the Balfour Declaration's stated policy in this regard. From April of 1920, when Mandatory Palestine was assigned to Britain by the League of Nations, until it assumed official control over the country in September of 1923, the post-war Occupied Enemy Territory Administration remained in charge. Sir Herbert Samuel stayed for five years as British high commissioner until 1925, during which time his attempts to create a representative legislative council were rebuffed, owing mainly to Arab objections. Ultimately, a lesser advisory council was established to act in its place. If, as has been suggested by the eminent scholar of empire, Wm Roger Louis, 'Palestine was the greatest failure in the whole history of British imperial rule' – and the continuing cycle of violence, oppression, and incivility in modern Israel that has befallen its resident Arab population provides ample evidence for this condemnatory statement – then where might the Cairo Conference intersect with this failure?[19]

In attempting to offer a retrospective of what remains today a highly charged and hotly contested episode in the modern history of the Middle East, one is supremely conscious of entering an historical – as well as an historiographical – minefield. So much intellectual energy has been expended, and so many words have been written, about what went wrong in Palestine, mainly for its Arab population, during the period of the British mandate until 1948, that it is difficult to know where to begin. The attempt here, therefore, is to restrict commentary to the salient events of the early- to mid-1920s that can be understood to have had a direct connection to the Cairo Conference. In this way the conference may be seen to have been part of a wider post-war British regional policy framework, the aspirations of which pointed ultimately to modern state-building, both Arab, as well as Arab–Jewish within Palestine.

For the British government, as well as for the governments of many other states, the Paris Peace Conference in 1919 had initiated a chain of events that would yield the establishment of the League of Nations, the convening of the San Remo Conference, the creation of the international Mandate System and the Treaty of Lausanne. These developments signalled a clear shift away from traditional-style territorial empire towards Great Power trusteeship in the 1920s by marking a new iteration in the Western domination of the international system.[20] In hindsight, the transition from empire to trusteeship, and then later to decolonization and independence, is seen often as a kind of flow-through phenomenon of twentieth-century history. But that is to place the imperial dynamic firmly within an historian's privileged, retrospective ambit. At the time, in the early 1920s, little such historical clarity was, or could be, discerned. Still, what *did* come to animate many contemporary decision-makers was the desire to create new states, or to sponsor the reconfiguration of existing ones, in ways that accorded with the nationalist-trustee model that had been endorsed widely first at Paris in 1919, and then elsewhere for many years thereafter.

This new-style paradigm, while certainly not exerting perfect control over the international system, was of strong and increasing appeal nonetheless to those who saw the continuation of contemporary empire as comprising mainly a tutelary function, if indeed it retained a useful function internationally to fill at all. In large part, the British response to this new late-imperial zeitgeist was to continue to act in accordance with its own long-established colonial precepts. That is, Britain chose to emphasise in those places where it retained imperial responsibility the practices of constitutional gradualism and devolutionary representative government. Sometimes this practice employed by the British came in response to the direct challenge of anti-colonial violence, and sometimes it did not. Examples of this British process at the time were, or would be soon, readily observable in India (the Montagu–Chelmsford Reforms of 1918–19); in Ireland (the Anglo-Irish Treaty of 1921); and in Egypt (the Allenby Declaration of 1922). A few years later, the Balfour Declaration of 1926 – leading as it did to the Statute of Westminster of 1931 – performed an analogous function for the senior members of the British Empire, the so-called dominions such as Canada and Australia, and would fall likewise into the category of what can be called tutelary empire. However, at the same time the British also kept a steady eye on whether their empire continued to serve particular national interests of a non-tutelary kind. Clearly it did, as maintaining their long-standing strategic control over the Suez Canal demonstrates. Accordingly, there can be no doubt that in seeking to help reorganize the post-First World War geopolitical map of the Middle East, the surest way to understand the actions of the British state at the time is to recognize the existence of these congeries of (inter-)national and imperial interests.[21]

In relation to the prospects for Mandatory Palestine in its earliest iteration therefore, the British would remain sanguine, as they would too for Iraq, as well as for Transjordan. Indeed, optimism reigned supreme in London that the cardinal problem of an ethnically and religiously divided Palestine could be solved ultimately through the same means of inter-ethnic accommodation and the gradual devolution of power that were understood to be effective features of traditional British rule overseas. Principled and pointed objections to the view that Mandatory Palestine was a soluble problem existed, certainly. But they were met by the existence of equally principled positions that it could be made to work as an emergent and modern civil polity. This measure of optimism is exactly what had powered the thinking behind the Middle East Department's view of what the future might hold for Mandatory Iraq, as well as for Transjordan. Retrospectively, such thinking may well seem impossibly naïve. Or, to view the situation differently, such thinking may well have been overweening in its Western arrogance, or in its paternalism, or in its exertion of imperial power. But at the time the aspirational position that Palestine could be transformed into an ordered and inclusive state where Arabs and Jews (and Christians) could live together in a society of constitutionally guaranteed mutual civility was firmly held by the British.

Discordant or warning voices within the British government existed nonetheless. Lord Curzon, for example, foreign secretary at the time, was one such critic of Britain's prevailing Palestine policy. In March of 1920 he bluntly wrote that 'The Zionists are after a Jewish State, with the Arabs as hewers of wood and drawers of water ... I want the Arabs to have a chance and I don't want a Hebrew State'.[22] He was not alone amongst powerful British policymakers in holding this position. As we know, Lord Allenby, with considerably more direct experience in the region than Curzon, agreed readily with the core elements of this view, although he would express himself much more circumspectly on the point.[23] But such was the surety of success held generally by the British that they pushed forward in Palestine anyhow. It is as if they were suffused with an air of invincible confidence in their own manifest abilities at state-making and political problem-solving regardless of where in the world they found themselves, or under which set of prevailing historical circumstances. Such a belief, for example, can be seen clearly in the highly-aspirational words of the former military Governor of Jerusalem, Sir Ronald Storrs. 'I do dare to believe', he stated in a speech in 1921 regarding the British Mandate in Palestine, '... if we can reconcile or unite at the source the chiefs and the followers of those three mighty religions, there may sound once more for the healing of the nations a voice out of Zion. If that should ever be, not the least of England's achievements will have been her part therein'.[24]

If the decision to partition Palestine was the worst one ever made in the history of the British Empire, as Louis would contend, then it was confirmed by having acted both naively and unrealistically in 1921 at Cairo. In attempting to solve a problem that has since then shown itself to be well-nigh insoluble, the mandatory British would falter badly. They would struggle with but fail ultimately in attempting to state-build in Palestine, brought down in part by the age-old imperial problem of how to enforce effective central control over a challenging periphery.[25] More pointedly, from 1917 onwards, unwavering support for the Balfour Declaration had committed Britain to a course of action that could end only in disaster for Palestine's Arabs. As Bell wrote presciently to her father in the summer of 1921, 'They regard us as their best hope in winning through to pan-Arabism . . . but I fear in the future we shall be hampered by our support of Zionism in Palestine and the French in Syria, neither of which is consistent with a pan-Arab policy'.[26]

In attempting to understand more fully the place of the Cairo Conference in the modern history of the Middle East it may be ultimately that the event serves mainly as a testament to Britain's irresistible imperative at the time to reshape and reinvigorate the politics of its mandatory territories. It would endeavour do so in ways that were aspirational theoretically, but would prove to be unachievable operationally. Mandatory Palestine, as it descended further into disorder later in the 1920s and then the 1930s, followed by episodic terrorism in the 1940s, would become a rueful example of the Cairo Conference's regional blueprint having been made a palimpsest of intransigent socio-political realities. In Iraq also, one can chart a similar pattern.

Only in Jordan can it be said that the Sherifian Solution lived up to its name fully and with considerable success. In attempting to inaugurate an acceptable and progressive course for a modern political future in the Middle East it is reasonable to consider the Cairo Conference to have been an enlightened and universalizing attempt at post-First World War state-building. As such, its assumptions were in line with the conference-centric approach taken following the war and into the 1920s to solving intractable international problems. In so doing, Cairo's delegates were no less confident about what the Middle East could become than had been those who gathered at the Paris Peace Conference two years earlier in 1919, and on an even broader plain believed themselves to be constructing a just and sustainable new world order. The impulse at the Cairo Conference may have been, as the historian David Cannadine suggests, both 'romantic' and 'hierarchical', but that did not make its outcome necessarily any less viable.[27]

Indeed, as Bell wrote to a friend while on board the train returning her to Baghdad from Cairo following the conclusion of the conference: 'It's going to be interesting! If we bring it off we shall make a difference in the world, for it will be the beginning of a quite new thing which will serve as an example – let's hope not as a warning'.[28] Today, a hundred years later, it is hard to avoid concluding that the multivalent failure of the Cairo Conference's geopolitical prescriptions for the post-war Middle East may well have been a grand opportunity missed, the dire implications of which remain with us still.

ENDNOTES

Abbreviations

AP Allenby Papers (Field Marshal Edmund Allenby, 1st Viscount Allenby of Megiddo), Liddell Hart Centre for Military Archives, King's College London

CHAR Sir Winston Churchill Papers, Churchill Archives Centre, Cambridge

CO Colonial Office Records, The National Archives, Kew, London

CP Captain Maxwell Henry Coote Papers, Liddell Hart Centre for Military Archives, King's College London

FO Foreign Office Records, The National Archives, Kew, London

GBA Gertrude Bell Archive, Newcastle University

HP Sir Maurice Hankey Papers, Churchill Archives Centre, Cambridge

JP Lieuenant Colonel Pierce Charles Joyce Papers, Liddell Hart Centre for Military Archives, King's College London

KP Philip Kerr Papers, National Records of Scotland, Edinburgh

LGP David Lloyd George Papers, Parliamentary Archives, London

LL T.E. Lawrence Letters, Bodleian Library, Oxford

ML Bishop Rennie MacInnes Letters, Middle East Centre Archive, St Antony's College, Oxford

RP General Sir William Robertson Papers, Liddell Hart Centre for Military Archives, King's College London

TEL Letters Malcolm Brown, ed., *Lawrence of Arabia: The Selected Letters*, London, Little Books, 2005

WP Sir Henry Wilson Papers, Imperial War Museum, London (WP)

WSC Companion Martin Gilbert, ed., *Winston S. Churchill: Companion Volume IV, Part 2 – July 1919–March 1921*, London, Heinemann, 1975

YP Sir Hubert Young Papers, Middle East Centre Archive, St Antony's College, Oxford

YP2 Sir Hubert Young Papers, Liddell Hart Centre for Military Archives, King's College London

Preface

1. See Aaron S. Klieman, *Foundations of British Policy in the Arab World: The Cairo Conference of 1921*, Baltimore, MD, Johns Hopkins University Press, 1970. It is a good but dated and less than comprehensive study of the Conference. The history of the Cairo Conference – examined in greater or lesser detail – is taken up in a large number of studies of the post-First World War Middle East, including Scott Anderson, *Lawrence in Arabia: War, Deceit, Imperial Folly and the Making of the Modern Middle East*, New York, 2013; James Barr, *A Line in the Sand: Britain, France and the Struggle That Shaped the Middle East*, London, Simon & Schuster, 2012; Christopher Catherwood, *Churchill's Folly: How Winston Churchill Created Modern Iraq*, New York, Carroll & Graf, 2004; Warren Dockter, *Churchill and the Islamic World*, London, I.B. Tauris, 2015; David Fromkin, *A Peace to End All Peace: Creating the Modern Middle East, 1914–1922*, New York, Henry Holt, 1989; Roger Hardy, *The Poisoned Well: Empire and Its Legacy in the Middle East*, New York, Oxford, Oxford University Press, 2016; Elie Kedourie, *In the Anglo-American Labryinth: The McMahon–Husayn Correspondence and Its Interpretations 1914–1939*, London, Frank Cass, 2000; Peter Mangold, *What the British Did: Two Centuries in the Middle East*, London, I.B. Tauris, 2016; and Karl E. Meyer and Shareen Blair Brysac, *Kingmakers: The Invention of the Modern Middle East*, New York, W.W. Norton, 2009.
2. C. Brad Faught, *Allenby: Making the Modern Middle East*, London, Bloomsbury, 2020.
3. Edmund Allenby to Catherine Allenby, 24 February 1921, AP 1/12/13. CHAR 17/19.
4. Barr, *A Line in the Sand*, p. 121.
5. See Susan Pedersen, *The Guardians: The League of Nations and the Crisis of Empire*, Oxford, Oxford University Press, 2015.
6. John Darwin, 'An Undeclared Empire: The British in the Middle East, 1918–39', *Journal of Imperial and Commonwealth History*, vol. 27, no. 2 (May 1999), pp. 159–76, p. 173.
7. Gertrude Bell to Florence Bell, 24 February and 25 March 1921, GBA.
8. T.E. Lawrence to Sarah Lawrence, 20 March 1921, *TEL Letters*, p. 197.
9. See Margaret MacMillan, *Paris 1919: Six Months That Changed the World*, New York, Random House, 2003. See also Pedersen, *The Guardians*.

Chapter 1 The First World War in the Middle East

1. The order of entry into the city would later be disputed. See Matthew Hughes, 'Elie Kedourie and the Capture of Damascus, 1 October 1918: A Reassessment', *War & Society*, vol. 23, no. 1 (2005), pp. 87–106.
2. Neil Faulkner, *Lawrence of Arabia's War: The Arabs, the British and the Remaking of the Middle East in WWI*, New Haven, CT, and London, Yale University Press, 2016, p. 449. Quoted in Jeremy Wilson, *Lawrence of Arabia: The Authorized Biography*, New York, Atheneum, 1990, p. 561.
3. 'The dreamers of the day are dangerous men, for they may act out their dream with open eyes, to make it possible. This I did.' T.E. Lawrence, *Seven Pillars of Wisdom: A Triumph*, Toronto, Penguin, 1990, frontispiece.
4. Edmund Allenby to Mabel Allenby, 3 October 1918, AP 1/9/12 and 17 October 1918, AP 1/9/15.
5. Lawrence, *Seven Pillars*, p. 683.
6. Lt-Gen Harry Chauvel, 'Meeting of Sir [*sic*] Edmund Allenby and the Emir Feisal at the Hotel Victoria, Damascus, on Oct. 3rd, 1918', AP 2/5/17.
7. Pierce Joyce, 'Reminiscences of T.E. Lawrence for the BBC, 14 July 1941', JP 2/19/1–4.
8. Lawrence, *Seven Pillars*, p. 683.
9. Joyce, 'Reminiscences', JP 2/19/1–4.

10. See, among many other titles, Corelli Barnett, *The Collapse of British Power*, Stroud, Sutton, 1997, ch. 1.
11. Rudyard Kipling, 'The Lesson' (1901). See Denis Judd and Keith Surridge, *The Boer War: A History*, London, I.B. Tauris, 2013, chs 1–2.
12. See Eugene Rogan, *The Fall of the Ottomans: The Great War in the Middle East*, New York, Basic Books, 2015, chs 1–2. See Peter Hopkirk, *The Great Game: On Secret Service in High Asia*, London, John Murray, 1990.
13. Chauvel, 'Meeting', AP 2/5/17.
14. Glen Balfour-Paul, 'Britain's Informal Empire in the Middle East', in Judith M. Brown and Wm Roger Louis, eds, *The Oxford History of the British Empire: Volume IV, The Twentieth Century*, Oxford, Oxford University Press, pp. 490–514. See also Rob Johnson, *The Great War and the Middle East*, Oxford, Oxford University Press, 2016, ch. 1.
15. See C. Brad Faught, *Gordon: Victorian Hero*, Washington, DC, Potomac Books, 2008, ch. 7.
16. See Nicholas J. Saunders, *Desert Insurgency: Archaeology, T.E. Lawrence and the Arab Revolt*, Oxford, Oxford University Press, ch. 4.
17. Richard A. Atkins, 'The Origins of the Anglo-French Condominium in Egypt, 1875–1876', *The Historian*, vol. 36, no. 2 (February 1974), pp. 264–82.
18. Martin Gilbert, *Churchill: A Life*, London, Heinemann, 1991, pp. 260–61.
19. See T.G. Otte, *Statesman of Europe: A Life of Sir Edward Grey*, London, Allen Lane, 2020.
20. C. Brad Faught, *Kitchener: Hero and Anti-Hero*, London, I.B. Tauris, 2016, pp. 190–91.
21. Quoted in Michael D. Berdine, *Redrawing the Middle East: Sir Mark Sykes, Imperialism and the Sykes–Picot Agreement*, London, I.B. Tauris, 2018, p. 19. Kitchener's understanding of contemporary Arabian geography was inaccurate as Kerbala (today's Karbala) is located in central Iraq about 60 miles south of Baghdad.
22. Ali A. Allawi, *Faisal I of Iraq*, New Haven, CT, and London, Yale University Press, 2014, p. 60.
23. Otte, *Statesman of Europe*, pp. 474, 55. See also Eliezer Tauber, *The Arab Movements in World War I*, London, Routledge, 1993.
24. For example, as Victor Kattan argues in *From Coexistence to Conquest: International Law and the Origins of the Arab–Israeli Conflict, 1891–1949*, London, Pluto Press, 2009. For an opposing view, see Kedourie, *In the Anglo-Arab Labyrinth*.
25. *Correspondence between Sir Henry McMahon, His Majesty's High Commissioner at Cairo and the Sherif Hussein of Mecca, July 1915–March 1916*, London, H.M. Stationery Office, Cmd 5957, Miscellaneous No. 3 (1939).
26. Allawi, *Faisal*, p. 74.
27. Studies of Lawrence's life are many. For this sketch of his formative years I have relied mainly on Wilson, *Lawrence of Arabia*, chs 1–4, and quoted in Anthony Sattin, *Young Lawrence: A Portrait of the Legend as a Young Man*, London, John Murray, 2015, p. 79.
28. See Sean McMeekin, *The Berlin–Baghdad Express: The Ottoman Empire and Germany's Bid for World Power*, Cambridge, MA, Belknap Press, 2013.
29. See Saunders, *Desert Insurgency*, p. 52. See also Rob Johnson, *Lawrence of Arabia on War: The Campaign in the Desert*, Oxford, Osprey, 2020, ch. 14.
30. Gertrude Bell to her family, 18 May 1911, Lady Bell, ed., *The Letters of Gertrude Bell, Volume 1*, London, Ernest Benn, 1927, p. 305.
31. Rogan, *The Fall of the Ottomans*, ch. 1.
32. On the vulnerability of the Ottomans at this time see Sean McMeekin, *The Ottoman Endgame: War, Revolution, and the Making of the Modern Middle East, 1908–1923*, London, Penguin, 2015.
33. T.E. Lawrence to Emily Rieder, 5 April 1913, David Garnett, ed., *The Letters of T.E. Lawrence*, London, Jonathan Cape, 1938, p. 152. T.E. Lawrence to anonymous, n.d., ibid., p. 181.

34. Lawrence, *Seven Pillars*, p. 661.
35. Malcolm Brown, ed., *The Letters of T.E. Lawrence*, London, J.M. Dent & Sons, 1988, p. 75.
36. T.E. Lawrence to his family, 5 October 1916, M.R. Lawrence, ed., *The Home Letters of T.E. Lawrence and his Brothers*, Oxford, Basil Blackwell, 1954, p. 115.
37. Quoted in Ronald Storrs, *The Memoirs of Sir Ronald Storrs*, New York, G.P. Putnam's Sons, 1937, p. 204.
38. Lawrence, *Seven Pillars*, p. 92. See Faulkner, *Lawrence of Arabia's War*, chs 9–10.
39. Pierce Joyce, 'Notes on Arab Tactics etc.', n.d., JP 2/17.
40. Faught, *Allenby*, p. 42. Lawrence, *Seven Pillars*, p. 330.
41. Edmund Allenby to William Robertson, 19 July 1917, RP 8/1/64.
42. See Stuart Hadaway, *From Gaza to Jerusalem: The Campaign for Southern Palestine 1917*, London, The History Press, 2015.
43. Edmund Allenby to Mabel Allenby, 11 December 1917, AP 1/8/32.
44. Rogan, *The Fall of the Ottomans*, pp. 350–53. See also Fromkin, *A Peace to End All Peace*, pp. 305–14.
45. See Shimon Lev, ed., *A General and a Gentleman: Allenby at the Gates of Jerusalem*, Jerusalem, Tower of David/Museum of the History of Jerusalem, 2017.
46. Joyce, 'Reminiscences', JP 2/19/1–4.
47. Michael Korda, *The Life and Legend of Lawrence of Arabia*, New York, HarperCollins, 2010, ch. 7. B.H. Liddell Hart, *History of the First World War*, London, Pan Books, 1970, p. 439.
48. Philip Mansel, *Aleppo: The Rise and Fall of Syria's Great Merchant City*, London, I.B. Tauris, 2018, p. 52.
49. Lawrence, *Seven Pillars*, p. 57. See Christopher Simon Sykes, *The Man Who Created the Middle East: A Story of Empire, Conflict and the Sykes–Picot Agreement*, London, HarperCollins, 2016.
50. See Berdine, *Redrawing the Middle East*, p. 20.
51. Faught, *Kitchener*, pp. 237–38. Barr, *A Line in the Sand*, p. 31.
52. Later, the victorious revolutionary Bolsheviks under Lenin would expose the Sykes–Picot Agreement to public criticism and then act to remove the new Soviet Union from being bound by its provisions.
53. Barr, *A Line in the Sand*, p. 33. Robert H. Lieshout, *Britain and the Arab Middle East: World War I and Its Aftermath*, London, I.B. Tauris, 2016, pp. 198–99.
54. Donald M. Lewis, *The Origins of Christian Zionism: Evangelical Support for a Jewish Homeland*, Cambridge, Cambridge University Press, 2010, p. 380. Christian Zionism grew steadily as a public cause during the Victorian era, as would be foreshadowed by the *Colonial Times* of Hobart, Tasmania, for example, in an article published on 23 February 1841 entitled 'Memorandum to the Protestant Monarchs of Europe for the Restoration of the Jews to Palestine'.
55. Roy Jenkins, *Asquith*, London, Collins, 1964, ch. 27. Don M. Cregier, *Bounder from Wales: Lloyd George's Career Before the First World War*, Columbia, University of Missouri Press, 1976, p. 13.
56. Norman Rose, *Chaim Weizmann: A Biography*, London, Penguin, 1989, pp. 320–21. Leonard Stein, *The Balfour Declaration*, London, Magnes Press, 1983, frontispiece. See also James Renton, *The Zionist Masquerade: The Birth of the Anglo-Zionist Alliance, 1914–1918*, New York, Palgrave Macmillan, 2007.
57. Wilson, *Lawrence of Arabia*, p. 502. King George V to Lord Allenby, 23 September 1918, AP 1/9/9.
58. See Michael Provence, *The Last Ottoman Generation and the Making of the Modern Middle East*, Cambridge, Cambridge University Press, 2017. *TEL Letters*, p. 164.

Chapter 2 'What a difficult world the war has bequeathed to us!' Middle East Diplomacy after 1918

1. Matthew Hughes, ed., *Allenby in Palestine: The Middle East Correspondence of Field Marshal Viscount Allenby June 1917–October 1919*, Stroud, Sutton, 2004, pp. 199, 201–2.
2. Edmund Allenby to Mabel Allenby, 17 October 1918, AP 1/9/15 and 15 October 1918, AP 1/9/14. Edmund Allenby to Henry Wilson, 23 October 1918, WP 2/33A/28.
3. Hughes, ed., *Allenby in Palestine*, p. 212.
4. Edmund Allenby to Henry Wilson, 19 October 1918, WP 2/33A/28 and 9 November 1918, WP 2/33A/29. Edmund Allenby to Catherine Allenby, 11 November 1918, AP 1/9/17.
5. Hughes, ed., *Allenby in Palestine*, p. 215. Wilson, *Lawrence of Arabia*, p. 571.
6. Quoted in Barr, *A Line in the Sand*, p. 69.
7. Brown, ed., *The Letters of T.E. Lawrence*, p. 161.
8. Wilson, *Lawrence of Arabia*, p. 571. Quoted in Allawi, *Faisal*, pp. 157, 167–8.
9. Quoted in D. Hunter Miller, *My Diaries of the Conference of Paris*, vol. 15, New York, Appeal, 1924, pp. 507–8.
10. Edmund Allenby to Henry Wilson, 19 October 1918, WP 2/33A/28.
11. Quoted in Allawi, *Faisal*, pp. 170–71. Quoted in Berdine, *Redrawing the Middle East*, p. 221.
12. Edmund Allenby to Henry Wilson, 9 November 1918, WP 2/33A/29 and 14 December 1918, WP 2/33B/4. Henry Wilson to Edmund Allenby, 7 December 1918, WP 2/33B/1.
13. Hughes, ed., *Allenby in Palestine*, pp. 220, 224.
14. Field-Marshal Viscount Wavell, *Allenby: Soldier and Statesman*, London, White Lion, 1974, pp. 258–59.
15. Mark Sykes, 'Appreciation of the Situation in Syria, Palestine, and lesser Armenia', KP GD40/17/37, ff. 28–9.
16. Berdine, *Redrawing the Middle East*, p. 230.
17. Edmund Allenby to Henry Wilson, 4 February 1919, KP GD40/17/37, f. 30.
18. Quoted in Wavell, *Allenby*, p. 259.
19. See MacMillan, *Paris 1919*, pp. 381–409.
20. Philip Kerr to David Lloyd George, 28 February 1919, KP GD40/17/1234.
21. MacMillan, *Paris 1919*, p. xxv.
22. Edmund Allenby to Mabel Allenby, 21 March 1919, AP 1/10/7.
23. Quoted in Lawrence James, *Imperial Warrior: The Life and Times of Field-Marshal Viscount Allenby 1861–1936*, London, Weidenfeld & Nicolson, 1993, p. 185.
24. MacMillan, *Paris 1919*, p. 394.
25. See Andrew Patrick, *America's Forgotten Middle East Initiative: The King–Crane Commission of 1919*, London, I.B. Tauris, 2015.
26. Hughes, ed., *Allenby in Palestine*, pp. 228–29, 232.
27. Quoted in John Darwin, *Britain, Egypt and the Middle East: Imperial Policy in the Aftermath of War 1918–1922*, London, Macmillan, 1981, p. 83.
28. Edmund Allenby to Mabel Allenby, 21 March 1919, AP 1/10/7.
29. Macmillan, *Paris 1919*, ch. 27; p. 392.
30. Allawi, *Faisal*, ch. 12.
31. Edmund Allenby to Henry Wilson, 17 May 1919, WP 2/33B/16.
32. D.K. Fieldhouse, *Western Imperialism in the Middle East 1914–1958*, Oxford, Oxford University Press, 2006, p. 61.
33. Edmund Allenby to Catherine Allenby, 28 December 1920, AP 1/11/44.
34. For a comprehensive treatment of the history of the League of Nations Permanent Mandates Commission see Pedersen, *The Guardians*. See also Cyrus Schayegh and Andrew Arsan, eds, *The Routledge Handbook of the History of the Middle East Mandates*,

London, Routledge, 2020, and Wm Roger Louis, *Ends of British Imperialism: The Scramble for Empire, Suez and Decolonization*, London, I.B. Tauris, 2006, pp. 251–90.

35. William Thwaites to Edmund Allenby, 5 May 1920, FO 141/624/1.
36. Faisal to Edmund Allenby, n.d. [probably June 1920], LGP F/59/10.
37. Allawi, *Faisal*, p. 294. Gertrude Bell to Edwin Montagu, 4 January 1920, KP GD40/17, f. 320.
38. The biographical information on Cox has been gleaned mainly from John Townsend, *Proconsul to the Middle East: Sir Percy Cox and the End of Empire*, London, I.B. Tauris, 2010, ch. 1.
39. See, for example, Rogan, *The Fall of the Ottomans*, ch. 10.
40. Roy Jenkins, *Churchill: A Biography*, Toronto, Plume, 2002, p. 220.
41. *Parliamentary Debates*, 17 June 1914. Quoted in Gilbert, *Churchill*, p. 261.
42. Quoted in David Gilmour, *Curzon: Imperial Statesman 1859–1925*, London, John Murray, 2003, p. 516.
43. Gertrude Bell to Hugh Bell, 17 October 1920, Lady Bell, ed., *The Letters of Gertrude Bell: Selected and Edited by Lady Bell, DBE, Volume 2*, New York, Boni and Liveright, 1927, p. 131.
44. Charles Tripp, *A History of Iraq*, Cambridge, Cambridge University Press, 2007, p. 43.
45. Winston Churchill to Aylmer Haldane, 7 February 1921 and Aylmer Haldane to Winston Churchill, 8 February 1921, *WSC Companion*, pp. 1337, 1339.
46. Quoted in Gilbert, *Churchill*, p. 433. Churchill's Cabinet meeting notes, 9 February 1921, *WSC Companion*, p. 1342.
47. Gertrude Bell to Edwin Montagu, 4 January 1920, KP GD40/17/40, ff. 320–6.
48. Gertrude Bell, *Review of the Civil Administration of Mesopotamia*, London, H.M. Stationery Office, 1920, Cmd 1061.
49. Gertrude Bell quoted in Sabine Krayenbühl and Zeva Oelbaum, dirs, *Letters from Baghdad*, Vitagraph Films, 2016. Gertrude Bell to Edwin Montagu, 4 January 1920, KP GD40/17/40, ff. 320–6.
50. Gertrude Bell to Sir Hugh Bell, 2 February 1922, GBA.

Chapter 3 Churchill at the Colonial Office: Towards the Cairo Conference

1. Quoted in Gilbert, *Churchill*, p. 426.
2. See Shereen Ilahi, *Imperial Violence and the Path to Independence: India, Ireland and the Crisis of Empire*, London, I.B. Tauris, 2016.
3. See Faught, *Allenby*, ch. 5. Gilbert, *Churchill*, pp. 425–26, 428.
4. Quoted in Martin Gilbert, *World in Torment: Winston S. Churchill 1917–1922*, London, Minerva, 1990, p. 505.
5. The chief architect of Port Lympne, Sir Herbert Baker, had designed South Africa's Union Buildings in Pretoria as well as Cecil Rhodes's spectacularly refurbished Cape Town house, Groote Schuur. He made his flat at 14 Barton Street available for Lawrence to use after the war.
6. See Damian Collins, *Charmed Life: The Phenomenal World of Philip Sassoon*, London, HarperCollins, 2016. David Stafford, *Oblivion or Glory: 1921 and the Making of Winston Churchill*, New Haven, CT, and London, Yale University Press, 2019, pp. 30–31.
7. See Ronald Hyam, *Elgin and Churchill at the Colonial Office 1905–1908: The Watershed of the Empire- Commonwealth*, London, Macmillan, 1968.
8. Maurice Hankey diary, 8 January 1921, HP 1/5.
9. Thomas had premiered his 'travelogues' – he produced six altogether but only two were used commercially – in New York City during March of 1919. He perfected them in Toronto later that spring and then moved on to the West End in July for what would be a six-month run. Later, Thomas would take his shows further afield to all the major capitals of the British Empire as well as to various cities throughout the United States.

All told it is thought that over 4 million people worldwide came to experience 'the legend of Lawrence of Arabia' by the end of the 1920s. See Ted Glenn, 'Lawrence of Canada', *Canada's History*, vol. 100, no. 6 (December 2020–January 2021), pp. 20–27.

10. *Strand Magazine* (April 1920). Allawi, *Faisal*, p. 180.
11. Quoted in Michael Korda, *Hero: The Life and Legend of Lawrence of Arabia*, New York, HarperCollins, 2010, frontispiece.
12. Wilson, *Lawrence of Arabia*, pp. 620–21.
13. See Faught, *Gordon*, pp. 79–80, and Faught, *Kitchener*, p. 194.
14. T.E. Lawrence to W.S. Blunt, 2 March 1921, *TEL Letters*, p. 196.
15. Quoted in Wilson, *Lawrence of Arabia*, pp. 621, 643. Eddie Marsh to Winston Churchill, 14 February 1921, CHAR 17/15.
16. Sonia Purnell, *Clementine: The Life of Mrs Winston Churchill*, New York, Viking, 2015, p. 138, and Mary Soames, *Churchill: His Life as a Painter*, London, Viking, 1990, p. 23.
17. See David Lough, *No More Champagne: Churchill and His Money*, London, Head of Zeus, 2015, and David Adams Richards, *Lord Beaverbrook*, Toronto, Penguin, 2011.
18. Purnell, *Clementine*, p. 138. Tragically, Marigold died of meningitis that summer.
19. The Great Offices of State are prime minister, chancellor of the Exchequer, foreign secretary and home secretary.
20. A.H.M. Kirk-Greene, 'Sir Ralph Dolignon Furse (1887–1973)' in H.C.G. Matthew and Brian Harrison, eds, *Oxford Dictionary of National Biography*, Oxford, Oxford University Press, 2004.
21. *The Manchester Guardian*, 16 February 1921 and *The Times*, 4 March 1921.
22. Winston S. Churchill, *Great Contemporaries*, London, Thornton Butterworth, 1937, p. 202. Gilmour, *Curzon*, p. 30.
23. Clementine Churchill to Winston Churchill, 9 February 1921, CHAR 1/139/11.
24. See, for example, Peter King, ed., *Lord Curzon: Travels with a Superior Person*, London, Sidgwick & Jackson, 1985.
25. Winston Churchill to Lord Curzon, 8 January 1921, *WSC Companion*, p. 1296.
26. G.H. Bennett, *British Foreign Policy during the Curzon Period, 1919–24*, New York, St Martin's Press, 1995, p. 109; Lord Curzon to Lady Grace Hinds, 14 February 1921, *WSC Companion*, p. 529.
27. Dockter, *Churchill and the Islamic World*, p. 119.
28. Lee, moving over from the Agriculture Ministry, was made first lord of the admiralty on the same day, 13 February, that Churchill became colonial secretary.
29. Quoted in Gilbert, *Churchill*, p. 432. Winston Churchill to Clementine Churchill, n.d., Mary Soames, ed., *Speaking for Themselves: The Personal Letters of Winston and Clementine Churchill*, New York, Doubleday, 1988, p. 224.
30. Lumley & Lumley, solicitors, to Winston Churchill, 7 May 1921, CHAR 1/151/29. Dockter, *Churchill and the Islamic World*, p. 141.
31. Quoted in Shane Leslie, *Mark Sykes: His Life and Letters*, London, Cassell, 1923, p. vii. Quoted in Barr, *A Line in the Sand*, p. 37.
32. Winston Churchill to David Lloyd George, 12 January 1921, CHAR 16/71. Gilmour, *Curzon*, p. 520.
33. *Illustrated Sunday Herald*, 25 January 1919. Quoted in Gilbert, *Churchill*, p. 947.
34. Winston Churchill to David Lloyd George (unsent), 25 January 1921, *WSC Companion*, p. 1324. Winston Churchill to David Lloyd George, 12 January 1921, CHAR 16/71.
35. Winston Churchill to Sir Percy Cox, n.d. [probably mid-February 1921], CHAR 17/18A–B; *Report on Middle East Conference Held in Cairo and Jerusalem, March 12th to 30th, 1921*, CO 935/1, p. 3.
36. Korda, *Hero*, p. 507. Fieldhouse, *Western Imperialism*, pp. 86–87. See also Sir Aylmer Haldane, *The Insurrection in Mesopotamia, 1920*, Edinburgh, William Blackwood & Sons, 1922.
37. Sir Henry Dobbs to Hubert Young, 5 October 1919, YP File 3.

38. Timothy J. Paris, 'British Middle East Policy-Making after the First World War: The Lawrentian and Wilsonian Schools', *The Historical Journal*, vol. 41, (September 1998), pp. 773–93, p. 791.
39. Allawi, *Faisal*, p. 315. Timothy J. Paris, *Britain, the Hashemites and Arab Rule 1920–1925: The Sherifian Solution*, London, Routledge, 2003, p. 2.
40. Winston Churchill to Clementine Churchill, 16 February 1921, *WSC Companion*, p. 1,355.
41. Allawi, *Faisal*, p. 320. Alan H. Brodrick, *Near to Greatness: A Life of the Sixth Earl Winterton*, London, Hutchinson, 1965, p. 19.
42. Evyatar Friesel, 'British Officials on the Situation in Palestine, 1923', *Middle Eastern Studies*, vol. 23, no. 2 (April 1987), pp. 194–210, p. 194.
43. YP2 File 2.
44. Hubert Young, *The Independent Arab*, London, John Murray, 1933. As Lawrence would be called in *St Nicholas* magazine (July 1927).
45. Allawi, *Faisal*, p. 317. Quoted in Korda, *Hero*, p. 510.
46. Winston Churchill to Arthur Hirtzel, 23 January 1921, *WSC Companion*, pp. 1320–21.
47. T.E. Lawrence to E.H. Marsh, 17 January 1921, ibid., p. 1314.
48. Richard Toye, *Churchill's Empire: The World That Made Him and the World He Made*, London, Pan Books, 2011, pp. 42–9. Robert Graves and B.H. Liddell Hart, eds, *T.E. Lawrence to His Biographers*, Garden City, NY, Doubleday, 1963, p. 143.
49. See, for example, Paul Gough, *A Terrible Beauty: British Artists in the First World War*, London, Sansom and Company, 2010. Quoted in Graves and Liddell Hart, eds, *T.E. Lawrence*, p. 143.
50. Hubert Young to W.H. Deedes, 30 December 1920, YP File 3.
51. John Shuckburgh to Edward Marsh, 25 February 1921, CHAR 17/18A–B. Brown, ed., *The Letters of T.E. Lawrence*, p. 256.
52. Quoted in Peter Sluglett, *Britain in Iraq 1914–1932*, New York, Columbia University Press, 2007, p. 63. Allawi, *Faisal*, p. 325.
53. Winston Churchill to Sir Percy Cox, n.d. [probably mid-February 1921], CHAR 17/18A–B; *Report*, CO 935/1, p. 3. Winston Churchill to Sir Percy Cox, n.d. [probably mid-February 1921], CHAR 17/18A–B. T. E. Lawrence to Winston Churchill, n.d. [*c.* 17 February 1921], CO 732/3, f. 402.
54. Martin Gilbert, *Winston S. Churchill, Volume Four: The Stricken World 1917–1922*, London, Heinemann, 1975, p. 540.
55. Ibid.
56. *Report*, CO 935/1, p. 156. Wilson, *Lawrence of Arabia*, pp. 647, 644.

Chapter 4 'Everybody Middle East is here': Ten Days in Cairo, Act I

1. Winston Churchill to Jennie Churchill, 1 March 1921, David Lough, ed., *Darling Winston: Forty Years of Letters Between Winston Churchill and His Mother*, London, Head of Zeus, 2019, p. 560.
2. Churchill's words in a note that he sent to Lloyd George thanking him for his letter of sympathy on the occasion of his mother's death. Ibid., p. 562.
3. Quoted in Purnell, *Clementine*, pp. 140, 432.
4. Winston Churchill to Edmund Allenby, 28 February 1921, CHAR 17/18A–B.
5. *Report*, CO 935/1, p. 4.
6. Quoted in Andrew Humphreys, *Grand Hotels of Egypt in the Golden Age of Travel*, Cairo, American University of Cairo Press, 2015, p. 29; Winston Churchill to Lord Allenby, 28 February 1921, CHAR 17/18A–B.
7. A series of threats issued by the Irish Republican Army against Churchill's life in the aftermath of his appointment as colonial secretary had spurred the assigning of Thompson to be his bodyguard. The two men made for a good match: Thompson

remained in Churchill's service until 1935. He resumed his post after being called out of retirement in 1939 and would serve Churchill until the end of the Second World War. Much has been written about their working relationship, especially by Thompson himself. See, for example, Walter H. Thompson, *Beside the Bulldog: The Intimate Memoirs of Churchill's Bodyguard*, London, Apollo, 2003.

8. *The Sunday Times*, 13 March 1921.
9. Quoted in Gilmour, *Curzon*, p. 524. Winston Churchill to George Curzon, 25 February 1921, *WSC Companion*, p. 1,378, and Edmund Allenby to George Curzon, 21 February 1921, ibid., p. 1369.
10. See Humphreys, *Grand Hotels of Egypt*, pp. 147–57.
11. Rudyard Kipling, *Letters of Travel: 1892–1913*, New York, Doubleday, 1920, p. 67.
12. Winston Churchill to Warren Fisher (Colonial Office), 18 March 1921, CHAR 17/19. Allenby saw that the hotel's location, with the river on one side, made it invulnerable to being surrounded by crowds. Churchill of course had come by his expensive tastes naturally. His mother Jennie's idea of economizing, for instance, was to move into the Ritz Hotel in Piccadilly, which she had done for a time beginning in 1908. Jennie Churchill to Winston Churchill, 5 December 1907, Lough, ed., *Darling Winston*, p. 471.
13. H.C.G. Matthew, *Gladstone 1809–1898*, Oxford, Clarendon Press, 1997, pp. 374–94.
14. See Roger Owen, *Lord Cromer: Victorian Imperialist, Edwardian Proconsul*, Oxford, Oxford University Press, 2004.
15. See Faught, *Allenby*, ch. 6.
16. T.E. Lawrence to Sarah Lawrence, 20 March 1921, *TEL Letters*, p. 196. T.E. Lawrence to Robert Graves [19 February 1921], [T.E. Lawrence], *T.E. Lawrence to His Biographer Robert Graves*, London, Faber & Faber, 1938, p. 10.
17. Gertrude Bell to Florence Bell, 24 February 1921, 12 and 16 March 1921, GBA. Gertrude Bell quoted in Krayenbühl and Oelbaum, dirs, *Letters from Baghdad*.
18. As attributed to the English composer Lord Berners (1883–1950).
19. *The Sunday Times*, 22 August 1920.
20. Edmund Allenby to Catherine Allenby, 24 February, AP 1/12/13 and 12 March 1921, AP 1/12/16.
21. T.E. Lawrence to Sarah Lawrence, 20 March 1921, *TEL Letters*, p. 197.
22. *Report*, CO 935/1, pp. 34–5. Where given names, initials, or appointments are not included none were provided in the written record of the Conference. The complete roster of the delegates who attended the Cairo Conference is listed in the *Report* as follows: British Mission: Churchill; Air-Marshal Sir Hugh Trenchard (chief of the Air Staff); Lt-Gen Sir Walter Congreve (general officer commanding, Egyptian Expeditionary Force); Sir George Barstow (His Majesty's Treasury); Maj-Gen Sir P.P. de B. Radcliffe (director of military operations, War Office); J.B. Crosland (director of finance, War Office); Sir Archibald Sinclair (private secretary to the secretary of state for the colonies); Lt-Col B.H. Waters-Taylor (secretary of the Military Committee); Col T.E. Lawrence (Middle East Department); Maj H.W. Young (Middle East Department); Wg Cdr E.L. Gossage (staff officer to chief of Air Staff); G. Myrrdin-Evans (private secretary to Sir G. Barstow); R.D. Badcock (secretary to the Conference). Mesopotamian Mission: Sir Percy Cox (high commissioner, Mesopotamia); Lt-Gen Sir J.A.L. Haldane (general officer commanding, Mesopotamian Expeditionary Force); Maj-Gen Sir Edmund Ironside (general officer commanding, Force in Persia); Maj-Gen E.H. de V. Atkinson (adviser of works and communications, Mesopotamia); S.H. Slater (financial adviser, Mesopotamia); Miss Gertrude Bell (political secretary, Mesopotamia); Col J.H.K. Stewart (General Staff 'A' Branch, Mesopotamian Expeditionary Force); Col G.R. Frith (General Staff 'Q' Branch, Mesopotamian Expeditionary Force); Wg Cdr Burrett (Mesopotamia); Maj J.I. Eadie (acting adviser to the Ministry of Defence, Mesopotamia). Palestine Mission: Sir Herbert Samuel

(high commissioner, Palestine); Air Vice-Marshal Sir G. Salmond (commanding Middle East Brigade, Royal Air Force); W.H. Deedes (civil secretary, Palestine); Maj the Hon. F.R. Somerset (British representative Trans-Jordania); Capt F.G. Peake (commandant Gendarmerie Trans-Jordania). Somaliland Mission: Sir Geoffrey Archer (governor of Somaliland); Maj Jebb (district commissioner, Berbera). Aden Mission: Maj T.E. Scott (resident and general officer commanding, Aden); Maj Barrett (first assistant). Persian Gulf Mission: Col A.P. Trevor (resident, Persian Gulf). Consultative Members: Sir Arnold Wilson (Anglo-Persian Oil Company); Col K. Cornwallis (Egyptian minister of finance); Lt-Col P.C. Joyce (adviser to minister of defence, Mesopotamia); Maj E.W.C. Noel; Jafar Pasha al-Askari (minister of defence, Mesopotamia); Sassoon Effendi [Eskell] (minister of finance, Mesopotamia).

23. Barr, *A Line in the Sand*, p. 121.
24. CHAR 17/18. *Report*, CO 935/1, p. 4.
25. Between 1915 and 1924 fifty-four such incidents created an atmosphere of acute fear amongst the British community in Cairo, as well as elsewhere in Egypt. AP 2/5/12. See Lanver Mak, *The British in Egypt: Community, Crime and Crises 1882–1922*, London, I.B. Tauris, 2012. See also Donald M. Reid, 'Political Assassination in Egypt, 1910–1954'. *The International Journal of African Historical Studies*, vol. 15, no. 4 (1982), pp. 625–51, pp. 625–6.
26. Gertrude Bell to [Florence Bell], 12 March 1921, GBA.
27. Georgina Howell, *Daughter of the Desert: The Remarkable Life of Gertrude Bell*, London, Macmillan, 2006, p. 120.
28. Gertrude Bell to Hugh Bell, 3 and 10 January 1921; Gertrude Bell to Florence Bell, 24 February 1921; Gertrude Bell to Frank Balfour, 25 March 1921, GBA.
29. Edmund Allenby to Catherine Allenby, 4 June 1920, AP 1/11/15 and 13 March 1921, AP 1/12/17.
30. Gertrude Bell to Frank Balfour, 25 March 1921, GBA.
31. *Report*, CO 935/1, pp. 34–5. CHAR 17/18A–B.
32. Winston Churchill to George Ritchie, 23 February 1921, CHAR 5/24/1.
33. *The Times*, 13 March 1921, and *Daily Herald*, 14 March 1921.
34. Quoted in Jenkins, *Churchill*, p. 359.
35. See William Facey and Najdat Fathi Safwat, eds, *A Soldier's Story: The Memoirs of Jafar Pasha Al-Askari*, Mustafa Tariq Al-Askaripage, trans., London, Arabian Publishing, 2003.
36. Quoted in *Times of Israel* (Jerusalem), 7 August 2016.
37. Gertrude Bell quoted in Krayenbühl and Oelbaum, dirs, *Letters from Baghdad*. Gertrude Bell to Florence Bell, 24 February 1921 and 12 March 1921, GBA.
38. *Report*, CO 935/1, p. 18.
39. See, for example, Catherwood, *Churchill's Folly*, p. 129. See also Meyer and Brysac, *Kingmakers*, pp. 160–3.
40. Gertrude Bell to Hugh Bell, 10 January 1921; Gertrude Bell to Frank Balfour, 25 March 1921, GBA.
41. Philby's exploits earlier as a desert explorer were many and he was duly lauded for them, including having been awarded the Royal Geographical Society (Founder's) Gold Medal in 1920. Always a maverick, however, his later life and career were marred by controversy, a mantle taken up even more demonstrably by his Soviet-defector son, the disgraced MI6 double-agent Kim Philby. A large number of books have been written about the Philby case and the so-called 'Cambridge Five'. For a recent example, passim, see Ben Macintyre, *The Spy and the Traitor: The Greatest Espionage Story of the Cold War*, Toronto, Signal, 2018.
42. *Report*, CO 935/1, p. 39.
43. Gertrude Bell to Florence Bell, 24 February 1921. Gertrude Bell to Frank Balfour, 25 March 1921, GBA.

44. *Report*, CO 935/1, p. 40. See also M.H. Coote diary, 13 March 1921, CP.
45. Allawi, *Faisal*, pp. 327–8.
46. *Report*, CO 935/1, p. 40.
47. Winston Churchill to David Lloyd George, 31 August 1920 (unsent), *WSC Companion*, p. 1,199.
48. Gertrude Bell to Hugh Bell, 2 February 1922, GBA.
49. See Faught, *Allenby*, ch. 6. See also ibid., p. 150.
50. MacMillan, *Paris 1919*, p. 390.
51. T.E. Lawrence to Sarah Lawrence, 20 March 1921, *TEL Letters*, p. 196.
52. Edmund Allenby to Catherine Allenby, 13 March 1921, AP 1/12/17.
53. Gertrude Bell to [Florence Bell], 12 March 1921, GBA.

Chapter 5 Ten Days in Cairo, Act II

1. T.E. Lawrence to Wilfrid Scawen Blunt, 2 March 1921, *TEL Letters*, p. 196.
2. Denis Boak, 'Malraux and T.E. Lawrence', *Modern Language Review*, vol. 61, no. 2 (April 1966), pp. 218–24, p. 220.
3. T.E. Lawrence and Gertrude Bell quoted in Krayenbühl and Oelbaum, dirs, *Letters from Baghdad*.
4. The first was Henry G.G. Cadogan (1859–93). A British Embassy staff member in Tehran at the time of Bell's visit as a young woman, Cadogan died there of pneumonia. The second was Charles 'Dick' Doughty-Wylie (1868–1915). A married British infantry officer of Bell's long and complicated acquaintance, he was killed at Gallipoli.
5. Winston Churchill to Edward Marsh, 13 March 1921, CHAR 17/18.
6. *Report*, CO 935/1, pp. 41–4.
7. Winston Churchill to David Lloyd George, 18 March 1921, CHAR 17/18A–B.
8. *Report*, CO 935/1, p. 46.
9. See Facey and Fathi Safwat, eds, *A Soldier's Story*, 2003.
10. Gertrude Bell to Florence Bell, 24 February 1921, GBA.
11. See Saad Eskander, 'Britain's Policy in Southern Kurdistan: The Formation and Termination of the First Kurdish Government, 1918–1919', *British Journal of Middle Eastern Studies*, vol. 27, no. 2, pp. 139–63.
12. *Report*, CO 935/1, pp. 35, 59.
13. See Peter Hopkirk, *On Secret Service East of Constantinople: The Great Game and the Great War*, London, John Murray, 1994. See also E.M. Noel, *Diary of Major E.M. Noel, on Special Duty in Kurdistan from June 14th to September 21st, 1919*, Basra, Office of the Civil Commissioner, 1920. As well, and more generally, see Priya Satia, *Spies in Arabia: The Great War and the Cultural Foundations of Britain's Covert Empire in the Middle East*, New York, Oxford University Press, 2008.
14. *Report*, CO 935/1, pp. 60–61.
15. Quoted in Janet Wallach, *Desert Queen: The Extraordinary Life of Gertrude Bell*, London, Weidenfeld & Nicolson, 1996, pp. 299, 59, 61.
16. Gertrude Bell to Hugh Bell, 10 January 1921. GBA.
17. *Report*, CO 935/1, pp. 60–61.
18. See Robert Olson, *The Emergence of Kurdish Nationalism and the Sheikh Said Rebellion, 1880–1925*, Austin, TX, University of Texas Press, 1989.
19. Howell, *Daughter of the Desert*, pp. 43–4.
20. Edmund Allenby to Catherine Allenby, 18 March 1921, AP 1/12/18. Kennington's original portrait of Allenby hung in Lawrence's Dorset cottage, Cloud's Hill, before being donated by his family to the National Portrait Gallery in London after his death. The bust of Allenby, sculpted by Abraham Melnikov (1892–1960), would be placed high atop a pedestal that stood at the centre of an Ottoman-built public garden in Beersheba that was renamed Allenby Park in honour of the success of the Palestine

Campaign. Damaged in the 1930s, a new bust was commissioned later, which continues to adorn the park today.
21. John Bowle, *Viscount Samuel: A Biography*, London, Victor Gollancz, 1957.
22. *Report*, CO 935/1, p. 97.
23. Allawi, *Faisal*, p. 330.
24. *Report*, CO 935/1, pp. 98–100.
25. Gertrude Bell to unknown [probably Florence Bell], 12 March 1921, GBA.
26. *Report*, CO 935/1, pp. 103–4.
27. Just prior to departing London for Cairo Churchill had requested that Allenby supply secretarial staff for the Conference, to which Allenby had replied that he could not do so: 'in view of developments here [a reference to the unsettled political atmosphere in Egypt] my staff is at present fully occupied'. In the end however, Allenby did release a small number of the Residency secretariat to assist at the Conference. Still, he wondered, 'could not assistance be furnished by Jerusalem?' Edmund Allenby to Winston Churchill, 1 March 1921, CHAR 17/18.
28. *Report*, CO 935/1, pp. 101–3.
29. Winston Churchill to David Lloyd George, 18 March 1921, CHAR 17/18A–B.
30. Winston Churchill to David Lloyd George, 18 March 1921, *WSC Companion*, pp. 1398–99.
31. *Report*, CO 935/1, pp. 51–2, 62–3, 74–5.
32. Much has been written on the topic. See, for example, David Killingray, '"A Swift Agent of Government": Air Power in British Colonial Africa, 1916–1939', *Journal of African History*, vol. 25, no. 4 (1984), pp. 429–44, and Priya Satia, 'The Defence of Inhumanity: Air Control and the British Idea of Arabia', *American Historical Review*, vol. 11, no. 1 (2006), pp. 26–32.
33. Robert Lacey, *The Kingdom: Arabia and the House of Saud*, New York, Harcourt Brace Jovanovich, 1982. See also David Holden and Richard Johns, *The House of Saud*, London, Sidgwick & Jackson, 1976.
34. *Report*, CO 935/1, pp. 188–9.
35. 'I have postponed my return', Churchill wrote to Edward Marsh in London just after departing Cairo, 'for one week to enable me to deal adequately with Palestine business'. Winston Churchill to Edward Marsh, 24 March 1921, CHAR 17/18A–B. Postponement was not correct exactly because, depending on how things went at Cairo, Churchill had planned to proceed to Jerusalem for a meeting with Abdullah about Transjordan's future.
36. *Report*, CO 935/1, pp. 5, 80.
37. Ibid., p. 194.
38. T.E. Lawrence to Sarah Lawrence, 20 March 1921, *TEL Letters*, p. 197.
39. Gertrude Bell to unknown [probably Florence Bell], 12 March 1921, GBA.
40. Gertrude Bell to Frank Balfour, 25 March 1921, GBA.
41. Gertrude Bell to Florence Bell, 24 February 1921, GBA.
42. Darwin, *Britain, Egypt and the Middle East*, p. 112.
43. Edmund Allenby to Catherine Allenby, 24 March 1921, AP 1/12/19. Even today, the completely re-built Semiramis (Intercontinental) Hotel remains a focal point for Cairo's cadres of regular anti-government protesters. In 2013, for example, it was reported widely that a 'group of 40 attackers' had 'stormed' the Semiramis. No casualties resulted from the incident but hotel guests were moved temporarily into a secure conference room while protestors entered the lobby. Afterwards, the lobby was left strewn with debris and broken glass. See Caitlin Dewey, 'Cairo Hotel Tweets for Help amid Clashes', *Washington Post*, 29 January 2013.
44. Purnell, *Clementine*, p. 140.
45. Quoted in Wallach, *Desert Queen*, p. 300.
46. Gilbert, *Churchill*, p. 434.

47. T.E. Lawrence to Winston Churchill, 18 November 1922, CHAR 1/157/79. Churchill had just lost his seat in the general election of three days earlier, which had seen the Conservatives under Andrew Bonar Law come to power. Lawrence had written to Churchill to offer his sympathies and to bolster his spirits by telling him that 'in guts and power and speech you can roll over anyone bar Lloyd George'. Contemplating the camel-riding scene today through the Orientalist filter provided later by the work of Edward Said, one might be tempted to see it merely as a demonstration of all that was wrong with the recent wartime encounter between the West and the Arab world: two powerful Englishmen appropriating a signature means of transport to reinforce their cultural bona fides as architects of a new and modern Middle East. Arguably, however, the scene is better understood as suggestive of Lawrence's abiding devotion to the Arabs, and of his desire to share with Churchill a level of respect and understanding for them, and of their aspirations for nation-building. See Edward W. Said, *Orientalism*, New York, Pantheon Books, 1978, and idem, *Culture and Imperialism*, New York, Knopf, 1993.
48. Humphreys, *Grand Hotels of Egypt*, p. 153.
49. No detailed account of the dinner exists although the author Mary Doria Russell offers a persuasive and evocative fictional one in her novel set at the time of the Cairo Conference, *Dreamers of the Day*, New York, Ballantine Books, 2008, pp. 81–92.
50. Humphreys, *Grand Hotels of Egypt*, p. 153. Faught, *Allenby*, ch. 7. Edmund Allenby to Catherine Allenby, 24 March 1921, AP 1/12/19.
51. Hubert Young to W.H. Deedes, 30 December 1920, YP File 3.
52. Quoted in Gilbert, *Winston S. Churchill*, p. 638.
53. T.E. Lawrence to Sarah Lawrence, 20 March 1921, *TEL Letters*, p. 197.
54. Gertrude Bell to Frank Balfour, 25 March 1921, GBA.
55. Howell, *Daughter of the Desert*, p. 399.

Chapter 6 Not Quite Finished at Cairo: On to Jerusalem

1. Quoted in Wilson, *Lawrence of Arabia*, p. 648.
2. T.E. Lawrence to Sarah Lawrence, 20 March 1921, *TEL Letters*, p. 197.
3. See Dotan Halevy, 'Toward a Palestinian History of Ruins: Interwar Gaza', *Journal of Palestine Studies*, vol. 48, no. 1 (autumn 2018), pp. 53–72.
4. Edmund Allenby to Catherine Allenby, 24 March 1921, AP 1/12/19. M.H. Coote diary, 24 March 1921, CP.
5. Edmund Allenby to Rennie MacInnes, n.d. [*c.* 25 November 1917]; n.d., [*c.* 29 December 1917]; 20 January 1918; 13 February 1918, ML.
6. Seth J. Frantzman, Benjamin W. Glueckstadt and Ruth Kark, 'The Anglican Church in Palestine and Israel: Colonialism, Arabization and Land Ownership', *Middle Eastern Studies*, vol. 47, no. 1 (January 2011), pp. 101–26. On the question of Christianity and Zionism more generally, see Lewis, *The Origins of Christian Zionism*. See also *New York Times*, 6 November 1922.
7. See Faught, *Allenby*, pp. 135–7.
8. Quoted in Gilbert, *Winston S. Churchill*, p. 559.
9. Lawrence, *Seven Pillars*, pp. 56–7.
10. Quoted in Korda, *Hero*, p. 353.
11. For a detailed treatment of this question see Isaiah Friedman, 'How Trans-Jordan Was Severed from the Territory of the Jewish National Home', *Journal of Israeli History*, vol. 27, no. 1 (2008), pp. 65–85.
12. See, for example, A.P. Thornton, *The Habit of Authority: Paternalism in British History*, London, Allen & Unwin, 1966. By the early part of the twentieth century Indirect Rule as imperial policy was meant to tutor developing states in the ways of local government in order to lessen the costs of administration borne by the British Treasury.

13. *Report*, CO 935/1, pp. 97–103.
14. Chaim Weizmann to David Lloyd George, 29 December 1919, KP GD40/17/40, f. 317.
15. Wilson, *Lawrence of Arabia*, p. 649.
16. Lawrence, *Seven Pillars*, pp. 66–7.
17. Philip Graves, ed., *Memoirs of King Abdullah of Transjordan*, London, Jonathan Cape, 1950, p. 170.
18. Mary C. Wilson, *King Abdullah, Britain and the Making of Jordan*, Cambridge, Cambridge University Press, 1987, p. 3.
19. T.E. Lawrence to Sarah Lawrence, 12 April [1921], *TEL Letters*, p. 197.
20. Wilson, *King Abdullah*, pp. 52–3.
21. FO 371/6343, 22 March 1921.
22. Wilson, *King Abdullah*, pp. 44, 48.
23. Winston Churchill to David Lloyd George, 23 March 1921, CHAR 17/18A–B.
24. Wilson, *King Abdullah*, p. 53.
25. Faulkner, *Lawrence of Arabia's War*, p. 165.
26. Allawi, *Faisal*, p. 331.
27. Lawrence, *Seven Pillars*, p. 68.
28. Robert Rhodes James, ed., *Winston S. Churchill: His Complete Speeches 1897–1963, Volume 3: 1914–1922*, New York, R.R. Bowker and Co., 1974, p. 3095.
29. Gilbert, *Winston S. Churchill*, p. 560.
30. Alec Seath Kirkbride, *A Crackle of Thorns: Experiences in the Middle East*, London, John Murray, 1956, pp. 26–7.
31. Wilson, *King Abdullah*, p. 53.
32. Efraim Karsh and Inari Karsh, *Empires of the Sand: The Struggle for Mastery in the Middle East, 1789–1923*, Cambridge, MA, Harvard University Press, 2001, p. 322.
33. Wilson, *King Abdullah*, p. 53.
34. Gilbert, *Winston S. Churchill*, p. 561.
35. *WSC Companion*, pp. 1419–21.
36. JP 1/0/9.
37. Faisal to Felix Frankfurter, KP GD40/17/40, f. 347, 1 March 1919.
38. Jehuda Reinharz, *Chaim Weizmann: The Making of a Statesman*, vol. 2, Oxford, Oxford University Press, 1993, p. 256.
39. A view maintained throughout the twentieth century by inheritors of the tradition such as the explorer-photographer-writer, Wilfred Thesiger (1910–2003). See, for example, Thesiger's book *Arabian Sands*, London, Longmans, 1959. This tradition would later be critiqued influentially by the Palestinian-born American Edward Said in *Orientalism* (1978).
40. *WSC Companion*, p. 1422. Richard Meinertzhagen, *Middle East Diary*, London, Cresset Press, 1959, pp. 99–100.
41. Quoted in Gilbert, *Churchill*, p. 435.
42. Winston Churchill to Eddie Marsh, 24 March 1921, CHAR 17/18A–B.
43. Lawrence, *Seven Pillars*, p. 283, note. *WSC Companion*, p. 1420.
44. See Richard W. Cogley, 'The Fall of the Ottoman Empire and the Restoration of Israel in the "Judeo-Centric" Strand of Puritan Millenarianism', *Church History*, vol. 72, no. 2 (June 2003), pp. 304–32.
45. Lawrence, *Seven Pillars*, p. 283, note.
46. Walter H. Thompson, *Assignment Churchill*, New York, Farrar, Straus and Young, 1955, p. 30.
47. Quoted in Wilson, *Lawrence of Arabia*, p. 649. T.E. Lawrence to Sarah Lawrence, 12 April [1921], *TEL Letters*, p. 197.
48. Quoted in Wilson, *Lawrence of Arabia*, p. 649.
49. Quoted in Fromkin, *A Peace to End All Peace*, p. 510.

50. T.E. Lawrence to Sarah Lawrence, 12 April [1921], *TEL Letters*, p. 197.
51. See Malcolm Brown, ed., *Secret Despatches from Arabia and Other Writings by T.E. Lawrence*, London, Bellew Publishing, 1991.
52. All quotes from Allawi, *Faisal*, p. 333.
53. T.E. Lawrence to Sarah Lawrence, 12 April [1921], *TEL Letters*, p. 198.
54. Edmund Allenby to Catherine Allenby, 20 April 1921, AP 1/12/24.
55. Lawrence, *Seven Pillars*, p. 659. T.E. Lawrence to Sarah Lawrence, 12 April [1921], *TEL Letters*, p. 198.
56. Quoted in Wilson, *Lawrence of Arabia*, p. 651.
57. T.E. Lawrence to Robert Graves, 21 May 1921, Lawrence, *T.E. Lawrence to His Biographer*, pp. 15, 80, 112, 117. See also Robert Graves, *Lawrence and the Arabs*, London, Jonathan Cape, 1927. Allawi, *Faisal*, p. 336.

Chapter 7 Cairo in Action: Implementing the Sherifian Solution

1. Gilbert, *Churchill*, pp. 437–8.
2. Undated and unsigned document, 'Miscellaneous Collection', GBA.
3. Gertrude Bell and Dorothy Van Ess quoted in Krayenbühl and Oelbaum, dirs, *Letters from Baghdad*.
4. Fieldhouse, *Western Imperialism*, p. 91.
5. Percy Cox to Gertrude Bell, 3 July 1921, Bell, ed., *The Letters of Gertrude Bell, Volume 1*, p. 428.
6. See H.St J. B. Philby, *Arabian Days*, London, Robert Hale, 1948.
7. Gertrude Bell to Hugh Bell, 2 May 1921, GBA. Bell, *Review*, p, 61.
8. Sir Gilbert Clayton quoted in Krayenbühl and Oelbaum, dirs, *Letters from Baghdad*. See also Timothy J. Paris, *In Defence of Britain's Middle Eastern Empire: A Life of Sir Gilbert Clayton*, Brighton, Sussex Academic Press, 2015.
9. Gertrude Bell to Edwin Montagu, 4 January 1920, KP GD40/17/40, f. 326.
10. For a recent example, see Meyer and Brysac, *Kingmakers*, pp. 251–2.
11. Gertrude Bell to Hugh Bell, 2 May 1921, GBA. Gertrude Bell quoted in Krayenbühl and Oelbaum, dirs, *Letters from Baghdad*.
12. Fieldhouse, *Western Imperialism*, p. 96. Indeed, Bell was of the opinion that US oil interests had contributed funds secretly to the leaders of the Iraqi uprising against British rule. Krayenbühl and Oelbaum, dirs, *Letters from Baghdad*.
13. Howell, *Daughter of the Desert*, p. 404.
14. Quoted in Allawi, *Faisal*, p. 364.
15. Townsend, *Proconsul to the Middle East*, 170–1. See also Philip Graves, *The Life of Sir Percy Cox*, London, Hutchinson, 1941.
16. Chaim Weizmann to the Executive of the Zionist Organisation, 25 March 1920, KP GD40/17/40, f. 353.
17. Gertrude Bell to Hugh Bell, 29 March, 3, 17, 25 April, 30 June 1921, GBA. Gertrude Bell quoted in Krayenbühl and Oelbaum, dirs, *Letters from Baghdad*.
18. For two such examples see Catherwood, *Churchill's Folly*, and James Barr, *A Line in the Sand*.
19. Gertrude Bell to Hugh Bell, 17 April 1921, GBA; Gertrude Bell to Florence Bell, 8 May 1921, GBA.
20. Howell, *Daughter of the Desert*, ch. 15, and Korda, *Hero*, p. 517. Also, Gertrude Bell to Hugh Bell, 23 June 1921, GBA.
21. Gertrude Bell to Hugh Bell, 19 June 1921, GBA. Bell's high-achieving Oxford experience had made her intolerant of un- and under-educated Western women. As her missionary friend in Baghdad, Dorothy Van Ess, put it when describing why she and Bell had got along so well: 'I do have a university degree, and I do speak Arabic'. Bell's 'arrogant side', as Van Ess commented also, may not have been her only side; neverthe-

less, it was the only one that 'many people saw'. Others who knew Bell spoke too about her acerbic manner. Sergeant Frank Stafford, for example, an Orderly Room staff member in Baghdad, remarked that Bell was 'snooty ... especially with other women, with whom she could be downright rude'. Dorothy Van Ess and Frank Stafford quoted in Krayenbühl and Oelbaum, dirs, *Letters from Baghdad*.

22. T.E. Lawrence to Emily Rieder, 7 July 1921, and to Wilfrid Scawen Blunt, 7 July 1921, *TEL Letters*, pp. 198–9.
23. The content (including Lawrence's quotes) for this narrative of events at Jeddah is drawn mainly from Wilson, *Lawrence of Arabia*, pp. 656–63.
24. Gertrude Bell to Hugh Bell, 21 and 30 June 1921, GBA.
25. Allawi, *Faisal*, pp. 347–9, 375, 377–8. The plebiscite to measure public opinion over Faisal's prospective enthronement had been preceded in 1918–19 by a similar attempt at national engagement to determine the nature of Iraq's government in the aftermath of the fall of the Ottomans. One of the questions asked then was whether Iraqis desired an Arab to be at the head of their new government. As unclear and imperfect as the results of this plebiscite would be, it is suggestive of the desire the British had to move the country along the road to indigenous leadership, self-government and independence.
26. Gertrude Bell to Hugh Bell, 7 July 1921, GBA.
27. Allawi, *Faisal*, pp. 376, 378. Winston Churchill to Percy Cox, 9 August 1921, CO 730/3/38478.
28. Gertrude Bell to Hugh Bell, 16 July and 6, 21, 28 August 1921, GBA.
29. See Faught, *Allenby*, chs 6–7. Allawi, *Faisal*, p. 385.
30. C.P. Stacey, *Canada and the Age of Conflict, Volume 2: 1921–1948, The Mackenzie King Era*, Toronto, University of Toronto Press, 1981, pp. 17–27.
31. See, passim, N. Masalha, 'Faisal's Pan-Arabism, 1921–33', *Middle Eastern Studies*, vol. 27, no. 4 (October 1991), pp. 679–93.
32. Gertrude Bell to Hugh Bell, 21 August 1921, GBA.
33. See, for example, Fieldhouse, *Western Imperialism*, p. 91.
34. Quoted in Allawi, *Faisal*, pp. 391, 474–6, 517, 520–1.
35. Winston Churchill to Percy Cox, 27 August 1922, CO 730/24/43045.
36. Quoted in Howell, *Daughter of the Desert*, p. 425. Gertrude Bell quoted in Krayenbühl and Oelbaum, dirs, *Letters from Baghdad*. Gertrude Bell to Hugh Bell, 4 June 1922, GBA.
37. See Myriam Yakoubi, 'Gertrude Bell's Perception of Faisal I of Iraq and the Anglo-Arab Romance', in Paul Collins and Charles Tripp, eds, *Gertrude Bell and Iraq: A Life and Legacy*, Oxford, Oxford University Press, 2017, pp. 187–213.
38. See Gerald de Gaury, *Three Kings in Baghdad: The Tragedy of Iraq's Monarchy*, London, I.B. Tauris, 2008.
39. Gertrude Bell to Hugh Bell, 6 August 1921, GBA. Gertrude Bell quoted in Krayenbühl and Oelbaum, dirs, *Letters from Baghdad*.
40. See Christopher Hitchens, 'The Woman Who Made Iraq', *The Atlantic* (June 2007). Dorothy Van Ess quoted in Krayenbühl and Oelbaum, dirs, *Letters from Baghdad*.
41. T.E. Lawrence to Hugh Trenchard, n.d. [January 1922], Brown, ed., *The Letters of T.E. Lawrence*, p, 193. T.E. Lawrence to R.R. Graves, 12 November 1922, [Lawrence], *T.E. Lawrence to His Biographer*, p. 23.
42. Winston Churchill to T.E. Lawrence, 16 May 1927, LL MS Eng. D. 3341. T.E. Lawrence to Winston Churchill, 18 November 1922, *TEL Letters*, p. 224.
43. See John Tosh, *Manliness and Masculinities in Nineteenth-Century Britain: Essays in Gender, Family and Empire*, Harlow, Pearson Longman, 2005. See also John E. Mack, *A Prince of Our Disorder: The Life of T.E. Lawrence*, Cambridge, MA, Harvard University Press, 1998.
44. Winston Churchill to T.E. Lawrence, 17 July 1922, LL MS Eng. D. 3341, f. 254.

45. Sir Herbert Samuel, 3 April 1926, British Library Sound Archive, 2004.
46. Winston Churchill to David Lloyd George, 1 September 1922, CHAR 17/27/31–2. Quoted in Gilbert, *Churchill*, p. 437.
47. Michael J. Cohen, *Churchill and the Jews, 1900–1948*, London, Routledge, 2003, p. 119.
48. Winston Churchill to John Shuckburgh, 15 June 1921, *WSC Companion*, p. 1508.
49. See Toye, *Churchill's Empire*, p. 149.
50. Chaim Weizmann to the Executive of the Zionist Organisation, 25 March 1920, KP GD40/17/40, f. 353.
51. Joseph B. Schechtman, *Rebel and Statesman: The Vladimir Jabotinsky Story*, New York, Thomas Yoseloff, 1956, pp. 279–82.
52. Winston Churchill to John Shuckburgh, 15 June 1921, *WSC Companion*, p. 1560.
53. *Palestine Correspondence with the Palestine Arab Delegation and the Zionist Organisation*, London, H.M. Stationery Office, 1922.
54. Fieldhouse, *Western Imperialism*, pp. 155–6. See also John McTague, *British Policy in Palestine, 1917–22*, Lanham, MD, University Press of America, 1983, p. 286.
55. See Sahar Huneidi, 'Was Balfour Policy Reversible? The Colonial Office and Palestine, 1921–23'. *Journal of Palestine Studies*, vol. 27, no. 2 (1998), pp. 23–41.
56. Quoted in Gilbert, *Churchill*, p. 438. Wilson, *King Abdullah*, p. 73–4.
57. Catherwood, *Churchill's Folly*. See also Toby Dodge, *Inventing Iraq: The Failure of Nation Building and a History Denied*, London, Hurst & Co., 2003.
58. Winston Churchill to David Lloyd George, 1 September 1922, CHAR 17/27/29, 32.

Conclusion: The Cairo Conference in Historical Retrospect

1. See Albert Hourani, *A History of the Arab Peoples*, Cambridge, MA, Harvard University Press, 1991, pp. 340–44.
2. David B. Abernethy, *The Dynamics of Global Dominance: European Overseas Empires, 1415–1980*, New Haven, CT, and London, Yale University Press, 2000, p. 406.
3. See, for example, Martin Meredith, *The State of Africa: A History of Fifty Years of Independence*, London, Free Press, 2005, or John Iliffe, *The African Poor: A History*, Cambridge, Cambridge University Press, 2009.
4. Gertrude Bell to Florence Bell, 28 August 1921, GBA.
5. Dexter Filkins, 'Among the Ghosts: Heroes and Grand Plans', *New York Times*, 9 July 2006.
6. T.E. Lawrence quoted in Krayenbühl and Oelbaum, dirs, *Letters from Baghdad*. Elie Kedourie, *The Chatham House Version and Other Middle-Eastern Studies*, Chicago, Ivan R. Dee, 2004, p. 239.
7. Gertrude Bell to Edwin Montagu, 4 January 1920, KP GD40/17/40, ff. 320–26.
8. See Allawi, *Faisal*, ch. 21. See also Fieldhouse, *Western Imperialism*, pp. 100–2.
9. Faisal quoted in Hanna Batatu, *The Old Social Classes and the Revolutionary Movements of Iraq: A Study of Iraq's Old Landed and Commercial Classes and of its Communists, Ba'thists, and Free Officers*, Princeton, NJ, Princeton University Press, 1978, p. 25.
10. Gertrude Bell to Edwin Montagu, 4 January 1920, KP GD40/17/40, ff. 320–26.
11. S.H. Longrigg, *Iraq 1900–1950: A Political, Social and Economic History*, Oxford, Oxford University Press, 1956, p. 224.
12. Gertrude Bell to Edwin Montagu, 4 January 1920, KP GD40/17/40, ff. 320–26.
13. Catherwood, *Churchill's Folly*. The term is used also by Scott Anderson in his book, *Lawrence in Arabia*. Quoted in C.E. Callwell, *Field Marshal Sir Henry Wilson: His Life and Diaries, Vol. II*, London, Cassell, 1927, p. 310.
14. Robert Rhodes James, ed., *Winston S. Churchill: His Complete Speeches 1897–1963, Volume 6: 1935–1942*, New York, R.R. Bowker & Co., 1974, p. 5715.
15. Abdullah I; Talal (who would rule briefly before abdicating); Hussein (Talal's son); and Abdullah II.

NOTES to pp. 207–215

16. Lawrence, *Seven Pillars*, p. 68.
17. See Eugene Rogan, *Frontiers of the State in the Late Ottoman Empire: Transjordan, 1851–1920*, Cambridge, Cambridge University Press, 1999.
18. There is much historiography examining these years of state consolidation in Jordan's history. See especially, amongst a large number of works, Wilson, *King Abdullah*; Wm Roger Louis, *The British Empire in the Middle East 1945–51: Arab Nationalism, the United States, and Postwar Imperialism*, Oxford, Clarendon Press, 1984; Philip Robins, *A History of Jordan*, 2nd edn, Cambridge, Cambridge University Press, 2019; and Paris, *Britain, the Hashemites and Arab Rule*.
19. Wilson, *Lawrence of Arabia*, p. 672. Fieldhouse, *Western Imperialism*, pp. 224, 227, 244, 530.
20. See Pedersen, *The Guardians*.
21. See Darwin, *Britain, Egypt and the Middle East*.
22. Quoted in Doreen Ingrams, ed., *Palestine Papers 1917–1923: Seeds of Conflict*, London, John Murray, 1972, p. 96.
23. In a telegram to David Lloyd George sent in May of 1920, Allenby had told the prime minister that the appointment of the Jewish Sir Herbert Samuel as high commissioner of Palestine would be 'highly dangerous', and that altogether both Muslim and Christian objections to such an appointment would make 'Government of any kind very difficult'. Allenby to Lloyd George, 6 May 1920, LGP LG/F/12/3/32(b).
24. Storrs, *The Memoirs*, 1937, p. 385. See also Roberto Mazza, *Jerusalem: From the Ottomans to the British*, London, I.B. Tauris, 2013.
25. For example, Mangold, *What the British Did*.
26. Gertrude Bell to Hugh Bell, 26 June 1921, GBA.
27. David Cannadine, *Ornamentalism: How the British Saw Their Empire*, Oxford, Oxford University Press, 2001, p. 73.
28. Gertrude Bell to Frank Balfour, 25 March 1921, GBA. See also Collins and Tripp, eds, *Gertrude Bell and Iraq*.

BIBLIOGRAPHY

ARCHIVAL SOURCES

Allenby Papers, Liddell Hart Centre for Military Archives, King's College London (AP)

Gertrude Bell Archive, Newcastle University (online) (GBA)

Cabinet Papers, The National Archives, Kew, London

Sir Winston Churchill Papers, Churchill Archives Centre, Cambridge (available online) (CHAR)

Colonial Office Records, The National Archives, Kew, London (CO)

Captain Maxwell Henry Coote Papers, Liddell Hart Centre for Military Archives, King's College London (CP)

Foreign Office Records, The National Archives, Kew, London (FO)

Sir Maurice Hankey Papers, Churchill Archives Centre, Cambridge (HP)

Lieutenant-Colonel Pierce Charles Joyce Papers, Liddell Hart Centre for Military Archives, King's College London (JP)

Kitchener Papers, The National Archives, Kew, London

T.E. Lawrence Letters, Bodleian Library, Oxford (LL)

David Lloyd George Papers, Parliamentary Archives, London (LGP)

Bishop Rennie MacInnes Letters, Middle East Centre Archive, St Antony's College, Oxford (ML)

Philip Kerr Papers, National Records of Scotland, Edinburgh (KP)

General Sir William Robertson Papers, Liddell Hart Centre for Military Archives, King's College London (RP)

Sir Henry Wilson Papers, Imperial War Museum, London (WP)

Sir Hubert Young Papers, Middle East Centre Archive, St Antony's College, Oxford (YP)

Sir Hubert Young Papers, Liddell Hart Centre for Military Archives, King's College London (YP2)

PRINTED PRIMARY SOURCES

Bell, Gertrude. *Review of the Civil Administration of Mesopotamia*, London, H.M. Stationery Office, 1920, Cmd 1061.

Bell, Lady, ed. *The Letters of Gertrude Bell, Volume 1*, London, Ernest Benn, 1927.

— *The Letters of Gertrude Bell: Selected and Edited by Lady Bell, DBE, Volume 2*, New York, Boni and Liveright, 1927.

Brown, Malcolm, ed. *The Letters of T.E. Lawrence*, London, J.M. Dent, 1988.

— *Secret Despatches from Arabia and Other Writings by T.E. Lawrence*, London, Bellew Publishing, 1991.

— *Lawrence of Arabia: The Selected Letters*, London, Little Books, 2005.

Churchill, Randolph, ed. *Winston S. Churchill: Companion Volume I, Part 2 – 1896–1900*, London, Heinemann, 1967.

Facey, William and Najdat Fathi Safwat, eds. *A Soldier's Story: The Memoirs of Jafar Pasha Al-Askari*, trans. Mustafa Tariq al-Askari, London, Arabian Publishing, 2003.

Garnett, David, ed. *The Letters of T.E. Lawrence*, London, Jonathan Cape, 1938.

Gilbert, Martin, ed. *Winston S. Churchill: Companion Volume IV, Part 2 – July 1919–March 1921*, London, Heinemann, 1975.

Graves, Philip, ed. *Memoirs of King Abdullah of Transjordan*, London, Jonathan Cape, 1950.

Graves, Robert and B.H. Liddell Hart, eds. *T.E. Lawrence to His Biographers*, Garden City, NY, Doubleday, 1963.

Haldane, Sir James Aylmer Lowthrop. *How We Escaped from Pretoria*, Edinburgh, William Blackwood & Sons, 1900.

Hughes, Matthew, ed. *Allenby in Palestine: The Middle East Correspondence of Field Marshal Viscount Allenby June 1917–October 1919*, Stroud, Sutton, 2004.

Ingrams, Doreen, ed. *Palestine Papers 1917–1922: Seeds of Conflict*, London, John Murray, 1972.

Kipling, Rudyard. *Letters of Travel: 1892–1913*, New York, Doubleday, 1920.

Lawrence, M.R. ed. *The Home Letters of T.E. Lawrence and His Brothers*, Oxford, Basil Blackwell, 1954.

Lawrence, T.E. *T.E. Lawrence to His Biographer Robert Graves*, London, Faber & Faber, 1938.

Leslie, Shane. *Mark Sykes: His Life and Letters*, London, Cassell, 1923.

Lloyd George, David. *War Memoirs*, vol. 1, London, Odhams Press, 1938.

Lough, David, ed. *Darling Winston: Forty Years of Letters Between Winston Churchill and His Mother*, London, Head of Zeus, 2019.

Matthew, H.C.G. and Brian Harrison, eds. *Oxford Dictionary of National Biography*, Oxford, Oxford University Press, 2004.

Meinertzhagen, Richard. *Middle East Diary, 1917–1956*, London, Cresset, 1959.

Miller, D. Hunter. *My Diaries of the Conference of Paris*, vol. 15, New York, Appeal, 1924.

Noel, E.M. *Diary of Major E.M. Noel, on Special Duty in Kurdistan from June 14th to September 21st, 1919*, Basra, Office of the Civil Commissioner, 1920.

O'Brien, Rosemary, ed. *Gertrude Bell: The Arabian Diaries, 1913–1914*, Syracuse, NY, Syracuse University Press, 2000.

Palestine Correspondence with the Palestine Arab Delegation and the Zionist Organisation, London, H.M. Stationery Office, 1922.

Rhodes James, Robert, ed. *Winston S. Churchill: His Complete Speeches 1897–1963, Volume 3: 1914–1922; Volume 6: 1935–1942*, New York, R.R. Bowker and Co., 1974.

Soames, Mary, ed. *Speaking for Themselves: The Personal Letters of Winston and Clementine Churchill*, New York, Doubleday, 1988.

Storrs, Ronald. *The Memoirs of Sir Ronald Storrs*, New York, G.P. Putnam's Sons, 1937.

Thompson, Walter H. *Beside the Bulldog: The Intimate Memoirs of Churchill's Bodyguard*, London, Apollo, 2003.

Wilson, Arnold T. *Mesopotamia, 1917–1920: A Clash of Loyalties, a Personal and Historical Record*, Oxford, Oxford University Press, 1931.

SECONDARY SOURCES

Books

Abernethy, David B. *The Dynamics of Global Dominance: Overseas Empires, 1415–1980*, New Haven, CT, and London, Yale University Press, 2000.

Aldous, Richard. *The Lion and the Unicorn: Gladstone vs Disraeli*, London, Hutchinson, 2006.

Allawi, Ali A. *Faisal I of Iraq*, New Haven, CT, and London, Yale University Press, 2014.

Anderson, Scott. *Lawrence in Arabia: War, Deceit, Imperial Folly and the Making of the Modern Middle East*, New York, Doubleday, 2013.

Barnett, Corelli. *The Collapse of British Power*, Stroud, Sutton, 1997.

Barr, James. *A Line in the Sand: Britain, France and the Struggle That Shaped the Middle East*, London, Simon & Schuster, 2012.

— *Lords of the Desert: Britain's Struggle with America to Dominate the Middle East*, London, Simon & Schuster, 2018.

Batatu, Hanna. *The Old Social Classes and the Revolutionary Movements of Iraq: A Study of Iraq's Old Landed and Commercial Classes and of Its Communists, Ba'thists, and Free Officers*, Princeton, NJ, Princeton University Press, 1978.

Bennett, G.H. *British Foreign Policy during the Curzon Period, 1919–24*, New York, St Martin's Press, 1995.

Berdine, Michael D. *Redrawing the Middle East: Sir Mark Sykes, Imperialism and the Sykes–Picot Agreement*, London, I.B. Tauris, 2018.

Bowle, John. *Viscount Samuel: A Biography*, London, Victor Gollancz, 1957.

Brodrick, Alan H. *Near to Greatness: A Life of the Sixth Earl Winterton*, London, Hutchinson, 1965.

Brown, Judith M. and Wm Roger Louis, eds. *The Oxford History of the British Empire: Volume IV, The Twentieth Century*, Oxford, Oxford University Press, 1999.

Brown, Malcolm. *Lawrence of Arabia: The Life, the Legend*, London, Thames & Hudson, 2005.

Callwell, C.E. *Field Marshal Sir Henry Wilson: His Life and Diaries*, vol. 2, London, Cassell, 1927.

Cannadine, David. *Ornamentalism: How the British Saw Their Empire*, Oxford, Oxford University Press, 2001.

Catherwood, Christopher. *Churchill's Folly: How Winston Churchill Created Modern Iraq*, New York, Carroll & Graf, 2004.

Churchill, Winston S. *Great Contemporaries*, London, Thomas Butterworth, 1937.

— *My African Journey*, London, Bloomsbury Academic, 2015.

Cohen, Michael J. *Churchill and the Jews, 1900–1948*, London, Routledge, 2003.

Collins, Damian. *Charmed Life: The Phenomenal World of Philip Sassoon*, London, HarperCollins, 2016.

Collins, Paul and Charles Tripp, eds. *Gertrude Bell and Iraq: A Life and Legacy*, Oxford, Oxford University Press, 2017.

Collins, Robert O. *The Nile*, New Haven, CT, and London, Yale University Press, 2002.

Cooper, Lisa. *In Search of Kings and Conquerors: Gertrude Bell and the Archaeology of the Middle East*, London, I.B. Tauris, 2016.

Cregier, Don M. *Bounder from Wales: Lloyd George's Career before the First World War*, Columbia, University of Missouri Press, 1976.

Darwin, John. *Britain, Egypt and the Middle East: Imperial Policy in the Aftermath of War 1918–1922*, London, Macmillan, 1981.

— *The Empire Project: The Rise and Fall of the British World System, 1830–1970* Cambridge, Cambridge University Press, 2009.

Davis, Paul K. *Ends and Means: The British Mesopotamian Campaign and Commission*, Ann Arbor, MI, University of Michigan Press, 1994.

de Gaury, Gerald. *Three Kings in Baghdad: The Tragedy of Iraq's Monarchy*, London, I.B. Tauris, 2008.

Dockter, Warren. *Churchill and the Islamic World*, London, I.B. Tauris, 2015.

Dodge, Toby. *Inventing Iraq: The Failure of Nation Building and a History Denied*, London, Hurst & Co., 2003.

Faught, C. Brad. *Gordon: Victorian Hero*, Washington, DC, Potomac Books, 2008.

— *Kitchener: Hero and Anti-Hero*, London, I.B. Tauris, 2016.

— *Allenby: Making the Modern Middle East*, London, Bloomsbury, 2020.

Faulkner, Neil. *Lawrence of Arabia's War: The Arabs, the British and the Remaking of the Middle East in WWI*, New Haven, CT, and London, Yale University Press, 2016.

Fieldhouse, D.K. *Western Imperialism in the Middle East 1914–1958*, Oxford, Oxford University Press, 2006.

Fromkin, David. *A Peace to End All Peace: The Fall of the Ottoman Empire and the Creation of the Modern Middle East*, New York, Henry Holt, 1989.

Gardner, Brian. *Allenby*, London, Cassell, 1965.

Gilbert, Martin. *Winston S. Churchill, Volume 4: World in Torment 1917–1922*, London, Minerva, 1990.

— *Churchill: A Life*, London, Heinemann, 1991.

Gilmour, David. *Curzon: Imperial Statesman 1859–1925*, London, John Murray, 2003.

Gough, Paul. *A Terrible Beauty: British Artists in the First World War*, London, Sansom and Company, 2010.

Graves, Philip. *The Life of Sir Percy Cox*, London, Hutchinson, 1941.

Graves, Robert. *Lawrence and the Arabs*, London, Jonathan Cape, 1927.

Hadaway, Stuart. *From Gaza to Jerusalem: The Campaign for Southern Palestine 1917*, London, History Press, 2015.

Haldane, Sir James Aylmer Lowthrop. *The Insurrection in Mesopotamia*, Edinburgh, William Blackwood & Sons, 1922.

Hardy, Roger. *The Poisoned Well: Empire and Its Legacy in the Middle East*, New York, Oxford University Press, 2016.

Holden, David, and Richard Johns. *The House of Saud*, London, Sidgwick & Jackson, 1976.

Holmes, Richard. *Sahib: The British Soldier in India, 1750–1914*, London, HarperCollins, 2005.

Hopkirk, Peter. *The Great Game: On Secret Service in High Asia*, London, John Murray, 1990.

— *On Secret Service East of Constantinople: The Great Game and the Great War*, London, John Murray, 1994.

Hourani, Albert. *A History of the Arab Peoples*, Cambridge, MA, Harvard University Press, 1991.

Howell, Georgina. *Daughter of the Desert: The Remarkable Life of Gertrude Bell*, London, Macmillan, 2006.

Humphreys, Andrew. *Grand Hotels of Egypt: In the Golden Age of Travel*, Cairo, American University of Cairo Press, 2012.

Hyam, Ronald. *Elgin and Churchill at the Colonial Office 1905–1908: The Watershed of the Empire-Commonwealth*, London, Macmillan, 1968.

Ilhahi, Shereen. *Imperial Violence and the Path to Independence: India, Ireland and the Crisis of Empire*, London, I.B. Tauris, 2016.

Iliffe, John. *The African Poor: A History*, Cambridge, Cambridge University Press, 2009.

James, Lawrence. *Imperial Warrior: The Life and Times of Field-Marshal Viscount Allenby 1861–1936*, London, Weidenfeld & Nicolson, 1993.

Jenkins, Roy. *Asquith*, London, Collins, 1964.

— *Churchill: A Biography*, Toronto, Plume, 2002.

Johnson, Rob. *The Great War and the Middle East*, Oxford, Oxford University Press, 2016.

— *Lawrence of Arabia on War: The Campaign in the Desert 1916–18*, Oxford, Osprey, 2020.

Karsh, Efraim and Inari Karsh. *Empires of the Sand: The Struggle for Mastery in the Middle East, 1789–1923*, Cambridge, MA, Harvard University Press, 2001.

Kattan, Victor. *From Coexistence to Conquest: International Law and the Origins of the Arab-Israeli Conflict, 1891–1949*, London, Pluto Press, 2009.

Kedourie, Elie. *In the Anglo-Arab Labyrinth: The McMahon–Husayn Correspondence and Its Interpretations 1914–1939*, London, Frank Cass, 2000.

— *The Chatham House Version and Other Middle-Eastern Studies*, Chicago, Ivan R. Dee, 2004.

King, Peter, ed. *Lord Curzon: Travels with a Superior Person*, London, Sidgwick & Jackson, 1985.

Kirkbride, Alec Seath. *A Crackle of Thorns: Experiences in the Middle East*, London, John Murray, 1956.

Klieman, Aaron S. *Foundations of British Policy in the Arab World: The Cairo Conference of 1921*, Baltimore, MD, Johns Hopkins Press, 1970.

Korda, Michael. *Hero: The Life and Legend of Lawrence of Arabia*, New York, HarperCollins, 2010.

Lacey, Robert. *The Kingdom: Arabia and the House of Saud*, New York, Harcourt Brace Jovanovich, 1982.

Lawrence, T.E. *Seven Pillars of Wisdom: A Triumph*, Toronto, Penguin, 1990.

Lev, Shimon, ed. *A General and a Gentleman: Allenby at the Gates of Jerusalem*, Jerusalem, Tower of David/Museum of the History of Jerusalem, 2017.

Lewis, Donald M. *The Origins of Christian Zionism: Evangelical Support for a Jewish Homeland*, Cambridge, Cambridge University Press, 2010.

Liddell Hart, B.H. *History of the First World War*, London, Pan Books, 1970.

Lieshout, Robert H. *Britain and the Arab Middle East: World War and Its Aftermath*, London, I.B. Tauris, 2016.

Longrigg, S.H. *Iraq 1900–1950: A Political, Social and Economic History*, Oxford, Oxford University Press, 1956.

Lough, David. *No More Champagne: Churchill and His Money*, London, Head of Zeus, 2015.

Louis, Wm Roger. *The British Empire in the Middle East 1945–51: Arab Nationalism, the United States, and Postwar Imperialism*, Oxford, Clarendon Press, 1984.

— *Ends of British Imperialism: The Scramble for Empire, Suez and Decolonization*, London, I.B. Tauris, 2006.

Macintyre, Ben. *The Spy and the Traitor: The Greatest Espionage Story of the Cold War*, Toronto, Signal, 2018.

Mack, John E. *A Prince of Our Disorder: The Life of T.E. Lawrence*, Cambridge, MA, Harvard University Press, 1998.

MacMillan, Margaret. *Paris 1919: Six Months That Changed the World*, New York, Random House, 2003.

Mak, Lanver. *The British in Egypt: Community, Crime and Crises 1882–1922*, London, I.B. Tauris, 2012.

Mangold, Peter. *What the British Did: Two Centuries in the Middle East*, London, I.B. Tauris, 2016.

Mansel, Philip. *Aleppo: The Rise and Fall of Syria's Great Merchant City*, London, I.B. Tauris, 2018.

Marlowe, John. *Late Victorian: The Life of Sir Arnold Talbot Wilson*, London: Cresset Press, 1967.

Matthew, H.C.G. *Gladstone 1809–1898*, Oxford, Clarendon Press, 1997.

Mazza, Roberto. *Jerusalem: From the Ottomans to the British*, London, I.B. Tauris, 2013.

McMeekin, Sean. *The Berlin–Baghdad Express: The Ottoman Empire and Germany's Bid for World Power*, Cambridge, MA, Belknap Press, 2013.

— *The Ottoman Endgame: War, Revolution, and the Making of the Modern Middle East, 1908–1923*, London, Penguin, 2015.

McTague, John. *British Policy in Palestine, 1917–22*, Lanham, MD, University Press of America, 1983.

Meredith, Martin. *The State of Africa: A History of Fifty Years of Independence*, London, Free Press, 2005.

Meyer, Karl E. and Shareen Blair Brysac. *Kingmakers: The Invention of the Modern Middle East*, New York, W.W. Norton, 2009.

Millard, Candice. *Hero of the Empire: The Boer War, a Daring Escape and the Making of Winston Churchill*, New York, Doubleday, 2016.

Olson, Robert. *The Emergence of Kurdish Nationalism and the Sheikh Said Rebellion, 1880–1925*, Austin, TX, University of Texas Press, 1989.

Otte, T.G. *Statesman of Europe: A Life of Sir Edward Grey*, London, Allen Lane, 2020.

Owen, Roger. *Lord Cromer: Victorian Imperialist, Edwardian Proconsul*, Oxford, Oxford University Press, 2004.

Pakenham, Thomas. *The Scramble for Africa*, New York, Random House, 1990.

Paris, Timothy J. *Britain, the Hashemites and Arab Rule 1920–1925: The Sherifian Solution*, London Routledge, 2003.

— *In Defence of Britain's Middle Eastern Empire: A Life of Sir Gilbert Clayton*, Brighton, Sussex Academic Press, 2015.

Patrick, Andrew. *America's Forgotten Middle East Initiative: The King–Crane Commission of 1919*, London, I.B. Tauris, 1919.

Pedersen, Susan. *The Guardians: The League of Nations and the Crisis of Empire*, Oxford, Oxford University Press, 2015.

Philby, H. St J.B. *Arabian Days*, London, Robert Hale, 1948.

Provence, Michael. *The Last Ottoman Generation and the Making of the Modern Middle East*, Cambridge, Cambridge University Press, 2017.

Purnell, Sonia. *Clementine: The Life of Mrs Winston Churchill*, New York, Viking, 2015.

Reinharz, Jehuda. *Chaim Weizmann: The Making of a Statesman*, vol. 2, Oxford, Oxford University Press, 1993.

Renton, James. *The Zionist Masquerade: The Birth of the Anglo-Zionist Alliance, 1914–1918*, New York, Palgrave Macmillan, 2007.

Richards, David Adams. *Lord Beaverbrook*, Toronto, Penguin, 2011.

Robins, Philip. *A History of Jordan*, 2nd edn, Cambridge, Cambridge University Press, 2019.

Rogan, Eugene. *Frontiers of the State in the Late Ottoman Empire: Transjordan, 1851–1920*, Cambridge, Cambridge University Press, 1999.

— *The Fall of the Ottomans: The Great War in the Middle East*, New York, Basic Books, 2015.

Rose, Norman. *Chaim Weizmann: A Biography*, London, Penguin, 1989.

Said, Edward W. *Orientalism*, New York, Pantheon Books, 1978.

— *Culture and Imperialism*, New York, Knopf, 1993.

Satia, Priya. *Spies in Arabia: The Great War and the Cultural Foundations of Britain's Covert Empire in the Middle East*, New York, Oxford University Press, 2008.

Sattin, Anthony. *Young Lawrence: A Portrait of the Legend as a Young Man*, London, John Murray, 2015.

Saunders, Nicholas J. *Desert Insurgency: Archaeology, T.E. Lawrence, and the Arab Revolt*, Oxford, Oxford University Press, 2020.

Schayegh, Cyrus and Andrew Arsan, eds. *The Routledge Handbook of the History of the Middle East Mandates*, London, Routledge, 2020.

Schechtman, Joseph B. *Rebel and Statesman: The Vladimir Jabotinsky Story*, New York, Thomas Yoseloff, 1956.

Schneer, Jonathan. *The Balfour Declaration: The Origins of the Arab–Israeli Conflict*, New York, Random House, 2010.

Sluglett, Peter. *Britain in Iraq 1914–1932*, New York, Columbia University, 2007.

Soames, Mary. *Churchill: His Life as a Painter*, London, Viking, 1990.

Stacey, C.P. *Canada and the Age of Conflict, Volume 2: 1921–1948, The Mackenzie King Era*, Toronto, University of Toronto Press, 1981.

Stafford, David. *Oblivion or Glory: 1921 and the Making of Winston Churchill*, New Haven, CT, and London, Yale University Press, 2019.

Stein, Leonard. *The Balfour Declaration*, London, Magnes Press, 1983.

Sykes, Christopher Simon. *The Man Who Created the Middle East: A Story of Empire, Conflict and the Sykes–Picot Agreement*, London, HarperCollins, 2016.

Tauber, Eliezer. *The Arab Movements in World War I*, London, Routledge, 1993.

Thesiger, Wilfred. *Arabian Sands*, London, Longmans, 1959.

Thompson, Elizabeth F. *How the West Stole Democracy from the Arabs*, New York, Atlantic Monthly Press, 2020.

Thompson, Walter H. *Assignment Churchill*, New York, Farrar, Straus and Young, 1955.

Thornton, A.P. *The Habit of Authority: Paternalism in British History*, London, Allen & Unwin, 1966.

Tosh, John. *Manliness and Masculinities in Nineteenth-Century Britain: Essays on Gender, Family and Empire*, Harlow, Pearson Longman, 2005.

Townsend, John. *Proconsul to the Middle East: Sir Percy Cox and the End of Empire*, London, I.B. Tauris, 2010.

Toye, Richard. *Churchill's Empire: The World That Made Him and the World He Made*, London, Pan Books, 2011.

Tripp, Charles. *A History of Iraq*, Cambridge, Cambridge University Press, 2007.

Wallach, Janet. *Desert Queen: The Extraordinary Life of Gertrude Bell*, London, Weidenfeld & Nicolson, 1996.

Wasserstein, Bernard. *The British in Palestine: The Mandatory Government and the Arab–Jewish Conflict, 1917–1929*, Oxford, Blackwell, 1991.

Wavell, Field Marshal Viscount. *Allenby: Soldier and Statesman*, London, White Lion, 1974.

Westrate, Bruce. *The Arab Bureau: British Policy in the Middle East, 1916–1920*, State College, PA, Pennsylvania State University Press, 1992.

Wilson, Jeremy. *Lawrence of Arabia: The Authorized Biography of T.E. Lawrence*, New York, Atheneum, 1990.

Wilson, Mary C. *King Abdullah, Britain and the Making of Jordan*, Cambridge, Cambridge University Press, 1987.

Winstone, H.V.F. *Gertrude Bell: A Biography*, London, Jonathan Cape, 1978.

Young, Hubert. *The Independent Arab*, London, John Murray, 1933.

Journal Articles

Atkins, Richard A. 'The Origins of the Anglo-French Condominium in Egypt, 1875–1876', *Historian*, vol. 36, no. 2 (February 1974), pp. 264–82.

Boak, Denis. 'Malraux and T.E. Lawrence', *Modern Language Review*, vol. 61, no. 2 (April 1966), pp. 218–24.

Bar-Josef, Eitan. 'The Last Crusade? British Propaganda and the Palestine Campaign, 1917-18', *Journal of Contemporary History*, vol. 36, no. 1 (January 2001), pp. 87–109.

Cogley, Richard W. 'The Fall of the Ottoman Empire and the Restoration of Israel in the "Judeo-Centric" Strand of Puritan Millenarianism', *Church History*, vol. 72, no. 2, (June 2003), pp. 304–32.

BIBLIOGRAPHY

Darwin, John. 'An Undeclared Empire: The British in the Middle East, 1918–39', vol. 27, no. 2 (May 1999), pp. 159–76.

Eskander, Saad. 'Britain's Policy in Southern Kurdistan: The Formation and Termination of the First Kurdish Government, 1918–1919', *British Journal of Middle Eastern Studies*, vol. 27, no. 2, pp. 139–63.

Frantzman, Seth J., Benjamin W. Glueckstadt and Ruth Kark. 'The Anglican Church in Palestine and Israel: Colonialism, Arabization and Land Ownership', *Middle Eastern Studies*, vol. 47, no. 1 (January 2011), pp. 101–26.

Friedman, Isaiah. 'How Trans-Jordan Was Severed from the Territory of the Jewish National Home', *Journal of Israeli History*, vol. 27, no. 1 (2008), pp. 65–85.

Friesel, Evyatar. 'British Officials on the Situation in Palestine, 1923', *Middle Eastern Studies*, vol. 23, no. 2 (April 1987), pp. 194–210.

Halevy, Dotan. 'Toward a Palestinian History of Ruins: Interwar Gaza', *Journal of Palestine Studies*, vol. 48, no. 1 (autumn 2018), pp. 53–72.

Hughes, Matthew. 'Elie Kedourie and the Capture of Damascus, 1 October 1918: A Reassessment', *War & Society*, vol. 23, no. 1 (2005), pp. 87–106.

Huneidi, Sahar. 'Was Balfour Policy Reversible? The Colonial Office and Palestine, 1921–23', *Journal of Palestine Studies*, vol. 27, no. 2 (1998), pp. 23–41.

Killingray, David. '"A Swift Agent of Government": Air Power in British Colonial Africa, 1916–1939', *Journal of African History*, vol. 25, no. 4 (1984), pp. 429–44.

Masalha, N. 'Faisal's Pan Arabism, 1921–33', *Middle Eastern Studies*, vol. 27, no. 4 (October 1991), pp. 679–93.

Paris, Timothy J. 'British Middle East Policy-Making after the First World War: The Lawrentian and Wilsonian Schools', *Historical Journal*, vol. 41 (September 1998), pp. 773–93.

Reid, Donald M. 'Political Assassination in Egypt, 1910–1954', *International Journal of African Historical Studies*, vol. 15, no. 4 (1982), pp. 625–51.

Satia, Priya. 'The Defence of Inhumanity: Air Control and the British Idea of Arabia', *American Historical Review*, vol. 111, no. 1 (2006), pp. 26–32.

Periodical Magazines

The Atlantic (Washington, DC)
Canada's History (Toronto)
The New Yorker
Strand Magazine (London)
St Nicholas (New York)

Newspapers

Colonial Times (Hobart, Tasmania)
Daily Herald (London)
The Manchester Guardian
Illustrated Sunday Herald (London)
New York Times
The Sunday Times (London)
The Times (London)
Washington Post

Novels

Russell, Mary Doria. *Dreamers of the Day*, New York, Ballantine Books, 2008.

BIBLIOGRAPHY

Documentary Films

Krayenbühl, Sabine and Zeva Oelbaum, dirs. *Letters from Baghdad*, Vitagraph Films, 2016.

Audio Recordings

British Library Sound Archive

INDEX